W9-AXJ-575

AFRICAN ISSUES

**Famine
Crimes**

Politics & the
Disaster Relief
Industry in Africa

AFRICAN ISSUES

Famine Crimes

Politics & the Disaster Relief Industry in Africa

ALEX DE WAAL
Co-director
African Rights

African Rights &
The International
African Institute
in association with
JAMES CURREY
Oxford
INDIANA UNIVERSITY PRESS
Bloomington & Indianapolis

African Rights
11 Marshalsea Road
London SE1 1EP
&
The International
African Institute
in association with

James Currey
73 Botley Road
Oxford OX2 0BS
&
Indiana University Press
601 North Morton Street
Bloomington
Indiana 47404
(North America)

British Library Cataloguing in Publication Data
De Waal, Alexander
Famine crimes: politics and the disaster relief industry
in Africa. – (African issues)
1. Disaster relief – Africa 2. Disaster relief – Political
aspects – Africa
I. Title II. International African Institute
363.3'48'096

ISBN 0-85255-811-2 (James Currey Cloth)
ISBN 0-85255-810-4 (James Currey Paper)

Library of Congress Cataloging-in-Publication Data
A catalog record for this book is available from the Library of Congress
ISBN 0-253-21158-1 (paper)
ISBN 0-253-33367-9 (cloth)

Typeset by
Exe Valley Dataset
Exeter, Devon
in 9/11 Melior with Optima display

Printed in Great Britain by
Villiers Publications
London N3

DEDICATION

To the Memory of
Ahmed Karadawi
1945–95

CONTENTS

PHOTOGRAPHS & MAPS

GLOSSARY & ACRONYMS

AMC	Agricultural Marketing Corporation (Ethiopia)
ARAP	Accelerated Rainfed Arable Production Programme (Botswana)
belg	short rains (Ethiopia)
CARE	Christian Action for Research and Education
Caritas	Italian originated third world charity
CRDA	Christian Relief and Development Association
DHA	UN Department of Humanitarian Affairs
DRP	Drought Relief Programme (Botswana)
Dergue	Provisional Military Administrative Committee (Ethiopia)
ECHO	Equipment to Charity Hospitals Overseas
EDP	externally displaced person
EPLF	Eritrean People's Liberation Front
EPRP	Ethiopian People's Revolutionary Party
ERA	Eritrean Relief Association
ERD	Emergency Relief Desk (Eritrea and Ethiopia)
ESAP	Economic and Social Action Plan (Zimbabwe)
FAO	UN Food and Agriculture Organization
FTC	Feed the Children
GMB	Grain Marketing Board (Zimbabwe)
ICRC	International Committee of the Red Cross
IDI	International Disasters Institute
IFI	international financial institution
IMF	International Monetary Fund
KANU	Kenyan African National Union
MEISON	All-Ethiopia Socialist Party
MSF	Médecins Sans Frontières
meher	long rains (Ethiopia)
NCPB	National Cereals and Produce Board (Kenya)
NIF	National Islamic Front (Sudan)
OLS	Operation Lifeline Sudan
REST	Relief Society of Tigray (Ethiopia)
RPA	Rwandese Patriotic Army
RPF	Rwandese Patriotic Front
RRC	Relief and Rehabilitation Commission (Ethiopia)

SCF	The Save the Children Fund
SDF	Social Development Fund (Zimbabwe)
SPLA	Sudan People's Liberation Army
SPM	Somali Patriotic Movement
SRCS	Somali Red Crescent Society
SRRA	Sudan Relief and Rehabilitation Association
SSU	Sudan Socialist Union
TPLF	Tigray People's Liberation Front (Ethiopia)
UNAMIR	UN Assistance Mission to Rwanda
UNDP	UN Development Programme
UNDRO	UN Disaster Relief Organization
UNEOE	UN Emergency Office for Ethiopia
UNHCR	UN High Commission for Refugees
UNICEF	UN Children's Fund
UNITAF	Unified Task Force (Somalia)
UNOSOM	UN Operation in Somalia
USAID	US Agency for International Development
USC	United Somali Congress
WFP	UN World Food Programme
ZANU	Zimbabwean African National Union

PREFACE

This book has been some six years in the writing. It began chiefly with a focus on the way in which respect for liberal civil and political rights could help deliver freedom from famine, and has since grown vastly in its empirical and theoretical scope. A focus on human rights as such has shifted to the political processes that can establish and guarantee them. The initial agenda was tied, implicitly at least, to widening the scope for humanitarian and human rights organizations to intrude (in certain ways) into the affairs of African countries. This has given way to a deeper analysis of the 'humanitarian international' – the transnational elite of relief workers, aid-dispensing civil servants, academics, journalists and others, and the institutions they work for – and its involvement in famines in Africa. The emergent critique of human rights organizations has yet to be written. Meanwhile, intermediate versions of the critique of humanitarianism, especially the paper *Humanitarianism Unbound* (African Rights, 1994a), have become widely known.

For understandable reasons, there has been most interest in the conclusions of the analysis – the suggestion that international humanitarianism is an obstacle rather than an aid to conquering famine in Africa – rather than in the course of the argument itself. This is unfortunate, because the critique of humanitarianism makes sense only in the context of an account of the political roots of famine and the political routes to its conquest. Without these earlier stages of the argument, the conclusion reads merely as a polemic, breaking a taboo for the sake of it. Hence the need to write a book which can cover the ground in a more sustained and comprehensive way, and which can allocate culpabilities more fairly between African governments and armed movements, Western governments and international financial institutions, the mass media, and the humanitarian agencies. Because the subject of inquiry – famine – is so central to the activities of the humanitarian agencies, they are more sharply in focus for much of the book than the other main players. Their faults are highlighted, but they can be understood and perhaps remedied only with attention to a wider context.

Judging from experience, there seem to be two powerful paradoxes at work. One is that, despite deeper and more extensive international humanitarian involvement in famines, these crises appear to be more intractable than before. Is this an illusion, simply because we know more? Is it due to extraneous factors, perhaps associated with the end of the Cold War, economic crisis and the rise of identity politics? Or could it be that the intrusion of the humanitarian institutions represents, in an insidious but profound way, a disempowerment of the people directly engaged in the crisis, which drains their capacity to find a solution? The idea that wars and political crises are like forest fires, which can burn themselves out 'naturally' if left alone, has been rightly ridiculed (see Slim, 1996: 10). But a recurring theme of the present book is the danger that external involvement, however well-intentioned, almost inevitably damages the search for local political solutions.

The second paradox is that the humanitarian international appears to have an extraordinary capacity to absorb criticism, not reform itself, and yet emerge strengthened. Books on famines and humanitarianism are almost by definition critiques of current practice. But, insofar as they are written by members (fully paid-up or honorary) of the humanitarian international institutions and published (or at least subsidized) by them and aimed at the authors' peers, they seem to have the effect of enriching the moral capital of these same humanitarian institutions. The legitimacy of Western relief agencies, donor institutions and even military forces seems to be enhanced by those who dispute their effectiveness. The humanitarian discourse itself, whatever its content, reinforces the humanitarians' moral ownership of famine and similar crises, at the expense of the people who are suffering.

This poses a dilemma. To whom should this book be addressed? Few if any African farmers and pastoralists and their representatives will read it. The obvious consumers are members of the humanitarian international, but will their consumption merely reinforce their hegemony, despite the present author's intentions and the goodwill of some of them? To deny that they (along with students and academics) will be the main readers would be a futile gesture. Instead, this book acknowledges that humanitarian agencies can be a genuine instrument of change in the international system for responding to large-scale human tragedies. Some of the provisos are elaborated in the text. Also, the argument does not shirk its logical conclusion: that most current humanitarian activity in Africa is useless or damaging and should be abandoned. Humanitarian action is too noble an enterprise to become debased and discredited in this manner.

ACKNOWLEDGEMENTS

The funds that made possible the completion of this book were generously provided by NOVIB (The Netherlands) and Diakonisches Werk (Germany), but it is also based on fourteen years of experience as a research student, relief consultant and 'human rights professional'. The people who have contributed to it in one way or another are very many: almost all the colleagues and friends who have accompanied me in the field or worked on one or other project deserve mention. The following I will pick out, at the risk of offending others (or indeed those I mention by name; the text contains analyses and opinions many of them will object to). I alone am responsible for errors of fact and analysis.

In Sudan, my work and understanding, such as it is, would have been impossible without, among others, Yoanes Ajawin, Suleiman Rahhal, Ordesse Hamad, Ruth Buckley, David Hughes, Michael Medley, John Ryle, and Wendy James. Mark Duffield deserves special mention, though his influences on my work range beyond Sudan. Others must remain anonymous for now, for reasons of security and lack of space. In Ethiopia, I owe particular thanks to Abadi Zemo, Tekleweyne Assefa, Gerezgerhe Bezabih, Gayle Smith, John Mitchell, Tony Vaux, and of course to a large number of rural Ethiopians whose names are buried in my notebooks. Jacques Willemse is living embodiment of the fact that a relief programme can work and be politically progressive. Barbara Hendrie has been my most thoughtful critic on Ethiopia, as well as on issues ranging from Foucault to the analytical structure of the book. Although Eritrea is scarcely mentioned, I cannot overlook the insights provided by Tekie Beyene, Paulos Tesfagiorgis and Habte Abreha. In Somalia, I have relied heavily on insights from Hussein Mursal, Abdi Baafo and Abdi Aden 'Dheere'. Lucy Hannan corrected some of my mistakes on Kenya. Joseph Mutaboba helped me to grapple with Rwanda. Others who have made important contributions to my thinking, across a range of countries and issues, include Aryeh Neier, Rae McGrath, Roger Briottet, Jeremy Swift, David Keen, Hugo Slim, Jeremy Benthall, John Seaman and Astier Almedom.

My colleague for seven years, Rakiya Omaar, has consistently been a touchstone for integrity, courage and judgement. Ahmed Karadawi, whose insight, honesty and friendship are irreplaceable, first set me off on this intellectual and personal journey. Lastly, my wife, Astier, and my son and daughter, Hiroë and Hannah, have been supportive, understanding and loving throughout.

Alex de Waal
London

INTRODUCTION

i

Famine is conquerable. It has been eradicated from most of the world. But in some countries in Africa human suffering seems to be getting more rather than less common. This is a tragedy and a scandal: setting it right is what motivates the best humanitarians. It is tempting to think of the expanding humanitarian enterprise as a heroic effort to keep up with a runaway juggernaut of war and natural disaster, which is somehow always too big and intractable to be stopped. Most thoughtful relief workers see humanitarian action as a neutral stop-gap – a brake on the out-of-control vehicle that may help the slower politicians and diplomats to catch up before it inflicts too much human damage. But, this book will argue, this view is mistaken. Humanitarian action *is* political action, of a certain kind. Unfortunately for the victims of famine, it can act less as a brake on the juggernaut of famine, and more as an element in the fuel that keeps the monster moving.

Mechanical metaphors can mislead. It is also inappropriate to begin an account of famine by examining humanitarian action; relief is generally merely a footnote to the story of how people survive famine. It is only by first studying famine, in its historical and political context, that humanitarianism can be put in its proper perspective. Hence the central subject of this book is not humanitarianism, but specifically the question of what kinds of political systems are effective in preventing famine. The argument moves through most of its important stages before modern-day humanitarianism makes any entrance at all. Some of the progenitors and siblings of humanitarianism also need analysis, including Malthusianism, neo-liberalism and indeed the whole enterprise of finding technical solutions to famine.

Much famine 'expertise' stops precisely at the point where politics begins; there is often a weak call for 'political will' to bridge the gap between knowledge of technical measures and action to implement them. This book rejects the technical-political dualism. The problem is not a 'missing link' but rather an entire political tradition, one manifestation of which is contemporary international humanitarianism.

1

Technical 'solutions' must be seen in political context, and politics itself in the light of the dominance of a technocratic approach to problems such as famine. This approach can be contrasted with a 'political contract' model of famine prevention, which is overtly political. An anti-famine political contract involves several things, including a political commitment by government, recognition of famine as a political scandal by the people, and lines of accountability from government to people that enable this commitment to be enforced. There are many different forms of anti-famine political contract, but the paradigm case is that of India, and a careful examination of the complexities and paradoxes of the conquest of famine in South Asia is a fertile ground from which to approach the current woeful state of affairs in Africa.

Can respect for liberal rights ensure protection from famine? The reverse case is clear: human rights abuses are invariably an intimate part of famine creation. Particular forms of warfare (most of them prohibited by the Geneva Conventions) are instrumental in creating war famines. Violations of the residence and property rights of small farmers, and the freedom of movement of pastoralists, have been important in many famines. The repression of freedoms of expression and association has prevented civil organizations from mobilizing to protest against or prevent famine, and has encouraged the abusive forces that create famine.

Does it follow that respecting these freedoms can prove a one-shot inoculation against famine? At the 'end of history' following the collapse of Communism, the triumph of political liberalism appeared, briefly, so incontestable that civil society and economic prosperity seemed ready, with state repression removed, to spring naturally into place. It was at this moment that Amartya Sen's thesis about the close interlinkage between basic freedoms and protection from famine awoke from its relative obscurity. According to Sen (1990), liberal democracies do not suffer famine:

> The diverse political freedoms that are available in a democratic state, including regular elections, free newspapers and freedom of speech, must be seen as the real force behind the elimination of famines. Here again, it appears that one set of freedoms – to criticize, publish and vote – are usually linked with other types of freedoms, such as the freedom to escape starvation and famine mortality.

Sen had first propounded this thesis in 1982, but it had not been widely taken up outside India until the end of the decade, when there was a flurry of interest. Sen himself wrote in the *New York Review of Books*, and liberal human rights organizations such as Article 19 (1990) and Human Rights Watch (1992) published reports. The present author, caught in the enthusiasm of the moment, also wrote widely, promoting variants of the same hypothesis (de Waal 1991a and b). The genesis of the present book was in fact a proposal to flesh out Sen's thesis with reference to Africa. This argument and these hopes were specific to the conquest of famine, but there was a more widespread expectation that the end of proxy wars and dictatorial governments would open up a new era of prosperity.

The optimism was, of course, premature. Much of this book is dedicated to explaining why. Three main arguments can be adduced.

One is that links between civil and political liberties and protection from famine are more tenuous and more specific than was anticipated. Even a cursory analysis of the political history of Indian famine prevention indicates that Sen's account needs important modifications, specifically the introduction of the notion of a political contract for famine prevention. This has ambiguous implications for human rights. The political contract itself is characteristically expressed in a human rights idiom, such as 'the right to food' or 'the right to be free from famine'. But it is liberal civil rights and the existence of independent institutions such as uncensored media and free political associations that enable people to fight for these social and economic rights. African 'success stories' (Kenya and Botswana both fall into this questionable category) illustrate how some political systems have delivered protection from famines, but also how fragile this protection tends to be.

Secondly, the obstacles to constructing anti-famine political contracts in Africa have been much more formidable than was appreciated. Internal political decay is by far the most important factor. Despite the 'democracy wave' of 1990–3, many African countries have witnessed deepening authoritarianism. Some have seen the growth of 'war economies', in which merchants and military commanders engage in the violent extraction of resources and stripping of assets as a commercial enterprise. Some rulers have adopted 'minimalist' state strategies, holding on to the symbols of sovereign government while allowing (or abetting) the decay of public services and civil structures.

External pressures have not been favourable. Paramount among them have been austerity measures invoked in the name of neo-liberalism. The prime concern here is not the economic impact of these measures, but the implications for the political process. Despite the commitment to 'democratization' and 'good governance' of the early 1990s, neo-liberalism tends to encourage authoritarianism, to reorient governmental accountability towards external financiers, and to weaken the mechanisms that mediate state responsibility for famine. The element of social Darwinism in neo-liberalism reduces the moral and political shock of famine: the end result of this process may be that famine is somehow considered inevitable or politically acceptable, in the way that Euro-American electorates have come to tolerate a certain degree of unemployment or homelessness.

A third, somewhat unexpected, obstacle has been the rapid growth in the power of the 'humanitarian international' – the cosmopolitan elite of relief workers, officials of donor agencies, consultant academics and the like, and the institutions for which they work. By extension it includes journalists and editors who faithfully propagate the humanitarian worldview. (Its growth is associated with the dominance of what might be called, to borrow from Foucault, a 'humanitarian mode of power'.[1]) The humanitarian international is avowedly dedicated to fighting famine, but does not in fact operate in a way that enables this to be achieved. There are 'successes' and 'failures', some of which are recounted here, but the unexpected consequences of humanitarian action are more significant. An exploration of the principles that drive 'actually existing humanitarianism' reveals that its power is exercised and its resources dispensed at the cost of weakening the forms of political accountability that underlie the prevention of famine.

About half of this book is concerned with 'actually existing humanitarianism' and its politically regressive implications. But humanitarianism, particularly when situated within a framework that includes dedication to technological mastery of social problems and neo-liberal economics, also has a powerful grasp over how we think. There is a powerful tendency to define famine in quasi-scientific terms, for example as a severe economic 'cooling', an epidemic of malnutrition, or a failure of food policy. Humanitarians operationally define famine as a state of affairs that they seek to relieve through aid.

This book implicitly adopts another theoretical level, examining both the 'problem' (famine) and the 'solution' (humanitarianism and related forms of public policy) together. The exercise of the humanitarian mode of power not only involves dispensing large sums of money and becoming intimately involved in distressed foreign societies, but also defining what is moral and what is true. It has won many converts in Africa. Humanitarianism is hugely self-justifying: it may even be the paradigm of a secular human enterprise that does not need to succeed in order to justify itself. Humanitarianism works, by definition. The eminent social theorist Russell Hardin has emphasized (in a different context – that of nationalism and group action) that:

> The most benign motivations can be coupled with perverse under-standing to produce dreadful results. And the most grasping, self-seeking motivations can produce massive, wonderful social benefits. *Motivations may explain but, because they need not correlate with the goodness or rightness of their effects, they do not justify.* . . . The important fact is that it is apparently true of all motivations of any significance that they can have grossly harmful effects (Hardin 1995: 15, emphasis in original)

It is the very *genuineness* of the humanitarian motive that is at the root of many of the complexities and problems of humanitarian action. Many

---

[1]This concept owes much to the 'philanthropic mode of power', as analysed with regard to camps for Burundi refugees in Tanzania by Liisa Malkki. See Malkki, 1995.

relief workers, and by extension the organizations they work for, have a real commitment to saving lives, reaching the poorest people, etc. They have discovered that this is not an easy task, and have responded to the challenges by developing ever more complex relief institutions and methods, and, above all, more effective means of raising money. Humanitarian agencies and their workers are often liberal and enlightened, and have helped the subjects of their concern to a fuller understanding of the problems of famine and other disasters – and indeed sometimes to an appreciation of the shortcomings of humanitarianism. But the struggle against famine has become professionalized and institutionalized. Technical mastery – especially in public health – is important. But these processes represent a leaching of power from those who suffer famine. Generalized, internationalized responsibility for fighting famine is far less valuable than specific, local political accountability. The struggle against famine cannot be the moral property of humanitarian institutions. An important step in that struggle is for those directly affected by famine to reclaim this moral ownership.

Humanitarianism does not prevent famine – a fact that is of concern primarily to the people variously described as its 'beneficiaries' and 'recipients'. But these people are excluded from having a significant voice should they decide to dispute its axioms. To borrow from Foucault again, humanitarianism is 'the detestable solution we seem unable to do without'. To be precise, the intractability of famine is the price that is paid for the ascendancy of humanitarianism.

This is familiar ground. More than 25 years ago, as described in the history of Oxfam (Black 1992: 182) Ivan Illich, in *Deschooling Society*, 'excoriated the humanitarians for being wide-eyed and gullible extensions of the system causing all the damage. For this he received their adulatory applause. . . . To help was to interfere, sometimes with unforeseen and negative consequences.' In the 1990s, some aid agency staff have also been avid consumers of critiques, and some of the points made by critics have been acknowledged, notably that relief agencies simply cannot solve the problems they face. From the 1970s debate, Oxfam's biographer concluded, 'But if even the humanitarian establishment contained more potential for social damage than repair, what hope on earth was there?' This conclusion is too lazy to get by today: non-'humanitarian' means are needed to meet humanitarian goals.

History is replete with successful methods of preventing famine. Common to them are versions of 'political contract' that impose political obligations on rulers. In the most effective anti-famine contracts, famine is a political scandal. Famine is *deterred*. The contract is enforced by throwing out a government that allows it to happen or otherwise punishing those in power.

In such political contracts, the charitable imperative is relegated to an ancillary role, a role that, importantly, does not claim the moral high ground. This is where human rights re-enter the picture, as a political idiom for exercising or curtailing power. For war famines, the challenge is to deter those who cause them. The Geneva Conventions contain strong provisions prohibiting the use of starvation as a method of warfare. Criminalizing the infliction of famine requires a further step, namely enforcing the prohibitions by prosecuting those guilty of the crime. This is to put famine into the category of offences requiring justice, and in particular war crimes.

When famine prevention is recognized as a human right, and fought for using the sorts of political structures that exist when human rights are respected, then famine can be conquered. This is not to abandon humanitarianism, which can again be a force for ethical progress. But a humanitarianism that sets itself against or above politics is futile. Rather we should seek a form of politics that transforms humanitarianism.

1

**Rights &
Entitlements**

The Conquest
of Famine in
South Asia

For almost a century there has been no excuse for famine. By 1907, the (revised) Indian Famine Codes became a charter for the effective prevention of famine (defined narrowly as mass death due to epidemic failure of food consumption) in South Asia, and by extension, other poor agrarian societies. Subsequent famines in Asia are all directly attributable to a catastrophic breakdown in government capacity or willingness to do what was known to be necessary to prevent famine. The well-known success of independent India in preventing famines has been due to the vigilance of its political institutions and electors in ensuring an adequate level of government accountability. This is a monumental achievement: until 25 years ago, 'famine' was virtually synonymous with one or other Asian country.

This chapter examines how and why the conquest of Asian famine was achieved, and also the limits of that success. It is important to begin in Asia because most modern famine theory and practice originate there, and because recent African failures provide such a compelling contrast with Asian success.

Most of the basic facts need no restating. In the nineteenth century, the Indian subcontinent suffered a notorious succession of famines. Well into the twentieth century, China was still 'the land of famine' (Mallory, 1926). This is history. Today, only Bangladesh, Cambodia and North Korea are (for very different reasons) considered vulnerable to famine. Economic reasons for the conquest of famine are important, though they will not be considered here. But it should be noted that South Asia is still extremely poor, and in particular, that the average food consumption of rural South Asians is below that of their African counterparts. The central reason for both the conquest of Asian famine, and the limits of that victory, is to be found in the political systems.

Amartya Sen has come up with a challenging explanation for India's success: respect for liberal civil and political rights – a free press, competitive elections and the other institutions of a liberal democracy

7

(Sen, 1990). The relationship between famine and human rights in South Asia is the starting point for the argument of this book. The first task is to analyse and refine Sen's hypothesis, and then see whether it fits the historical facts. The conclusion is that a deeper level of explanation is required, locating human rights within political processes, and identifying a specific 'political contract' that has ensured an enforceable freedom from famine in India.

Before returning in the following chapter to the main thread of the argument, in Africa, it will be necessary to digress briefly into an account of the development of famine theory and anti-famine practice. The link between the two is not simple (on occasions the theory and practice have been in open contradiction), and their relationship to human rights is not straightforward either.

Human rights and freedom from famine

There are three main approaches to the links between human rights and freedom from famine. One is the formulation of a 'right to food'. The second is respect for liberal civil and political rights, on the grounds that a transparent and accountable government cannot let famine occur. The third utilizes the laws of war, also known as international humanitarian law, which seek to prevent hunger during wartime. The issue of the legality of starvation as a means of waging war has concerned legal scholars for decades, with little effect on the way in which wars are waged. This issue will be taken up in later chapters.

The right to food

The Chinese Government, in its attempts to rebut liberal criticisms of its human rights record, has advocated a right to food: 'It is a simple truth that, for any country or nation, the right to subsistence is the most important of all human rights, without which the other rights are out of the question' (Government of China, 1991: 9). This has been characterized as the 'full belly view': liberal rights can only be enjoyed by people who are already endowed with basic subsistence. A hierarchy of rights is established, with social and economic rights at the top.

The formulation of a 'right to food' might appear to be one of the most unproblematic of human rights. It has repeatedly been the focus of international human rights legislation; 120 international instruments have been adopted during the period 1921–87 dealing with human rights and food (Tomasevski, 1994). In 1989, the UN Special Rapporteur on the subject, Asbjorn Eide, gave the most complete definition yet:

> Everyone requires access to food which is (a) sufficient, balanced and safe to satisfy nutritional requirements, (b) culturally acceptable, and (c) accessible in a manner which does not destroy one's dignity as human beings. (Eide, 1989)

This has not been followed up, perhaps because since 1989 the heat has been taken out of the advocacy of socialist theories of human rights. At the 1993 UN Conference on Human Rights in Vienna, there was no mention of the right to food (Tomasevski, 1994).

There are serious theoretical problems with the right to food. The very manner in which food is one of the sinews of social and political relations makes it complicated and awkward to instumentalize the 'right to food'. The verb 'to starve' has both transitive and intransitive senses. One person can starve another, or someone can starve.[1] To outlaw the act of starvation, inflicted by one person on another, requires corrective justice: it is akin to criminalizing murder. To outlaw non-culpable starvation is a different matter: it implies a positive right to food which in turn requires a form of distributive justice if it is to be fulfilled. This leads to a set of profound questions about the nature of government that is required to wield the necessary redistributive power. There is a huge potential for abuse of such power, as illustrated by the excesses of revolutionary regimes, including the Chinese.

Another problem with the right to food is that it is significantly different from the right to be free from famine. Famine is much more than hunger: it includes social breakdown, economic deprivation and health crisis. Famine is more appropriately seen as the converse of the 'right to development', a right that is considerably more problematic even than the right to food.

The right to food is commonly seen as an aspirational right: it cannot be judicially enforced and its avowal by governments is merely a statement of intention towards their citizens. The basic question to ask is not, 'does it exist?' or even, 'can it be enforced?' but rather, 'has it ever worked?' The answer, elaborated below, is that it may sometimes have contributed to overcoming famine.

Liberal rights and famine

There is a contrasting liberal view of human rights and freedom from famine. This comes in several versions.

The weakest claim is that all famines are in part or wholly caused by abuses of a range of human rights, including fundamental human rights, liberal civil and political rights, and the laws of war. This argument is implicit throughout this book: all the case studies demonstrate the violation of rights in the creation of famine. Identifying these violations does not, however, entail a simple agenda for freedom from famine.

An alternative and very strong claim is that upholding liberal rights is not only the best protection against famine, but also prevents a wide range of material deprivations including chronic hunger and poverty.

---

[1]Very occasionally the word 'hunger' has been used in a similar sense. E.g. 'The Mahdi spent five months hungering out Obeid' (*The Daily Telegraph*, 12 May 1884).

This argument gained popularity at the end of the Cold War. It will not be discussed here, but the revolutionary Chinese Government's prodigious achievements in conquering poverty should be grounds enough to question this view.

An intermediate version is the substantive claim that upholding liberal rights is not only desirable in its own right, but also provides protection from famine. Amartya Sen was not the first, but he was the most influential, proponent of this view. He presented it in the 1982 Coromandel lecture (shortly after developing his twin 'entitlement approach' to famine), whereupon it was largely neglected until the end of the decade. The triumph of liberalism at the end of the Cold War gave the theory a new lease of life, and Sen returned to publicizing it, along with human rights organizations and liberal commentators.

This intermediate thesis is the most important. To summarize, it holds that democratic institutions can operate in a number of ways to make famine prevention effective. They ensure that credible information exists as to the nature of any impending crisis, so that famines cannot develop in secret. A much simplified line is 'censorship causes famines'. In addition, they ensure that governments respond to this information in a timely and effective manner. The failure of 'triggering' is the greatest problem with technical early-warning systems. In a system with democratic accountability, this role is played by the very sources of credible information themselves, namely civil organizations and the press. By playing an adversarial, critical role, calling to account those politicians and administrators who are failing to respond, civil organizations and the press can ensure that the government responds appropriately and quickly. In turn, elected representatives have a powerful incentive to respond: their positions depend upon popular support. A member of parliament who allows a famine to occur in his or her constituency will face serious difficulties in getting re-elected.

Finally, democracies have institutions to examine the record (a point omitted by Sen). Famine relief and prevention is an evolving practice. Mistakes are invariably made; it is essential to learn from them. In a democratic country, each time there is a disaster, some form of public inquiry is launched into what went wrong, who was to blame, what can be learned – and also, what was done correctly. This may take the form of an official commission of inquiry or scrutiny by the press or the legislature.

One of the main attractions of this thesis is that liberal rights are enforceable. The account leads directly to a political agenda that could, in principle, deliver freedom from a huge social and economic evil at low cost.

There is much going for the liberal theory. Where there is respect for civil and political rights there are more safeguards against needless disaster than is the case with repressive government. The number, variety and resilience of liberal institutions make it more difficult for famines to recur.

But, for liberal democratic government in a poor country to provide a robust protection against famine, other preconditions need to be met. To begin with, the state must have the administrative capacity to deliver famine prevention and relief. This capacity cannot be built overnight, so there must be a sustained commitment to famine prevention. Furthermore, the most famine-vulnerable citizens must be regarded as worthy of full consideration. Those who are at most risk of famine are inevitably the poorest and most marginal citizens, whose rights and welfare are most easily ignored. The existence of liberal institutions does not guarantee equality of treatment for all citizens, even in the provision of the most elementary services. Most importantly, famine must be regarded as an issue worthy of publicity and debate in the political domain; in short, a famine should be seen as a political scandal. The liberal rights theory explains *how* democratic institutions can help prevent famine, but not *why* they sometimes do so. There are other huge social tragedies, such as high rates of infant mortality, that have not been resolved by democratic institutions. What makes famine special?

The question of how and why the preconditions are met must be addressed by examining political history. The key concept here is that of 'political contract'.

Famine and political contract
The idea of a social or political contract dedicated to famine prevention constitutes an attempt to infuse social and economic rights into civil liberties, i.e. to explain why some social and economic rights are considered sufficiently important that they are guaranteed by political process. 'Political contract' is not used in the sense of the 'social contract' of Locke or Rousseau. Instead, it is the result of a popular movement successfully articulating a new right, and forcing a reluctant government to comply with its claims. Rough parallels include non-violent independence movements, the civil liberties movement in the United States, the women's movement, and pro-democracy and human rights movements in Eastern Europe since the 1975 Helsinki Treaties. Following the success of each of these 'primary movements', governments have recognized that maintaining their legitimacy rests on respecting certain democratic rights. These gains are defended by the 'secondary activism' of specialists such as journalists, lawyers, elected representatives, etc., who have (at least in principle) the opportunity to fall back upon popular mobilization.

Famine is so self-evidently wrong and so visible that it readily offers itself as a political cause. It has often provided the impulse for mass mobilization. Sometimes it has been a scandal among the political classes. Occasionally, it has been both, but only rarely has it proved the basis for an enduring coalition that can enforce a long-term change in governments' political priorities. (This also requires famine prevention and relief policies that *work* – a key requirement that should not be overlooked.) In such cases one can truly speak of an anti-famine political contract. One of these exceptional cases is that of India.

The conquest of famine in India

Ceding an anti-famine political contract was the price paid by Britain for maintaining imperial rule in India. In the second half of the nineteenth century, by its reluctance to take on responsibility for famine relief, the British Government discredited itself and so nurtured the nationalist movement, which in turn sought to use famine as an issue for mass mobilization. Sustained political agitation forced the government to take serious anti-famine measures, implicitly accepting a political contract. When the British Government broke that contract in Bengal in 1943, it strengthened the nationalist momentum and helped bring on Independence four years later. In turn, post-imperial governments have respected the anti-famine contract, under the vigilance of the press and elected representatives.

Forging the contract
Nineteenth-century famine relief in India was, by and large, parsimonious, poorly organized and informed by austere doctrines of economic liberalism and Malthusian population theory. Many British administrators maintained that famine was the lesser of two evils; the alternative being relentless impoverishment brought about by unchecked population growth. 'In this context, the argument would run somewhat like this: what is the use of saving lives when once again the people so saved would suffer later in the same way?' (Ambirajan, 1976: 5). For example, Governor-General Lord Lytton (1876–80) believed that India's 'natural limit' to population had been reached, and that the provision of famine relief would merely tax the industrious to reward the idle, thereby ensuring that future famines would be greater and more deadly.

Such doctrines conflicted with the political imperative of maintaining British rule. The 1857 Indian 'mutiny' and subsequent growth in nationalism rapidly led the Raj to the conclusion that mitigating hardship and preventing political unrest were two sides of the same coin. Anti-famine measures began in 1867 and were developed alongside political repression. The 1878 Vernacular Press Act which banned criticisms of the state was related to newspaper coverage of famines.

At the same time, within the rarefied circle of high-ranking administrators, a debate on famine was opened. It was conducted with theoretical sophistication as well as political and fiscal acuity (Hall-Matthews, 1996). It involved two famine commissions and a series of experiments in famine relief. In 1874, an expensive famine campaign in Bihar prevented famine mortality, while a famine in south India was estimated by the official inquiry to have cost over 5 million lives. 'Success' was measured as much by fiscal expenditure as by lives saved, and stringent measures were adopted in the 1876 Bombay famine. The discussion culminated in the second Famine Commission of 1880 and the promulgation of its renowned Famine Code.

On paper, the Famine Codes of the 1880s were comprehensive and sophisticated. (They compare well with many relief systems drawn up a century later.) According to the 1898 Famine Commission (Bhatia, 1967: Ch. IX) and some later analysts such as Drèze (1990a) they performed as well as could have been expected, when faced with severe drought in 1896–7. Others have argued that this famine presented the Codes with their first major test, which they failed, having been taken as a charter for financial stringency and minimalist intervention (Bhatia, 1967). In the 1899–1901 famine the response was more generous, but again did not prevent mass mortality.

At this point, the British Government rediscovered why it needed a famine prevention system (Hall-Matthews, 1996). In 1896 the Indian National Congress passed two resolutions linking poverty and hunger to the burdens of British rule, and urged the government to go further in saving lives in famine. The turn of the century saw a spate of polemics from Indian nationalists and British philanthropists and socialists accusing the Raj of immiserating the subcontinent. George Lambert's *India: The Horror-Stricken Empire* was published in 1898, Romesh Dutt's *Famine in India* in 1900 and his *Economic History of India* in 1904, and Dadabhai Naoroji's *Poverty and Un-British Rule in India* in 1901. These were as embarrassing in Britain as they were threatening in India.[2]

The reality contrasted with the noble intentions stated in the 1880 Report, which spoke grandly of the 'paramount *duty of the State* to give all practicable assistance to the people in time of famine, and to devote all its available resources to this end' (Report of the Famine Commission, 1880: 31, emphasis in original). The aim of the words 'practicable' and 'available' was to vitiate the assumption of the state's duty to prevent starvation, but a crevice was opened which was subsequently to be levered wide apart.

Between 1901 and 1907 the Famine Codes were drastically revised. The Famine Commission provided a mechanism for the government to do this without an overt backing down: it was both a self-correcting

[2]There is an interesting parallel with the way the Indian and international outcry over the Amritsar massacre in 1921 impelled the British army to adopt a doctrine of minimum force in dealing with civil unrest. See Mockaitis, 1990.

mechanism and a means of evaluating the civil service. While the resulting Codes were superficially similar to their predecessors, in reality they were much more substantial. Economy in expenditure remained important, but was balanced by a clear statement of the duty 'to relieve actual distress wherever it is found'. The Madras Code of 1905 struck a balance:

> It has been recognized as incumbent on the State to take steps to avert the loss of human life. . . . The object of state intervention is to save life and all other considerations should be subordinated to this. . . . At the same time it should be remembered that, though the State is bound to protect the people from starvation in times of distress, it is no part of its duty to maintain them at their normal level of comfort or to insure them against all suffering, and .hat its interference should impair as little as possible the traditional and family obligations of the social system of the country. (Madras Presidency, 1905: 1)

The government had now taken on a responsibility for effective relief to prevent starvation. It was determined that this should not imply a reciprocal *right* on the part of the population to be free from famine or comparable distress: relief was merely an administrative *duty*. The government (like its independent successors) also used a relatively narrow definition of famine, equating it with mass starvation and associated epidemic diseases. There was no duty to arrest the economic processes of impoverishment that led to famine or to overcome poverty and chronic malnutrition. Nonetheless, the anti-famine contract was in place.

Enforcing the contract
For 35 years, regular and relatively generous famine relief had the dual effects of dampening political agitation and creating a widespread belief that relief had become a civil right. When, in 1943, the government decided not to implement the Famine Codes during the Bengal famine, the anger among nationalists and their sympathizers was all the greater. Two main factors appear to have impeded an official response. One was that the famine was not related to any shortfall in food production (which confused administrators). The second was that fear of a Japanese invasion from Burma panicked the administration into preventing free movement of the fishing fleet and other water-borne transport. This not only halted movement of food by river and sea at a critical moment, but left a large section of the population without gainful employment. Traders panicked (and speculated) and withheld stocks from the market: the resulting price rise created famine virtually overnight.

The Bengal famine became a *cause célèbre* of the nationalist movement. It was a vindication of the Famine Commissioners' insight that effective famine prevention would be a brake on anti-British sentiment.

That sentiment was now unleashed with a vengeance. For the Viceroy's Council, allowing the famine was not only a crime, it was also a blunder. It caused the largest loss of life in British-ruled territory during the war years, and four years later India was independent.

With such a legacy, governments in independent India have had a strong motive to prevent famine. The post-colonial Scarcity Manuals embody essentially the same approach to famine prevention and amelioration as their predecessors, but with important innovations. One of these is the readiness to intervene in the grain market; others are public food distribution systems and employment guarantees. Thus they have moved from the prevention of starvation among the destitute towards the protection of basic entitlements. The Employment Guarantee scheme in Maharashtra is the most notable example of this: it provides an income from labouring for all who need it, whether or not there is a crisis.

The provisions of the Scarcity Manuals have frequently been implemented, most notably in 1966–7, 1971–3, 1979–80 and 1987–8. In all cases, they have prevented mortality arising from severe food shortages, although sometimes only by a narrow margin. But even a poor quality relief programme, such as in Bihar in 1966–7, prevented the descent to epidemic starvation. The 1970–3 drought relief response in Maharashtra stands as a model of effective famine prevention by utilizing the provisions of the Scarcity Manuals to the full. Over 5 million people obtained an income from relief works at the height of the drought (Drèze, 1990a: 89–90).

While food remains the most potentially explosive political issue, epidemic disease is not far behind. Malaria, smallpox, cholera and other diarrhoeal diseases were by far the major causes of famine mortality during imperial rule. Improvements in public health, spurred in part by political pressure, were instrumental in bringing these threats under control.

At the centre of this continuing success is the anti-famine political contract, still intact and strengthened and widened over time. The means of enforcement have changed: rather than nationalist agitation and imperial rulers' calculations of interest, mediated by Famine Commissions, there is now robust public debate.

India's independent press has played a key role. It has displayed a greater degree of sophistication in dealing with the issue of famine than any other media, including the Western press. At crucial moments, it has influenced the public mood and triggered governmental action, as described by the editor and journalist N. Ram (1990). In each of the main post-independence famine relief programmes, newspapers have distinguished themselves by determined investigation and critical analysis. Famine is an issue in a wide range of papers, ranging from the local vernacular press to the quasi-academic journal *Economic and*

Political Weekly. Hence coverage is not only thorough, but theoretically well-informed (better than in the British or North American press, for example).

The preparedness of the press to take up the issue of famine has meant that politicians and administrators are vigilant to the signs of distress, and rural people are ready to make public protests about their conditions. These are possible because India remains a liberal democracy, albeit a flawed one, with regular multi-party elections, so that any representative who has clearly failed to act on behalf of his or her constituents is in danger of being removed by the electorate, and also because trade unions, farmers' associations and other special interest groups can be organized to protest about impending famine. Famine is thus politicized: it is a key concern for ordinary people, and in a country where some basic political liberties can be enjoyed, this means that it is also a concern for politicians.

The competence of the Indian civil service remains an important element. The Scarcity Manuals are a system which professional administrators can take pride in implementing. A relief programme can be an opportunity for ambitious civil servants to prove their worth. The combination of concerned civil servants and self-interested politicians is powerful.

The greatest strength of the anti-famine contract lies in the recognition by the government, by other civil and political leaders and by the vulnerable people themselves that this political contract exists. With reference to the Maharashtra relief programme, Drèze writes:

> Direct public pressure on the part of the drought-affected populations also deserves emphatic mention. Employment for all was not only a clear instruction in the Bombay Scarcity Manual, it was also a *perceived right* which millions of poor men and (especially) women were determined to claim – if necessary by marching, picketing, and rioting. As one labourer aptly put it, 'they would let us die if they thought we would not make a noise about it'. (Drèze, 1990a: 92–3, emphasis in orginal)

The contract is not maintained by tradition or symbolism, but by power and interest. Famine is deterred.

It is important to note the narrowness of this political contract. The government is obliged to prevent famine, under the narrow definition of mass death due to epidemic failure of food consumption. It is not required or expected to prevent the wider process of impoverishment, and so does not help what Amrita Rangasami (1985) has called the 'famine process' itself. It has not overcome the marginalization of large sections of Indian society, who in all other respects remain without any form of political contract. Neither does the contract include the conquest of chronic malnutrition or other social ills such as female infanticide. Famine is a legitimate, even obligatory, subject for political advocacy, but these are not.

Other Asian comparisons

The operation of the Indian anti-famine contract presents human rights theory with an irony: liberal freedoms are operational in preventing famine precisely because those who take advantage of them espouse a basic economic right, namely freedom from famine. The above analysis has shown some of the complex history involved in establishing and maintaining the contract. Subsequent case studies will examine the different forms that such political contracts can take, and the threats that they face.

Bangladesh

The only post-independence famine in the subcontinent struck in Bangladesh in 1974. Given the political significance of the 1943 Bengal famine, a particularly strong political commitment to fighting famine might have been expected to be in place. It was not, and the reasons can be sought in the turbulent political history of East Bengal, later East Pakistan, and then from 1971 the independent state of Bangladesh, in the intervening decades.

In 1943, observers were struck by the fatalism with which destitute Bengalis faced famine. There were no riots, let alone insurrection. It was Indian nationalists who made the famine into a political scandal: their agenda was a secular state uniting the whole subcontinent. For the Muslim League, however, the overriding aim was achieving a separate state of East and West Pakistan; the famine operated less strongly in their idiom of legitimization. After 1947, the democratic institutions that enforced the anti-famine contract in India were much weaker in authoritarian Pakistan.

This weakness was compounded by the Bangladeshi war of independence in 1971, followed by a violent internal crisis. When the famine struck in 1974, the government of Sheikh Mujibar Rahman was nominally democratic, but was struggling to survive, and in January 1975 Mujibar abrogated the constitution and assumed presidential powers, banning all opposition. Bangladesh was also internationally isolated: in one of Henry Kissinger's cruellest decisions, the United States blocked food aid. Foreign-exchange reserves were rapidly running down. Floods, compounded by traders speculatively withholding grain from the market in anticipation of a shortage, caused sharp price rises and, almost immediately, famine (Ravallion, 1985; Osmani, 1991). Meanwhile, as in 1943, rural Bangladeshis suffered and died with scarcely a hint of political unrest (Currey, 1978). In these circumstances, the government's priority was its own survival.

The Public Food Distribution Scheme (PFDS) had the capacity to deliver food to famine-stricken people if the government chose either to deprive other recipients or to import more food. It was a highly effective rationing system and a major supplier of food to the populace. Its standard priorities were to the army and civil service; industrial workers, university students and school teachers; and other urban dwellers – an accurate reflection of the relative political power of the three groups. Food aid was also used as a reward for political support: 'the nationalist movement saw national independence as an opportunity to get a much larger share of the aid cake' (Sobhan, 1982: 6). Faced with a shortfall of food supplies into the PFDS, the government chose to maintain supplies to the priority beneficiaries in the urban areas and cut off the marginal rural people, and also not to use up its meagre foreign exchange on food imports.

Implicitly, the 1974 famine reflected triage on the part of a desperate government. Its priority was to placate politically significant urban constituencies, even at the cost of famine.

China

Comparisons between China and India are fascinating and often fruitful. The starting point for much of Amartya Sen's analysis of the political economy of hunger and famine is the contrast between the world's two largest nations.

Between the revolution and the end of the 1970s, communist China established an enviable record for the improvement of living standards among the rural poor. This achievement was marred, however, by one appalling episode: the famine of 1958–61, the largest in recorded history, and estimated to have claimed between 15 and 30 million lives. The genesis and progress of the famine are now well-documented, though they remain so extraordinary as to beggar belief (Kane, 1988). By far the most important cause was Chairman Mao's 'Great Leap Forward', coming on the heels of the collectivization of agriculture. Food production collapsed, but such was the loyal dedication of party cadres throughout the country that they universally proclaimed the programme a success. The government did not act to mitigate the famine, nor to provide famine relief, nor even to try to learn the lessons of the disaster afterwards. The government learned (belatedly) of the famine, when one of the most respected cadres, Peng Duhai, confronted Chairman Mao with his experiences following a visit to his home area; Mao listened, ignored the evidence, and then purged Peng. The very fact of the disaster was concealed for two decades and was only officially admitted in the 1980s.

Judged by official policy statements, the Chinese Government had a far deeper commitment to conquering hunger than any government in India. There was much evidence to support its claims. During their long guerrilla war, the Communists mobilized against famine in Yunan in 1942. In power, they achieved extraordinary increases in life expectancy and decreases in malnutrition. The weakness lay in the dictatorial political system and the absolute power of Chairman Mao. The commitment to the hungry was a *promise*, not a *contract*. Whether or not it was made in good faith, the promise could not be enforced.

Amartya Sen (1990) has described the Chinese famine as the greatest loss of life attributable to the absence of respect for civil and political liberties. This is correct: only in a dictatorship could the disastrous policies of the Great Leap Forward have been implemented unchallenged, and the subsequent disaster gone unrelieved. This particular famine would have been impossible in a political system allowing freedom of information and of association, but it does not follow that these liberties alone would have been enough to ensure protection from (other) famines.

The politics of famine theory

Fighting famine is both a technical and a political challenge. Effective prevention and relief measures require sound planning, implementation and assessment; the necessary skills include economics, demography, nutrition and epidemiology, as well as management and logistics. Academic theory plays an important role, both in determining the technical response to the political decision to combat famine, and in shaping the political discourse that can forge or deny an anti-famine political contract. For example, the narrow definition of 'famine' accepted by the British Raj and the Indian nationalists was rooted in Malthus's theory of famine.

The relationship between famine theory and practice is not straightforward. This is not surprising, as immediate political considerations often directly shape famine prevention and relief policies, but only indirectly influence famine theory, which develops according to its own (usually slower) rhythms. In addition, famine theory and practice have themselves become institutionalized, and exercise power through a range of specially created technical institutions and professions. This expertise can contribute to the conquest of famine, but its own autonomous exercise of power can also become an obstacle to the negotiation of anti-famine political contracts.

The Malthusian revolution
Before the last quarter of the eighteenth century and the writings of Adam Smith and Thomas Malthus, the distinction between famine theory and practice was barely meaningful.

Modern English anti-famine practice dates from the Elizabethan era, when the first systematic secular attempts were made to deal with the problems posed by poor and hungry people (Leonard, 1900). The 'Scarcity Book of Orders' (first issued in 1587) instructed local authorities to respond to the threat of famine by controlling the market in grain, providing work for the able-bodied unemployed, and giving free assistance to the 'deserving poor'. The Elizabethan Privy Council was less concerned with welfare as such than with the political unrest invariably associated with famine or food shortage: 'measures of organized relief were seen to be the most effectual method of repression [of disorder], and closer study of the subject resulted in greater care for the poor' (ibid.: 91). Its other main fear was epidemic disease transmitted by wandering vagrants.

Power was manifestly central to early English anti-famine measures. Two centuries later, a 'scientific' theory was broached which obscured this relationship, claiming to reduce famine to arithmetical laws that were beyond governmental control. It also had the advantage of blaming the starving for their plight. This was the population theory of Thomas Malthus, who in 1798 published *An Essay on the Principle of Population* (Malthus, 1926). Malthus identified famine as a shortfall in the supply of food in a given area and, simultaneously, the death by starvation[3] of a substantial proportion of the inhabitants. It was a bold theory of compelling logic. It was also wholly without empirical foundation, as Malthus himself was to discover when he belatedly began to research the topic, *after* having published the first edition of his famous work.

Malthus' theory must rank as one of the most monstrous intellectual aberrations of all time. On a purely academic level, Malthusian theory is itself disabled by a simple problem. There is a contradiction in Malthus' writing between his theory and the evidence he presented about actual famines (de Waal, 1989a: Ch. 1). He wrote, 'gigantic inevitable famine stalks in the rear, and with one mighty blow levels the population with the food of the world' (Malthus, 1926: 140). Famines simply do not kill enough people to fit his theoretical requirements (Watkins and Menken, 1985). As his *Essay* progressed through successive editions and the empirical evidence for (actual) famines increased, the prominence given to (theoretical) 'famine' declined. But the notion of 'gigantic inevitable famine' caught the popular imagination and became part of political discourse. The scientific pretensions of Malthusianism provided a charter for the government to abandon responsibility for the welfare of the poor, and to refuse to assume responsibility for famines in colonized countries such as Ireland and India.

Malthusianism went hand in hand with the liberal economics of Adam Smith. In *The Wealth of Nations*, published in 1776, Smith was concerned with the way in which governments had too readily succumbed to popular pressure to regulate the grain trade. Echoing Karl Polanyi's (1946) observation that market forces need the protection of a strong and intrusive state, Arnold has noted:

---

[3]The word 'starvation' was itself of recent coinage, first recorded in 1775 (Oxford English Dictionary).

Smith's economic reasoning was not without its political ironies. On the one hand, governments were sternly rebuked for meddling in the grain trade and for not allowing market forces to operate free from artificial constraint. But, stripped of its ancient role as 'victualler of last resort', the state was summoned back as policeman instead, for how else could the freedom of trade be guaranteed but by the presence of policemen and soldiers to prevent or discourage looting and seizures of grain? (Arnold, 1988: 110)

In short, Smithian political economy and Malthusian demographics were the ideological justification for the first industrial state tearing up a pre-existing social contract.

The English Industrial Revolution generated profound threats to the livelihoods of artisans. It was a period of widespread food riots, which were not only the result of increasing hardship but a response to a perceived abrogation of a pre-existing moral economy in which the wealthy and powerful had clear obligations to the poor. Resistance combined the idioms of food and power. An 1817 insurrection promising a 'provisional government' gained at least one follower who believed that it was to do with providing food (Thompson, 1980: 732) and 'bread or blood' was a slogan of rebellion in the 1830s. Malthusian precepts, together with Smithian political economy, provided an ideological legitimation for crushing such resistance and ignoring its social ethics.

As early as 1806, 'Malthusian doctrine had become as much an oral tradition as a written one' (Smith, 1951: 63). As a result, people contributed to the debate in ignorance of the nuances of Malthus' actual writings. One of these was Nassau Senior, who became infamous for allegedly saying that he 'feared the famine of 1848 in Ireland would not kill more than a million people, and that would scarcely be enough to do any good' (Woodham Smith, 1962: 375–6). Senior later 'confessed with penitence that he had trusted more to his ears than his eyes for a knowledge of Malthusian doctrine, and had written a learned criticism, not of the opinion of Mr Malthus, but of that which "the multitudes who have followed and the few who have endeavoured to oppose" Mr Malthus, have assumed to be his opinion' (Bonar, 1895: 3–4).

Whether based soundly on Malthus' writings or not, 'Malthusian' doctrines were adopted not just by 'the multitudes' – which in this context emphatically excludes those who might suffer from famine – but also by the British Government. This helped inform official policies towards Ireland in the 1840s, when a series of famines killed over a million people and forced many others to emigrate. The story of the Irish famine is complex and remains controversial, but there is little doubt that British political economy is implicated. Believing that unalterable economic forces were at work, which should on no account be interfered with, London provided very modest and belated relief and even allowed food to be exported from the island. The government may not have directly unleashed the famine, as some Irish nationalists subsequently claimed, but its smug and callous response fully deserved the moral revulsion heaped upon it. Its prophet, Thomas Malthus, should also shoulder the blame.

The Indian Famine Codes and the entitlement approach

The East India Company appointed Malthus as Professor of Political Economy at its college at Haileybury, and his doctrines became highly influential among the Britons who ruled India. But by the time of the 1880 Famine Commission, there had been a subtle shift away from doctrinaire Malthusianism. The Commissioners had surveyed enough empirical evidence to see that the simple version of the theory, at least, did not fit the reality. Having identified the famine-prone as chiefly agricultural labourers and rural artisans, the Commissioners wrote:

> As a general rule, there is an abundance of food procurable, even in the worst districts at the worst time; but when men who, at the best, merely live from hand to mouth, are deprived of their means of earning wages, they starve, not from the impossibility of getting food, but for want of the money to buy it. (Report of the Famine Commission, 1880: Appendix 1: 205)

Hence, at the heart of the Famine Codes was a commitment to employing the destitute and hungry. The theory of famine was changing, although only implicitly. The government congratulated itself on abolishing famine in its 'true meaning' of 'extreme and general scarcity of food', and instead claimed that ' "Famine" now means a prolonged period of unemployment, accompanied by dear food' (Fraser, 1911: 281). But, in the absence of an overarching theory to elaborate such an insight, Malthusian precepts were kept alive long after they should have died. For instance, the view that famine follows a collapse in food availability remained common (and contributed to complacency in Bengal in 1943).

Legitimation for the theory implicit in the Famine Codes came only in 1981, when Amartya Sen published *Poverty and Famines*. Sen's main immediate target was the still prevalent view that famine was caused by a decline in food availability within a certain area. His opening statement echoes the Famine Commissioners of a century earlier:

> Starvation is the characteristic of some people not *having* enough food to eat. It is not the characteristic of there not *being* enough food to eat. While the latter can be a cause of the former, it is but one of many possible causes. Whether and how starvation relates to food supply is a matter for factual investigation. (Sen, 1981: 1, emphasis in original)

Sen demonstrated that famines have occurred despite there being no shortfall of available food compared with previous, non-famine years.

Other years of decline in food availability have, conversely, not seen famine.

A second (and not explicit) rationale for *Poverty and Famines* was to protect the state intervention model of famine prevention that had been practised since the beginning of the century in India. Lacking academic legitimation, the practice was threatened by neo-liberal economic doctrines. So the missing overall theory was at last provided: Sen called his central concept 'entitlement'.

Sen uses the word 'entitlement' in purely economic terms, to refer to command over food. He rejects any normative connotations, contrasting his usage with Robert Nozick's 'entitlement theory' of justice: 'The two exercises are thus differently motivated and must not be confused with each other' (ibid.: 2, fn. 4). However, entitlement theory has often been presented in ways that would surprise its author. Sen's theory has become part of a wider discourse, and confusion with the lay meaning of 'entitlement' is one reason for its mystique and its attraction.

Instead, Sen's moral and political theory is found in his quite separate account of how civil and political rights protect from famine – the theory outlined at the start of this chapter. The separation of the technical/economic from the moral/political says much about the politics of famine theory. *Poverty and Famines* was commissioned by the International Labour Organization: it is a technical study for a specialist readership. By contrast, Sen has presented his political theory in non-specialist magazines.

Power and theory

Few economists' writings are as accessible as those of Amartya Sen, while even specialists struggle to understand some publications on the economics of famine. 'Famine' (and related subjects such as food policy, nutrition, early warning and emergency logistics) have become a subject for technical institutions and specialized professions. This is an immensely important development. Although its origins can be traced back to Malthus and Smith, the most spectacular growth of the 'citadel of expertise' (a phrase borrowed from Hewitt, 1983: 5) has taken place since the 1950s. The institutionalization and professionalization of fighting famine have slowly but radically changed the balance of power between those who suffer famine and those holding institutional power. The implications are a recurring theme throughout this book.

Academic theory can play different roles. It can legitimize and thereby protect successful practice; the way in which Sen's writings have done this is a case in point. By the same token, theory can also help fossilize practice and thereby impede innovation. Radical critics of Sen have pointed out that entitlement theory, like the Famine Codes, is concerned solely with the final, mass-death stage of the process of famine, and ignores the earlier processes of impoverishment (e.g. Rangasami, 1985). They argue that this carries regressive political implications: while mass death is scandalous, impoverishment itself is made somehow normal and unproblematic.

Theory reaches much wider than academia: there is a technocratic elite that dominates research, policy and practice to do with famine. Some theoreticians wield power directly as government advisers. Governments and international institutions employ an army of consultants to advise or assess policies. There is a revolving door between academia, consultancy and jobs in government and international agencies. Many members of the technocratic elite would describe themselves as 'practitioners' and decry theory and avow pragmatism. But such anti-theorism contains its own implicit theory, which is almost invariably the view that famine reflects an economic, managerial and logistical malfunctioning, and can be remedied by better economics, management and logistics.

The existence of a technocratic elite does not entail homogeneity or consensus. In India, specialist debate on famine is dominated by economists. In Africa, a range of technologies, such as early-warning systems based on satellite imagery and nutritional surveillance, play a more dominant role. There are often sharp differences of opinion, such as the disagreements among economists over the liberalization of food markets and among nutritionists and epidemiologists as to the relative roles of undernutrition and disease in causing mortality. But one universal tendency stands out: technical solutions are promoted at the expense of political ones. In evaluations, a caveat is sometimes inserted stating that politics lies beyond the scope of the study. In recommendations, lip service is paid to the need for 'political will'. These amount to formulaic dismissals: energy, money and prestige are devoted to the technical sphere. This is an insidious form of political theory.

Technical specialities are beyond the reach of most laypeople, including those who are at risk of famine. In turn, most technicians do not consider the views and experiences of ordinary famine-vulnerable people. Local information is considered only insofar as it is technically relevant. This approach carries the risk of undermining any existing anti-famine political contract.

The technocratic elite not only influences governments but has itself developed a mode of exercising power. The technical specialities become self-justifying, so that institutional priorities drive practice. There are examples of how the international agenda for food aid, development assistance and population policy is driven by the institutional needs of the specialist bureaucracies (Uvin, 1994). (Much of the second half of this book is concerned with a particular case of this, international humanitarian organizations.) These institutions are not themselves subject to any anti-famine political contracts; directors, professors and consultants do not lose their jobs if there are famines. On the contrary, the more frequent the famines, the more needed the specialists appear to be.

Some social anthropologists and Marxist political economists have tried to develop analyses of famine that avoid these traps. There is a vibrant little tradition of studying indigenous concepts of famine, and showing how these are subjective, normative and much more sensitive to local realities than the concepts deployed by Western economists. Some scholars have also criticized the role of academic theory as part of the exercise of power, both during the colonial era and in the context of institutional development aid. These remain dissenting views; their insights are generally incorporated only when they come up with specific 'practical' suggestions. Such exercises (and this book is one) generally wield little power: they may be persuasive but they change little.

The political role of famine theory as an instrument of power is less blatant now than in the nineteenth-century heyday of Malthusianism. On one occasion (entitlement theory), famine theory has proved (mildly) emancipatory. But there are no poor, famine-vulnerable Africans or Asians within the 'citadel of expertise' of famine theory: the institutions and professions are partly owned by governments and partly exercise their own autonomous, but self-serving, power.

2

Africa 1900–85

A Fragile Obligation to Famine Relief

Compared with South Asia, those who fight famine in Africa have blunt weapons. The quality of empirical evidence for mortality, for example, is far inferior in contemporary Africa than in India a century ago, and the theoretical analysis is similarly poorer. Most importantly, there have been few sustained political alliances founded on the fight against famine, and hence few anti-famine political contracts.

This chapter looks at the development of famine prevention and relief systems in Africa from about 1900 to 1984/5. This period saw a slow and very uneven improvement in the capacity of African institutions to fight famine, starting with the first reluctant attempts of colonial governments and reaching its height in the Botswana drought relief programme of 1982–4. Ironically, these systems in Africa were probably at their strongest on the eve of the notorious famines of 1984–5. In some places, at some moments, the idea of freedom from famine developed a right, promising the creation of an anti-famine political contract. On the whole, however, African anti-famine systems remained based on administrative obligation rather than hard-won political right. There is a cut-off in 1985, chosen somewhat arbitrarily as the historical moment when a conjunction of events threw this slow evolution in wholly different directions.

Colonial famine policies in Africa

The colonial powers did not introduce sophisticated anti-famine systems in Africa, because they were never compelled to do so. The history of famine policy reflects the exploitative nature of colonialism and its reliance on military power, and only towards the very end of the era and in some territories a sense of administrative responsibility towards colonial subjects. Meanwhile, African resistance rarely forged strategic anti-famine alliances.

In the first generation of colonialism, the conquerors often created famine. Early colonial warfare unashamedly employed extremely brutal methods. In his 1896 treatise *Small Wars – Their Principles and Practice*, Charles Callwell wrote

> [W]here there is no king to conquer, no capital to seize, no organized army to overthrow . . . the objective is not so easy to select. It is then that the regular troops are forced to resort to cattle lifting and village burning and that the war assumes an aspect which may shock the humanitarian. (Callwell, 1996: edn. 40)

Some peoples were subjugated with the intention of forcing them off land wanted for European plantations and farms. In Rhodesia in 1896, the South Africa Company deliberately destroyed grain stocks and prevented the rebellious Ndebele from harvesting, ultimately forcing them to surrender rather than face starvation (Iliffe, 1990: 23–4). In the Sudan, especially in the South, punitive patrols confiscated large herds of cattle and destroyed villages during two decades of intermittent but savage violence against the resisting pastoral peoples (Collins, 1971). In Tanganyika, the violent suppression of the Maji Maji rebellion caused serious famine in 1906–7, and the forced recruitment of porters for the military campaigns of World War I had a similar effect. Scorched-earth tactics by the retreating German army in Ruanda-Urundi also created famine in 1916–17. These depredations were mild compared with the savagery inflicted on the inhabitants of the Congo 'Free State' in the last decades of the nineteenth century, which caused a halving of the population in many areas and the shattering of an entire political tradition.

In the second colonial generation, some famine relief systems were implemented, but they remained elementary. This was for several reasons. Africa was not considered prone to famine and the techno- logical, transport and administrative infrastructure was not sufficient to support an Indian-style system. Most importantly, the political threats did not warrant expenditure on relief. African rebellions rarely presented a major military threat, and there was little chance of political embarrassment at home. Of all the colonial wars in Africa, only the Boer war caused a major outcry in Europe – undoubtedly because the victims of the first concentration camps were white. (The *Manchester Guardian*'s opposition to the 1896–8 reconquest of the Sudan was a minority cause.)

In Africa, the conquerors' Malthusian anxiety was chiefly focused on the supposedly reckless and destructive African farming and herding practices, rather than on impending famine itself. Colonial land-use policies and their political legacy will be examined below.

In 1913–14, following severe drought, there was widespread famine across the Sahel and Sudan. The colonial governments were unpre- pared. Further food crises in the immediate post-war years led to serious examination of famine relief proposals in Nigeria (Watts, 1983: 302) and the Anglo-Egyptian Sudan.

The Sudan Famine Regulations of 1920

For the British in Sudan, the first decades after their reconquest in 1898 felt precarious. Neo-Mahdism remained a real military threat well into the twentieth century, recalling the Mahdi's victories over British-led armies in the 1880s. The southern and western peoples resisted occupation fiercely, while Egyptian-fostered nationalism was a force in the cities and the North. Political fragility was compounded by the vulnerability of the Nile Valley to famine: agriculture relied on pumping water from the river and towns were dependent on imported food. Both the severe famine of 1913–14 and the food crisis of 1919 caused hardship, migration and unrest.

The British rulers responded by transplanting an Indian Famine Code to Sudan. Shortened and with extra measures to protect irrigation pumps and oxen, the Sudan Famine Regulations were promulgated in 1920 (de Waal, 1989b; Shepherd, 1988). But conditions in Sudan were very different from those in Madras (the model adopted). First, the civil service consisted of a tiny number of British administrators overseeing local chiefs: there was no capacity to carry out the demanding tasks of collecting information to establish an 'intelligence' system, let alone to administer the complex relief works envisaged.

A second set of problems was the generic difference between (most) South Asian famines and (most) African ones. In India, agricultural labourers and rural artisans could be rendered destitute and hungry overnight by a collapse in employment or a rise in prices. In Sudan, those at risk were largely rural farmers and herders, low in income but high in assets, and with access to a variety of sources of income and food, including wild foods. This meant that famines were less easy to predict, but also slower to develop, so that there was less of a premium on instant response. The lack of transport infrastructure and the absence of an integrated market in basic foodstuffs also meant that the deference of the regulations to classical economics was inappropriate; indeed it was quickly abandoned, as the first response of the administrators to scarcity was immediately to intervene in the grain market. As practised, the regulations were greatly pared down and gave enormous discretion to district officers. One revealing remark on the intelligence system runs: 'But it should be remembered that in the Sudan where the population is small and scattered it will be safer to rely on personal inspection of the people themselves than on any symptoms or tests' (Government of Sudan, 1920: para. 7).

The Famine Regulations were, in fact, primarily a response to a political threat, and served that purpose well. Their implementation reflected the political hierarchy of colonial Sudan. Government employees and townspeople were the highest priority for subsidized food; those in the riverain regions came next, while people living in remote regions were lucky if they received any assistance at all. Relief was ignored altogether when government finances were low.

Politics dictated relief. Immediately after food riots in Khartoum in 1926, cheap food was issued. In 1932, famine relief was used to help pacify the rebellious natives of Jebel Tullishi in the Nuba Mountains. A famine in the Funj (southern Blue Nile) in the same year caused political embarrassment because the local sheikh, Yusuf el Agab, bankrupted himself providing relief to hungry people on the understanding that the government would reimburse him, which it subsequently refused to do. Sheikh Yusuf was dismissed from his post, and fasted (Ramadhan style) in protest until he was reinstated. Egypt eagerly used the episode to curry favour among the Sudanese and cast the British administration in a bad light. The Famine Regulations were implemented in the drought of 1941–2, when there was a need for labour to build military airfields and roads. Large relief programmes were started in the drought of 1948–9, when the government feared that nationalist politicians in Khartoum and their Egyptian allies would exploit the famine for political leverage.

With larger and more frequent relief programmes and a different strategy on the part of the Sudanese political elite, an anti-famine political contract encompassing rural people might have emerged in Sudan. But early nationalist politics was too closely bound up with issues of national identity, internal sectarian divisions and tactics of playing off the British, Egyptians and Americans against each other to make anything other than opportunistic use of rural hardship.

Other colonial relief policies

British-ruled Tanganyika had an enlightened if elementary anti-famine policy. A primary duty of an administrative officer was to ensure that his district was fed: 'peasant food security was the linchpin of district policy, to ignore it was to commit gross negligence' (Bryceson, 1990: 69). This meant encouraging the cultivation of drought-resistant crops, building food stores and enforcing their use, restricting the export of foodcrops from the district, and if necessary importing food for sale at subsidized prices or general distribution in times of crop failure. In central Tanganyika, more than 100,000 people were in receipt of famine relief on three occasions in the years 1953–63 (Brooke, 1967). Such benevolence reflected the absence of countervailing political interests (such as European settlers or mine owners) and was a dramatic change from the period of German rule. But generosity was also rigidly circumscribed:

Peasantries were supposed to produce a surplus, not to cost money. A profusion of arguments were therefore developed to underplay the seriousness of famines and to try to show that they were caused by the irresponsibility and lack of foresight of peasants themselves. (Bantje, 1980: 15)

The duty to prevent famine was closer to an administrative ethic than a directive. Above all, there was never an intention to nurture a corresponding right to relief. However, over the decades, a government obligation to prevent hunger came to be recognized. Post-independence Members of Parliament in Tanzania are expected by their constituents to ensure that they are provided with emergency food.

In colonies dominated by European-owned farms and labour-hungry mines, colonial administrators had different priorities. In Rhodesia, both the mass expropriation of land and controls on grain marketing to benefit settler farmers had the effect of deepening rural misery and increasing vulnerability to famine in the 1930s and 1940s (Iliffe, 1990). Responses to scarcities became dominated by settler interests, and accordingly became simpler and less comprehensive. A programme of public works was implemented in response to the famine of 1922, before the development of a capitalist settler economy, but not in later famines. Employment opportunities in the wage-earning economy were seen as sufficient protection against famine.

The worst famine of the second colonial generation struck Rwanda in 1943–4 and killed an estimated 300,000 people. A major cause was the attempt of the wartime Belgian governor to make the administration economically self-sufficient. Cattle were requisitioned, food was compulsorily purchased at low prices, and (most seriously) forced labour was demanded for crops and projects such as road-building. These exactions continued unremittingly despite a blight on the 1943 harvest, and only modest amounts of food relief were imported very late in the day. Most of the responsibility for relief fell on the Catholic missions, which played a dominant social and political role, but they were neither able to provide for the huge numbers of needy people nor willing to pressurize the administration to halt the policies instrumental in creating the famine.

It is a testimony to the extraordinary obedience to authority that prevails in Rwanda that this calamity – on a scale without parallel in Africa at that time – led only to what missionaries described as 'a steady deterioration in the morale of the country' (Linden, 1977: 207). Many peasants emigrated to Uganda and others turned to banditry, but the cataclysm played no role in either nationalist mobilization or the political ideology of post-colonial Rwanda. The main political pressure for the reform of Belgian agricultural policies after the war came from fear of adverse publicity at the United Nations (which took over supervision of the Rwanda mandate from the League of Nations). The comparison with simultaneous events in Bengal is striking: famine relief had become a right in India, but not in Africa, where it remained at best an administrative obligation.

The case of urban food subsidies and related privileges is markedly different. Keeping the cities fed, especially with the growth of trade unionism and nationalist sentiment among the salaried classes, always remained a political imperative, and duly became perceived as a right. It is here that we find the strongest political contracts, and hence powerful explanations for the thrust of much colonial and post-colonial food policy. Different colonial administrations followed laissez-faire or interventionist policies, but the security of urban food consumption remained politically sacrosanct (Guyer, 1987). The fact that city dwellers have been immune from famine is a striking indication of the relative strengths of urban and rural political contracts.

Environmental and health policies and political mobilization

The politics of fighting famine in colonial Africa is complicated by the politics of land use and soil conservation. An exaggerated anxiety about environmental deterioration led colonial governors to impose more or less draconian regulations for preserving what was seen as a very fragile environment, and restraining what were regarded as reckless and damaging farming practices. This analysis suited the colonial powers well, as it justified their control of natural resources: for example, European companies could be awarded monopolistic control of forests on the grounds that their exploitation would be more 'rational' (see for example, Monson, 1996). Both the fact of the interference and the measures themselves were deeply resented, and resistance to them contributed to nationalist politics in no small measure.

A well documented case is that of the Usambara mountains of Tanganyika (Feierman, 1990). The British rulers saw erosion control not only as desirable in its own right but as a means of helping to maintain stable communities and prevent migration. Local resistance to erosion control focused on 'traditional' institutions such as rain-makers, rather than on the bureaucracy: it was silent and often politically invisible protest. This strategy enabled the resistance to survive, but also hampered the emergence of a strategic alliance between peasants and nationalist politicians.

Even when a broader alliance was forged – as in Malawi in 1949 – famine remained a problematic issue for nationalists.

> In so far as the famine brought about an increased intervention on the part of the Department of Agriculture in cultivation practices of ordinary people, so it can be said that it contributed to the

development of an effective nationalist movement in Malawi. Agricultural, and especially conservation, policies became the focuses of popular agitation and opposition throughout Malawi, and united strategically the educated elite with the mass of the rural population. (Vaughan, 1987: 153)

Conservation measures were even (astutely) interpreted as a 'punishment' for the famine by some peasants. After independence, President Hastings Banda repeatedly used the 1949 famine as a means to discredit his colonial predecessor, contrasting this with independent Malawi's good reputation for food security. But in fact Banda made few substantive changes to agricultural or land-use policy: it was a propaganda point only.

While epidemic disease has always been prominent in African famine mortality, the political salience of public health has been low – far lower than in India. Outside major towns, public health measures have rarely been a political priority. On the contrary, programmes to control diseases such as sleeping sickness and relapsing fever were implemented in an authoritarian manner (involving relocating whole communities by force) that undermined any popular support they might otherwise have had. Political and specialist debate on African famine remains almost wholly couched in terms of food and income rather than disease; even when famine is politicized, it is politicized in a very narrow manner.

Rural Africans had good reason to grow sceptical about the rhetoric of fighting famine. The fact that the most widespread and sustained 'anti-famine' policies were both ineffective and unpopular has had a profound legacy. These measures also discredited more effective anti-famine practices, such as forcing farmers to maintain food reserves. A political contract is founded on trust, and rural Africans have sound historical reasons for distrusting avowedly anti-famine initiatives that come from above.

Post-colonial welfare promises

No nationalist movement in Africa put the conquest of famine at the centre of its political programme. A host of other issues ranging from racial identity to civil service jobs were far more central to the legitimacy of newly independent governments. This reflected a number of factors, including the relative absence of mass civic mobilization of rural people and the troubled legacy of 'anti-famine' land-use controls. There was instead a *promise* of economic development and social welfare. This promise was undoubtedly sincere in many cases, but it was not enforceable.

Fortuitously, the first decade of independence saw no need for large-scale famine relief in most of Africa, apart from war-stricken Congo and

Biafra. Many countries abandoned whatever anti-famine systems they had inherited. The developmentalist promise, plus a healthy macro-economic environment and good weather, made it seem as though there was a short cut to a famine-free future.

Tanzania: fragile benevolence

The Tanzanian drought-relief system is typical of Africa. Independence came with 600,000 people receiving food relief, chiefly in the central regions. Relief programmes were seen as an interim measure, something of an embarrassment, that would soon be made redundant by rapid economic development. There is no doubt that President Julius Nyerere's government sincerely believed that rapid and equitable development lay within its grasp. The previous commitment to safe-guarding peasant food supply, which had provided a foundation for the rural economy, was abandoned. In its place came ambitious promises of social and economic transformation, while actual food policy was guided by the immediate commercial demands of the National Milling Corporation, which was given monopoly powers over marketing national grain production (Bryceson, 1980). Meanwhile a host of independent associations (notably the Ruvuma Development Association) were disbanded, as the state took over exclusive responsibility for service delivery.

In common with many African countries, Tanzania relearned the necessity of an anti-famine policy a decade later. In 1974, poor harvests coincided with high grain prices on the world market and the oil price shock. Tanzania faced a serious food crisis, and the national trade deficit doubled in a single year because of the need to import maize. Immediately afterwards, a national maize programme was started and long-term planning for a national food strategy resumed. This picked up where the colonial system had left off. It was based on the principle of district-level relief, given to all the residents of a district declared to be at risk of famine. This was founded on the assumption that if a district is stricken by drought, then about 90 per cent of the non-salary-earning population will be in need of assistance; the effort and delay involved in identifying the 10 per cent not needing assistance is not an economic proposition, and a general ration is therefore given. Lobbying by the local MP – seen as the patron of his constituents and under pressure to provide them with basic needs – became the key element in compelling local relief programmes to start. Even during Tanzania's era as a one-party system, seats were contested by different candidates, and a large proportion of MPs were voted out at elections. There was a modest system for enforcing local-level food security.

In parallel, a national-level technical early warning system was developed, funded by foreign aid and operated in conjunction with the UN. This collected and analysed monthly data from 400 field stations and the National Milling Corporation, passing it on to the crop monitoring and early warning system office, which in turn passed its summaries to the Ministry of Agriculture (Kashasha, 1989). This system has operated essentially unchanged for two decades. Its technical sophistication is offset by a major flaw: response cannot be enforced by the populace. The early warning information is not normally made public. This contributed to the system coming close to breakdown on at least one occasion. In 1981, the famine early warning system predicted that 170,000 tons of maize would have to be imported. This information was not passed on in the normal manner, possibly because senior officials hoped to profit from private food aid deals. National food stocks dwindled to two months' consumption, with 8 months to wait before the next harvest. The extent of the crisis only became known only when an expatriate in the early warning system office spoke to a foreign journalist, whose inquiries alerted the President. Famine was averted only when the Western donors responded quickly (Bryceson, 1990: 208–9).

Meanwhile, residents of Dar es Salaam, who had experienced periodic food supply crises over the years, had developed their own response mechanisms (such as widespread urban gardening and unofficial food marketing), which gave the government unexpected leeway (Bryceson, 1987: 188–91). Tanzania's 'alternative' informal economy provided a buffer for formal political and economic structures which would otherwise have descended even more deeply into crisis.

Radical transformations: the Horn of Africa
The main countries of the Horn of Africa illustrate the same themes as Tanzania, in far more extreme versions. In the mid-1970s all possessed, briefly, some of the most ambitious, participatory and professional anti-famine institutions on the continent. All have since suffered exceptionally severe famines (which will be taken up as case studies in later chapters).

In the mid-1970s revolutionary Ethiopia and socialist Somalia were briefly committed to radical social and economic transformation. They both set up anti-famine systems from scratch. Ethiopia's was prompted by the political scandal of the unrelieved 1973 famine in Wollo which helped to discredit Emperor Haile Selassie. As well as creating a specialist anti-famine institution (the Relief and Rehabilitation Commission), the government enacted some of the most radical social and economic reforms witnessed in Africa, aimed at consigning famine to oblivion. Somalia's involved mass participation; tens of thousands of young people who had been mobilized in a mass literacy campaign were employed in distributing relief. Many did so with enthusiasm, and at the end of the decade Somali refugee programmes benefited from a cadre of experienced and dedicated professionals. Sudan's government was less radical but it also pinned its legitimacy on the promise of development, through a professional bureaucracy. The country survived the 'Sahelian' drought of the 1970s without suffering famine and in 1975 also coped with an influx of Eritrean and Ethiopian refugees with meagre international aid.

These successes were all achieved in countries with minimal liberal-democratic credentials. Instead, there were commitments to national economic development and social welfare, to be achieved through the mobilization of technocratic zeal. The commitments may have come from unelected leaders, but they enjoyed genuine popularity and captured the energies of both educated citizens and rural dwellers. Relief institutions briefly reached a zenith in their popularity.

The welfare promises proved fragile. Authoritarian politics are partly to blame: all three national governments undermined their own relief institutions, and the famine-vulnerable populace could not protect them. Urban-centred political processes and institutions such as newspapers were too little concerned with rural poverty. The environmentalist orthodoxy remained largely unchallenged, ineffective in both meeting its stated aims and legitimizing heavy-handed government interference in rural society (Leach and Mearns, 1996). In retrospect the decline looks all too inevitable. But it is important to recall that these radical developmentalist or welfarist promises did bring tangible benefits: they actually prevented some famines. What could have made them more robust, to warrant being considered as a form of anti-famine political contract? The remainder of this chapter examines two case studies which illuminate the limits of accountability. The first – Kenya in the 1980s – is an example of an authoritarian government that knows exactly on whom its survival depends, and therefore selectively prevents famine. The second, Botswana, is a case of the most enduring anti-famine system on the continent.

Deterring famine in 1980s Kenya

Kenya is not popularly associated with famine or humanitarian relief. Famine prevention is neither a subject of popular debate nor a foundation for government legitimacy. This can be partly attributed to the government's success (at least until the mid-1980s, the concern of this section) in preventing a famine that might threaten its grip on power. This was not a matter of luck or favourable climate, because in 1984–5 Kenya faced a huge national food deficit. Its success in escaping famine was largely attributable to the political astuteness of President Daniel arap Moi, who recognized a rudimentary and implicit political contract: feed the central highlands and (most importantly) the cities, and the government will survive. Moi further turned the relief programme to his own advantage.

Meanwhile, many semi-nomadic pastoralists in the dry northern and north-eastern lowlands suffered chronic impoverishment and regular famine for decades. It suited the government to blame famine on aridity and backwardness – an account that does not stand up to even cursory scrutiny. The roots of famine in these areas lie in decades of political marginalization punctuated by violent repression.

The following account does not go beyond the mid-1980s; analysis of subsequent developments must await another occasion.

Relief and political survival in the highlands
From the beginning of the colonial era, inhabitants of all parts of Kenya were subjected to restrictions, exactions and abuses that left them highly vulnerable to famine. In the highlands, the mass expropriation of land for settler agriculture left farmers and pastoralists impoverished. Colonial land seizures created classes of landless labourers and 'squatters' on settler farms. These people were not only poor but deeply aggrieved by the historical injustice inflicted upon them, and played an important role in the 1950s Mau Mau insurrection that threatened the colonial state.

The British began to allow moves to independence only when Mau Mau had been defeated and the future of settler agriculture had been assured through the co-operation of the leaders of the Kenyan African National Union (KANU). Hence, the political dispensation at independence sundered the potential major coalition between the nationalist leaders and the rural poor. Many of the governing elites themselves joined the landowning class, perpetuating the same structural causes of rural poverty in the highlands. Palliative measures have failed to dampen the explosive potential of the land question. However, the delivery of some services, including 'development', was central to the legitimacy of Kenya's first President, Jomo Kenyatta. The institution of *Harambee* ('self-help development') was simultaneously a means of popular mobilization and a channel for political patronage. An emphasis on 'development' became a pretext for disallowing political pluralism.

The situation became more polarized after Daniel arap Moi took over the Presidency on Kenyatta's death in 1978. Moi lacked the nationalist credentials of the founding President. In the ethnic-political coalitions of the time, Moi's origins as a Tugen (a member of the 'Kalenjin' group) and a former leader of KANU's pre-independence rival, the Kenyan African Democratic Union (KADU), also denied him ready support among KANU's main ethnic power base of the Kikuyu of the central highlands, while also making him more acceptable to many non-Kikuyu. At first it seemed as though Moi could not succeed: a coup attempt in 1982 confirmed the President's sense of insecurity.

After the coup attempt, Moi embarked upon a mix of repression and measures to ensure that the central highlands remained politically quiescent. An extensive and expanding security apparatus was deployed, and the structures of political patronage were reshaped. Kenyatta's patrimonialism was hardened into a much more conformist and monolithic political culture, appropriately summed up in Moi's public call on members of his governments to 'sing like parrots'. Moi made KANU the sole legal party and began to develop it as a mass political movement. But mass membership did not entail mass solidarity; the party was used precisely to prevent the emergence of rural-urban or pan-ethnic coalitions.

Much of the legitimacy of the post-colonial Kenyan state has rested on the ability of those in power to deliver material benefits, especially 'development', to their constituents. Beginning in 1983, Moi began to reshape the structures used to deliver 'development'. The District Focus for Rural Development initiative set up new local-level 'developmental' institutions, notably the District Development Committees, which opened up new channels for government patronage. Provincial officials and politicians took control of *Harambees*, and forced contributions became a feature (Kanyinga, 1995: 71). Simultaneously, KANU, which had become virtually defunct as an organ for political mobilization, was reinvigorated and its membership massively expanded. Full-time officials such as district party chairmen were appointed for the first time. Alongside appointments and propaganda, various means such as preferential supply of basic goods were used to encourage or coerce people to join.

District administrators, who came to play a central role in Moi's structures of control, were expected to act like chiefs, dispensing patronage and safeguarding local food supplies. Acting as a super-patron, the government was expected to ensure that timely relief was supplied when necessary. The role of MPs as patrons for their constituents began to decay as Moi undermined parliament. In the 'snap' elections of 1983 many Kenyatta loyalists were removed. The independence of the judiciary was also undermined and the security forces, notably the Special Branch, became in effect the KANU security police.

In early 1984, highland Kenya suffered a severe though brief drought which resulted in a large national food deficit. Maize production fell from an average of 2.2 million tonnes to just 1.4 million, proportionally a greater fall than that in either Sudan or Ethiopia at the time. The government reacted with exceptional speed. Before the end of April, a harvest failure in the central highlands was evident. Although the formal report of the national early warning system was still two months in the future, the President's Office asked several government departments to prepare evaluations of the situation (Borton, 1989). In May, sales from the National Cereals and Produce Board (NCPB) were increased, and by the middle of June the government had inaugurated a National Famine Relief Fund (for private donations) and also made a comprehensive request for food assistance to international donors. The donors responded rapidly; they pledged in August (World Food Programme, 1989). But even earlier, in July, the government tendered for commercial imports of food, reversing the 1983 policy which had been to export surpluses. Free food reached 1.57 million people, most of them in Eastern Province.

Despite the speed of the international reaction, by September Kenya was close to running out of food, as food aid deliveries fell behind schedule. If it had been forced to rely on food aid alone, the country would have suffered famine. But of the 420,000 tonnes of cereals imported by January 1985, only 7 per cent was international food aid. The import programme prevented famine. The government took no risks and also prepared for the contingency that the 1985 rains would also fail. When the growing season was good, it was left with stocks of 200,000 tonnes of maize, much of which it had to re-export (at a loss) (Borton, 1989: 35–6). Internally, the government initiated a general ration in the worst drought-affected areas, employed 25,000 people in employment-creation projects, and restricted the internal movement of grain. It was a textbook case of how prompt government action could avert a major crisis.

It was also a textbook case of a government turning a crisis into an opportunity. Failure to respond would have provided a pretext for all manner of dissenting activism, from speeches in parliament (still with a vestigial potential to criticize) to food riots. The chains of patronage in KANU, the development structures and parliament might have been broken, and a legitimate idiom of dissent provided. Moi recognized this at once. He not only pre-empted the threat, but turned the relief programme to political advantage. Food aid became an important instrument of patronage in KANU's nationwide mobilization and Moi's reshaping of the patronage structures that underpinned his rule. Peter Gibbon, an astute analyst of Kenyan politics, summed up the ways in which Moi deftly turned the 1984 drought to his benefit (along with, to a lesser extent, its predecessor in 1979–80):

> The grain crises . . . were used as an excuse for appointing a large number of inefficient cooperatives in Luhya areas as agents for the NCPB, to the benefit of certain Luhya populist politicians. It was also used to break the power of the Kenya Farmers' Association, the main base of the politicians in the Rift Valley independent of Moi. It was thirdly used to consolidate the bases of Moi's 'home area' allies in Nandi by tripling the number of NCPB employees there and increasing farmgate prices to uneconomic levels. Finally, the cost of this predation was transferred to the coffee and dairy farmers in Kikuyu areas, who were forced to transfer the savings accounts of their cooperatives to the Cooperative Bank, which had run up large losses in covering the NCPB's grain purchases. (Gibbon, 1992a: 17)

In addition, the food crisis was a 'specious pretext' for indefinitely delaying the implementation of grain marketing reform (Mosley *et al.*, 1991: 290). Senior government officials benefited both politically and commercially from the monopolistic position of the NCPB, and were strenuously resisting pressure from the World Bank for a deregulation of agricultural marketing. Although a formal agreement to relax licensing controls on maize marketing had been reached in 1980, the drought provided the most powerful in a string of reasons for freezing reform. The NCPB remained one of the most powerful instruments of state patronage for a further decade (Ikiara *et al.*, 1995) and Kenya adopted a structural adjustment programme only in the 1990s. Famine in the highlands would also have raised the land question again, with smallholders challenging the entrenched privileges of white and elite Kenyan commercial farmers: this danger was pre-empted. In short, the crisis provided a major opportunity for the government to distribute favours to clients, while making actual and potential opponents bear the costs.

Like parliament, the Kenyan press played virtually no role in the relief response. There was very little reporting of the drought, and after the government appealed for assistance, local media reporting largely consisted of lauding government efforts and asking the public to contribute to the National Famine Relief Fund. The initiative for the food imports and relief programme came entirely from the highest political level.

Pauperization and State violence in the north and north-east
The story of famine in Kenya's north and north-eastern peripheries is radically different. In the space of a generation, the pastoralists of these areas have been reduced from prosperity to penury, even chronic famine. This is graphically described by the anthropologist Paul Baxter:

> A few years ago, I stayed in a village near the Uaso Nyiro River in Isiolo District, northern Kenya. The villagers, who were Oromo-speaking Boran and Sakuye, had until recently lived proudly and independently with their herds of cattle and camels and flocks of sheep and goats. In 1982, only a few fortunate ones still maintained themselves through stock pastoralism. Some 40 per cent of the Boran and Sakuye of the District had been driven to peri-urban shanty villages in the new administrative townships. There, they eked out a bare subsistence, hanging around the petrol stations for odd jobs, hawking for *miraa* (a mild stimulant better known as chat), making illicit alcohol, engaging in prostitution and the like. (Baxter, 1993: 143)

The current period is known colloquially as 'the time of stop'.

> I had worked in the same Uaso Nyiro River area in 1953. Then, the Boran and the Sakuye were well nourished and well clothed and, though a pastoral life is always physically demanding, people led a dignified and satisfying life. . . . They had clearly been prospering for some years. In 1940 the District Commissioner commented in his Handing Over Report: 'The Ewaso Boran have degenerated through wealth and soft living into an idle and cowardly set'. . . .

The people who some thirty years ago were probably the wealthiest and most productive pastoralists of the Horn are now among the poorest. (ibid.: 145–6)

Periods of hardship and famine are nothing new for pastoralists such as the Boran. However, Baxter stresses: 'What has been strikingly new and awful in recent years has been the *extent and duration* of famine, and the slow rate of recovery from them' (ibid.: 150, emphasis in original). This is a dramatic problem, for which the blame is conventionally attached to the weather and the environmental depredations of the pastoralists themselves. Failed aid projects are also the targets of much criticism. Baxter is dismissive: 'To blame sorcerers would be more logical' (ibid.: 152).

The explanation must be sought in political relations. Contemporary Kenyan pastoralism is shaped by violent and exploitative political relationships which have, if anything, intensified since the ending of European colonialism. At the very moment of independence, the out-going British and the incoming Kenyan Governments flouted any form of political contract with the ethnic Somali pastoralists and their neighbours. Since then, violence, human rights abuses and a range of social and economic restrictions have led to relentless impoverishment. It is a textbook case of a 'human rights violations' account of vulnerability to famine.

In 1963, Kenyan Somali community leaders made clear their overwhelming desire to join the Somali Republic. Jomo Kenyatta made the opposite demand, and Britain went back on its promise to honour the outcome of the vote. A guerrilla army then began an armed struggle: the so-called 'shifta war'. As the name 'shifta' (meaning bandit) itself indicates, the official view of the insurrection was that it was an outbreak of criminality, not a political movement. A State of Emergency was decreed and later augmented by further powers, which allowed the security forces to detain people without trial for up to 56 days, confiscate assets from entire communities in reprisal for acts of violence, and restrict freedom of assembly and movement. A 'prohibited zone' along the Somali border was created. The death penalty was made mandatory for unauthorized possession of firearms. Special courts without guarantees of due process of law were established. As a 'Special District', the north-east was subjected to even more far-reaching government powers, including the right to arrest, detain and move entire tribes, and alienate any land. The 1960s saw a military onslaught on the entire pastoral way of life. Vast numbers of animals were confiscated or slaughtered, partly in order to deny transport to the guerrillas, and much of the population was confined to a few population centres, where an underclass of destitutes developed. Many enterprising and educated Kenyan Somalis fled to Somalia. Some of those who remained turned to banditry.

The war, and more significantly, the repressive measures, ranged much wider than the ethnic Somali population. A large proportion of the Isiolo Boran was condemned to penury as a result of decades of 'pacification' (Hogg, 1985). During the 1963–7 war, the Kenyan army concentrated the Boran in three urban centres and prevented them from migrating freely. This led to stock losses and pauperization. Boran society was irretrievably altered. The wealthiest were able to prosper by diversifying into trade and farming. The poor, no longer able to survive as herders, were largely reduced to labouring for wages locally or in the Kenyan cities. Many others were still further reduced to dependence on relief, caught in poverty ratchets (Hogg, 1986). A similar story of deracination, sedentarization and dependency holds for nearby Samburu areas (Sperling, 1987).

In 1968 the Somali Republic abandoned its claims to north-east Kenya. But insurrection, brigandage and violent repression continued. Routine police and military operations, including a 'shoot to kill' policy aimed at suspected poachers, were punctuated by large-scale massacres. The worst single incident was in February 1984 when at least 2,000 people were killed at Wajir, chiefly at the town's airstrip. Sweeping powers over livestock and land remained, and government officials stated on more than one occasion that 'Nomadism will no longer be tolerated' (Survival International, no date: 13). Meanwhile, systematic discrimination against ethnic Somalis made it difficult for them to obtain urban employment. This reached its height in 1989 with the nationwide 'screening' of Somalis and the forcible deportation of all who did not have Kenyan identity cards in their possession, a category that included many Kenyan citizens. The State of Emergency was lifted only in November 1991, but military operations against alleged raiders from Somalia were then used as a pretext for continuing *de facto* military rule.

Elsewhere on Kenya's northern periphery, military repression was eased in the 1970s, but the cycle of pastoral impoverishment was then driven by continuing pressures, notably restriction on movement. In his study of the Rendille and Ariaal, Neal Sobiana (1988: 221) charts how migrations were gradually restricted over the decades, so that by 1980 herders were covering only a tiny fraction of the distances their fathers and grandfathers had travelled. The regulation of migration, fencing of rangeland and water development led to a tighter radius of movement and severe environmental damage within this circle. In turn, this has meant that herders are less able to respond to each successive drought, entailing higher and higher livestock losses, and ultimately the abandonment of pastoralism altogether. Sobiana concludes (1988: 239):

> As a result, famine relief has become a permanent subsistence mode for many in northern Kenya. With the ever-widening circles of desertification there exists an ever-increasing possibility that the once

self-sufficient herdsman and his family will become permanent welfare recipients.

Herd ownership is increasingly concentrated in the hands of absentee ranchers, townsmen and livestock traders. Absentee 'part-time pastoralists' with their different economic priorities have intensified the cycle of environmental decay (Little, 1985).

The threat of extreme government violence is ever-present and underpins the decay of pastoralism. Using the pretext that nomads are inherently warlike and beyond the civilized pale, the government has mounted occasional punitive expeditions. For example, in the Ilemi Triangle (annexed from S̆udan) in 1988, following the murder of fifteen policemen by Nyangatom raiders, the Kenyan army mounted colonial-style reprisals in which several hundred Toposa and Nyangatom were killed.[1]

Continuities between colonial and post-colonial policies are evident. The assumption of power by Daniel arap Moi, who is from a Rift Valley pastoral group, did not change this. (Developments since 1991 will not be discussed here.) The army chief of staff, General Mohamed Mahmoud, is a Kenyan Somali. The ascent to power of these men has seen more 'development' resources directed to some pastoral areas, but chiefly in the form of patronage to urban centres and agricultural projects, plus food aid. They did not change basic policy towards pastoralists; they were political opportunists rewarding their clients and securing their own power base, rather than displaying accountability to the needs of their constituents.

In this environment of extreme dislocation and chronic violence, even a small economic downturn can lead to widespread famine. This happened in 1979–80 and again in 1983–4. Famine relief, which was meagre and belated in many areas in 1980, had the minimum effect of preventing major mortality, but did not halt the relentless impoverishment. Even outside drought periods, chronic nutritional problems remain.

Implications
Understanding vulnerability to famine in Kenya means focusing on the contours of political accountability and the political strategy of President Moi. The Government of Kenya has avoided tackling the structural causes of poverty and vulnerability in both the highlands and the lowlands. A modest impulse towards accountability – namely the government's fear of civil unrest – mitigated the worst consequences of this neglect for the highlands in 1984–5, thereby escaping a potentially serious famine. The cities remained fed at all times. *Contra* Jean Drèze (1990b), this should be seen only as a rather superficial success, as

---

[1] Information collected by Lucy Hannan.

illustrated by the analysis of the north-east peripheries. Subsequent history, including the political reconfigurations of 1990–2 and the 'land clashes' of 1992–3, shows that no anti-famine political contract emerged, and that the government's political commitment to fighting famine weakened as circumstances changed.

Welfare and patronage in Botswana

Botswana is an anomaly in sub-Saharan Africa: a country that has enjoyed a functioning multi-party political system since independence, and a chronically food-deficit drought-stricken country that has consistently averted famine. Throughout the 1980s, Botswana's harvests were grossly inadequate compared to need, reaching a low of 13 per cent of requirements in 1984. (Sudan and Ethiopia both harvested about 80 per cent of normal harvests in that year.)

Botswana's enduring multi-party electoral system, the high levels of professionalism and accountability in its civil service and its success in famine prevention have been intimately linked. They provide a powerful illustration of how democratic accountability is at the centre of famine prevention. But the story is also more complex: it would be wrong to fall back on simple formulas that equate the institutions of liberal democracy with immunity from famine. Botswana's anti-famine political contract has been the most robust such system in Africa, anchored by political commitment, a sense of administrative obligation and accountability through participatory structures and electoral politics. It is made possible by wealth: Botswana is by far the richest of the countries considered in this book. But it is weakened by the absence of popular mobilization to assert rights.

The immediate origins of Botswana's anti-famine system lie in the government's response to a conventional and modestly successful drought relief programme in 1979–80. Child malnutrition and mortality rates rose slightly and much food aid was poorly used in blanket distributions. In an echo of nineteenth-century practice in India, the government commissioned an independent evaluation from the private consulting firm Gooch–MacDonald, which produced a painstaking and remarkably frank appraisal. The reports recommended the setting up of a famine-prevention system roughly along the lines of the Indian Scarcity Manuals (Gooch and MacDonald, 1981a and b). But similarities with India conceal an important difference: in Botswana there was no mass popular agitation, but instead a government with a sense of obligation and a shrewd sense of where its electoral interests lay.

Bureaucratic integrity is to be valued. Eleven reports were commissioned in all, and the government took the recommendations seriously and discussed them in public. In January 1982 it formally adopted a set of guidelines for a Drought Relief Programme (DRP) based closely on the

Gooch–MacDonald recommendations, and then opened another series of discussions on structures for their local implementation (Tabor, 1983). The reorganized and renamed Department of Food Resources was given an increased budget and increased responsibilities, and food and other forms of assistance were to be guaranteed to those in need as a matter of right.

> Most critical to allowing this growth process to go forward is that the Government sought frank, expert evaluations of the problems and then encouraged open public comment on the recommendations. The debate has given local officials opportunity to modify national policy proposals, and to respond to the grass-roots realities, e.g. income needs, training of staff and public opinion. (Holm and Morgan, 1985: 475)

A 'right' that is granted is less real than one that is won through popular struggle. But it is not a chimera. Members of Parliament and the elected Village Development Committees took their roles seriously. It was an example of the characteristically Botswanan process of consultation and consensus-making, not a case of adversarial vigilance. The electoral dominance of the Botswana Democratic Party (BDP) was never under threat and there was no opposition media to speak of (largely for commercial reasons). It was also patronage politics in the BDP's established tradition. Election years (e.g. 1974, 1979) normally saw generous rural development or relief programmes, decried by the BDP's critics as 'pork-barrel politics' (Otlhogile, 1991).

DRP, first phase 1982–4
When drought struck in 1982, and continued for six years, the government was prepared. Its commitment to drought relief was remarkable. Relief expenditure peaked at 15 per cent of total government development expenditure by 1984. Around 20 per cent of the rural working population was employed on the Labour-Based Relief Programme. While the results of the labour projects were of uneven value, their prime role in maintaining employment proved effective. Supplementary feeding programmes for children were also begun, reaching 45 per cent of the whole population. These proved an effective form of income transfer, blunting the impoverishing effect of the drought (Buchanan-Smith, 1990; Valentine, 1993). Thus, while the drought was both more severe and prolonged than that of 1979–80, the human suffering was far less. Malnutrition rates rose slightly, and then fell to levels better than before the drought. No increased mortality was reported, and infant and child death rates fell by over one-third between 1980 and 1984 (Jespersen, 1992: 44–5).

The DRP is arguably the greatest success of famine prevention in Africa. In the hands of its enthusiastic advocates it combined a professionalism matched only by the Indian relief systems with a strong political contract based on the government's obligation to provide the basic needs of the rural poor. More than 90 per cent of the finance for the programme came from the government's own revenues, though Botswana's high reputation with international donors means that it can make such expenditures confident that it can later recoup the money in foreign aid.

DRP, second phase 1984–9

The success of the DRP in preventing famine is a considerable achievement under any circumstances. But from 1984/5 onwards the DRP began to serve the demands of Botswana's commercial and bureaucratic elites, entrenched in power through the continued electoral dominance of the BDP, increasingly at the cost of the needs of those most vulnerable to famine. The priorities of the DRP became distorted, and by 1989 it was beginning to undermine protection against famine.

The electoral calculations behind the DRP became evident in the election year 1984 when relief expenditure rose by 145 per cent (Food Studies Group, 1990b: 8), and the Ministry of Finance had to resist proposals by the cabinet to spend even more. (The BDP duly won a handsome majority.)

After the election, the character of the DRP changed substantially. Until 1985 it had concentrated almost exclusively on 'human relief programmes'; thereafter the stress was on agricultural programmes. These were more expensive and economically regressive: the benefits were largely monopolized by commercial herders, tractor owners and other elites (Food Studies Group, 1990b: 16). Some relief measures were specifically aimed at protecting agricultural capital. One was writing off a number of agricultural loans taken out during the drought; only larger farmers had access to commercial credit, and they were the beneficiaries of this programme. A second measure was assistance to livestock to maintain herd sizes, which succeeded in preventing major cattle losses by the distribution of subsidized livestock feed, but was chiefly taken up by the larger herders. Vaccination programmes were more effective in reaching smaller herds, but even there some significant failures were admitted. Overall, large cattle herds suffered much lower mortality rates than smaller ones (Buchanan-Smith, 1990: 55). Jacqueline Solway, an anthropologist who worked with Kgalagadi in central Botswana over a seventeen-year period, noted the polarization of cattle ownership. In 1977, only 8.6 per cent of households in the area owned no cattle; by 1986 that rate had doubled (Solway, 1995: 478).

The major expenditure in the last years of the drought (and the two-year extension of the programme into the post-drought 'recovery' phase) was on the Accelerated Rainfed Arable Production Programme (ARAP) begun in 1985. This was scarcely an anti-famine measure at all, but rather a subsidy for rural elites. In contrast to normal practice in Botswana, it was designed in secret and announced over the radio without any prior consultation with the public or officials in the Ministry of Agriculture. Originally heralded as a single-year programme, it was in fact extended for four years, and spent well over half of the overall DRP annual expenditure (Food Studies Group, 1990a: 23). Three-quarters of ARAP expenditure was taken up by a 100 per cent ploughing subsidy to tractor owners, and most of it was taken by commercial contractors, who ploughed huge areas – far more than were ever properly cultivated (Buchanan-Smith, 1990: 53). The expansion of commercial tractor ownership was socially regressive; the ploughing subsidy was awarded to the individual in whose name the land was registered, thus overriding customary land tenure in which many relatives had claims on the land in favour of the single claim of the most prominent individual. The growth of tractor ploughing also obliterated similarly complicated customary arrangements over oxen ownership and loans of ox-plough teams from richer to poorer households. As a consequence, ox-ploughing by small farmers contracted sharply. In Solway's study area, 90 per cent ploughed in 1977, but – despite the subsidy programmes – that number had halved by 1986 (Solway, 1995: 480). Hence rural food production became highly polarized, with a few larger farmers harvesting large crops but many growing little or nothing. Lastly, in contrast to the usually high standards of public administration in Botswana, there was misappropriation of funds 'on a significant scale' in the ploughing subsidy programme (Buchanan-Smith, 1990: 54).

As before, the government commissioned an independent evaluation of its programme. The review, led by the Food Studies Group of Queen Elizabeth House, Oxford, was highly critical of the ARAP, but otherwise generally favourable. The very fact that it was commissioned at all indicates an enduring sense of government obligation for rural welfare.

> The emphasis on political accountability has meant that the abuses which have occurred elsewhere [in Africa] have been less likely to happen in Botswana. Examples of politicians attempting to interfere in implementation for their own ends are rare and well-controlled, even though the programmes themselves are often politically-motivated. (Wallis, 1990: 3)

The review concluded by recommending a 'fundamental reorientation' of the DRP. It proposed that famine prevention and agricultural programmes should be delinked, and that the government should address itself to lasting solutions to the economic vulnerability of the poorest.

The shortcomings of the second phase of the DRP were concealed by extraordinary economic growth. Between 1985 and 1990, Botswana's GDP grew at an astonishing 18 per cent per annum, up from 3 per cent in the first half of the decade. The increase is largely accounted for by diamond mining. The Food Studies Group review recommended that in future the DRP should be much more carefully targeted, especially if resources were to become more limited in future (Food Studies Group, 1990a: 17). The implication was that a less financially secure government would be unable to maintain such a wide array of relief programmes. This implies that Botswanans escaped famine in the later 1980s because of the prosperity of the exchequer rather than through the policies of the DRP itself.

Botswana's capacity to respond to this threat was quickly tested. In 1991–2, the country suffered a very severe, but short drought; which combined with a fall in income from diamonds, as world prices fell with the ending of the Cold War and unregulated mining in Angola. The self-regulation in the Botswanan political system, manifest in the independent 1990 review, largely worked. The ARAP, which had been stopped in 1990, was not restarted. The government had planned to switch agricultural support to credit for small farmers but, under strong pressure from large ranchers and farmers, adopted an untargeted ploughing subsidy as in previous years (Thompson, 1993: 32). In terms of human relief, the model of the early 1980s was adopted, but the government response was less speedy. There was an increase in malnutrition in early 1992, followed by a fall. The overall performance of the drought relief programme still compared well with that of other countries in southern Africa (ibid.).

Implications

Botswana's DRP is founded on its own version of an anti-famine political contract. Its strengths lie in the integrity of the public administration and the BDP's astute use of patronage and local institutions to ensure popular legitimacy while still pursuing policies aimed at enhancing the power and wealth of a commercial-governmental elite (Molutsi, 1991). Its weakness is the absence of mass political mobilization to enforce the government's commitment to relief: poor people still rely on structures of representation (Village Development Councils, general elections) in which they have little power to set the agenda. While the ARAP exacerbated economic inequalities, the human relief of the DRP enhanced state power *vis-à-vis* the rural poor, by gradually recasting patronage to focus power on state structures rather than customary networks. This was partly masked by the fact that the drought provided a convenient scapegoat for income inequalities and other social problems that were in fact caused by government policy.

More than a decade of generous drought relief possibly provides the foundation for an emerging anti-famine political contract in Botswana. But it is no more than a foundation: famine relief is hostage to a patrimonial style of government, albeit a relatively benevolent one. The profound differences in political culture between Botswana and India are as important as the superficial similarities between their technical famine relief systems and democratic institutions; we cannot assume that Indian 'solutions' can be transferred to Africa. The weaslth of Botswana also cautions against generalizing this solution to other countries on the continent.

The basic challenge for effective African anti-famine systems is: What safeguards are there to protect them? Botswana's experience in the early 1980s was the swan song of national famine-prevention systems. Ten years later, despite economic growth, governments capacity to resist famine was weaker. In Botswana as elsewhere, freedom from famine has not emerged as a political right.

3

**Retreat from
Accountability: I**

Neo-Liberalism
& Adjustment

The most important reason for the decay of famine-prevention and relief systems is governments' abuse of power. International influences have also contributed to the decline, not so much by weakening the capacity of a committed government to implement public policy as by influencing the nature of government itself – specifically, by encouraging authoritarianism rather than domestic accountability. One international development has been the imposition of the neo-liberal doctrines of structural adjustment programmes and a second has been the internationalization of emergency public welfare. The two are linked: they amounted to a change in the international moral economy which, abetted by internal political decay, undermined developmentalist or welfarist contracts (where such existed) and did nothing to foster their creation (where they did not).

This chapter considers some of the implications of neo-liberalism. It deals not with the mixed economic record of structural adjustment and stabilization policies, but rather with some their political implications. While every case is different, a general trend is evident: neo-liberalism did not promote democratic accountability, and in important ways helped to undermine it. The case of Zimbabwe is presented to illustrate some of the themes. Having largely escaped the drought of the 1980s, Zimbabwe was brought to the brink of major famine in 1992. The impact of internationalized humanitarianism will be examined in succeeding chapters.

Structural adjustment in Africa

From the late 1970s, advocates of neo-liberal economic doctrines gathered confidence, promoting first economic stabilization (i.e. austerity) plans and then structural adjustment programmes. This was the most important post-independence shift in the moral economy of African government; the redrawing of state responsibility has been

49

compared to the ideological transformations that accompanied the Industrial Revolution. There was an ideological onslaught on the notion of the state, under which poor and financially dependent governments had no option but to submit to the new orthodoxy. The 1976–92 period saw widespread urban protests: popular anger was directed as much at the withdrawal of what were seen as political entitlements as against austerity itself (Walton and Seddon, 1994). Rural people rarely protested; they were less well mobilized and their political entitlements were weaker.

Although some of its theoretical economic precepts have proved remarkably durable, neo-liberalism has not been homogeneous in practice, and has (modestly and belatedly) adapted to African realities. It moved through various manifestations and political colours. Its association with political liberalization arrived late, and may have departed early.

By the late 1970s, African economies needed major reform in order to survive – and in order to achieve better protection from famine. Some form of adjustment was imperative. The first phase of neo-liberal reform was a mixture of *ad hoc* responses to the specific financial difficulties of particular governments, rapidly evolving into more comprehensive programmes recommended across the continent. The World Bank's 1981 report, *Accelerated Development in Sub-Saharan Africa: An Agenda for Action*, is representative of this period. It identified major structural problems common to African development policies, such as 'urban bias' in economic (including food) policy and grossly inefficient public service delivery.

Urban bias was real. A recurring theme of this book is how urban groups in Africa have established strong political contracts (enduring through both colonial and nationalist dispensations) that have protected their food entitlements. Often this has been at the expense of rural political contracts. There has been little political pressure to protect rural people from famine, and small farmers have received below-market prices for their crops. The most consistent economic benefit of structural adjustment programmes is that farmers have, often for the first time, achieved fair prices for their produce. Some technically proficient drought contingency planning systems have also been set up. But without rural political contracts to create an imperative to make them work properly, they are not sufficient to ensure protection from famine.

The problem of structural adjustment was that it addressed the economic symptoms of urban bias and not its political causes. Urban bias arose from urban-centred political contracts, and was best over-come by political processes that forged rural contracts as well. Instead, the political corollary of economic reform was simply to dismantle urban entitlements.

The provision of public services had often become a channel for patronage and abuse of state power. Amongst other things, as the cases of Kenya and Botswana illustrate, this left anti-famine measures vulnerable to manipulation by those in power. Again, the proposed solutions were narrowly economic: austerity and privatization. In principle, privatization need not have been politically regressive, provided that any regulatory authorities were sufficiently accountable to the people. In practice, the neo-liberals' overriding concern was with pushing and cajoling governments into taking resolute and unpopular measures.

In the early days, the World Bank openly leaned towards authoritarian government. Its 1981 report speaks coyly of 'special constraints' that may impede reform, by which it means the political imperatives of governments to respond to influential interest groups, which may, for example, defend urban food or housing subsidies. In the long term, the neo-liberals argued, reform was in everyone's interest, but in the short term some powerful groups stood to lose. In a much-quoted phrase, Deepak Lal wrote: 'A courageous, ruthless and perhaps undemocratic government is required to ride roughshod over these newly-created special interest groups' (quoted in Toye, 1992: 109). The transitional process of abrogating existing urban political contracts made governments less accountable, and the absence of a countervailing process of establishing a wider political contract tended to create more remote and arbitrary rule.

First attempts
First results varied. In the late 1970s and early 1980s, the World Bank and the International Monetary Fund had considerable difficulty in persuading African governments to adopt these measures. Some, like Tanzania, were adamantly opposed to the austerity measures that were entailed. With the Cold War at its second peak, the strategic interests of the United States constrained the extent to which austerity packages were imposed. The US State Department knew perfectly well that it would endanger its political clients if it compelled them to cut back social expenditure too far or insisted on unrestricted access for humanitarian organizations. Hence, for the major US clients (Sudan, Zaire, Liberia), strategic concerns dictated generosity while economics dictated firmness and austerity; governments quickly found that there was an ambiguous space that could be exploited, and that failure to implement the policy conditionalities need not lead to financial sanctions. Another constraint was the limited capacity of some major international institutions to reorient their policies. For example, the food aid lobby in the United States continued to exercise considerable influence, on occasions simultaneously contradicting both strategic policy and neo-liberal doctrine (Uvin, 1994).

What did this stage of neo-liberalism mean for protection against famine? Theoretically, neo-liberalism has affinities with social Darwinism, with the implication that the weak fail (i.e. starve) (cf. Archer, 1994: 29). The implementation of neo-liberal policies coincided with drought in many countries and famine in several. But in none of the specific cases examined in this book is it possible to point to a simple relationship in which structural adjustment contributed directly either to food crises or to the incapacity of governments to respond. Only in Sudan is there the full combination of structural adjustment, the privatization of social welfare, and famine. To some extent the opposite occurred: drought impeded structural adjustment. In Kenya, food shortage was used as a pretext for delaying the deregulation of food marketing.

The African food crisis of 1984–5 and the widespread failure of the first generation of adjustment policies led to some revisions to the neo-liberal project in Africa. Two initiatives stand out. One was a critique by UNICEF leading to the proposal of 'adjustment with a human face' (Cornia *et al.*, 1987). The second was the adoption and formalization of the 'food security approach' by the World Bank (1986).

'Adjustment with a human face'
The UNICEF proposal of 'adjustment with a human face' was both a critique and an attempt to sugar the neo-liberal pill. UNICEF was modest and realistic in the concessions it hoped to extract from the World Bank and the IMF, and it was moderately successful in influencing policy. Frances Stewart, one of the authors of the UNICEF report, describes the impact:

> Since 1987, the World Bank's staff guidelines have required Policy Framework Papers for low-income countries to include 'a brief description and assessment ... of the social impact of the government's intended adjustment program', and all President's Reports supporting structural adjustment to pay particular attention to 'the short-term impact of the adjustment program on the urban and rural poor, and measures proposed to alleviate negative effects'. (Stewart, 1995: 7)

Much of the energy of international institutions over the following years was dedicated to building programmes to cushion the blows of stabilization and adjustment. Typically this took the form of a social fund, intended either as a very basic form of social welfare, or as a compensation package for those who lose out, for example from job cuts in the state sector. The latter, the 'new poor', have a greater political significance, while the chronic or 'old poor' may face greater overall hardship. Some social funds have been pre-existing programmes, such as Botswana's Drought Relief Programme, while others have been specially designed as part of the adjustment package. A review has found that pre-existing, nationally designed programmes have generally been more effective at reaching both the 'old' and the 'new' poor than specially designed programmes (ibid.: 126–7).

Many international NGOs joined in the criticism of structural adjustment. They have been bolder but less influential than UNICEF (e.g. Oxfam, 1995). They have rarely presented a coherent alternative economic course that could be taken by pre-adjustment states in crisis. This, however, is not the NGOs' major role; the combination of neo-liberalism and advocacy of a 'human face' has created a new role for international NGOs as subcontractors in the large-scale delivery of basic services such as health, agricultural extension and food rations. They have found both an institutional opportunity and an ideological opening. Often, the larger service-delivery NGOs (CARE, Catholic Relief Services, Save the Children Fund) have been drawn in when there has been a crisis such as famine or institutional collapse, and have stayed on afterwards. In other cases, NGOs have placed advisers in ministries (health is the favourite) and occasionally have even taken over responsibility for entire services. The entire basic drug supply for clinics in the capital of Sudan, primary health care in rural Uganda and almost all TB and leprosy programmes in Tanzania are just three of the 'national' health programmes largely directed by international NGOs using funds from Euro-American institutional donors.

Michael Camdessus, Managing Director of the IMF, defended his policies before the UN Social and Economic Council on 11 July 1990:

> The [Fund] programs involve, first and foremost, macroeconomic discipline, beginning with the reductions of fiscal deficits and monetary measures aimed at achieving price stability and realistic exchange rates . . . . Let me say outright: these policies serve the poor, and we must do our utmost to implement them if we are to be efficient in the fight against poverty. (quoted in Stewart, 1995: 213–14)

An overview of the record in Africa suggests that both adjusting and non-adjusting countries have suffered an increase in poverty. Factors such as debt, the international terms of trade, and internal political crises all played their role. The criticism of the World Bank and the IMF is less that their policies intensified poverty, but rather that, contrary to their claims, they failed to prevent this deterioration. In fact, in their attachment to doctrine and their unwillingness to face up to empirical complexities, especially before 1987, the IMF and the World Bank deliberately ignored evidence of increasing poverty in adjusting countries. This was partly motivated by the hope that adjustment would be vindicated in the longer term, and that a premature admission of problems would be counterproductive: adjusting governments merely needed to keep their nerve under pressure. This attitude has three main ramifications. One, it has parallels in the way in which the international financial institutions ignored the political consequences of adjustment; they must bear some responsibility for these too. Two, it delayed responses to deepening social problems and made it harder to deal with poverty. Three, it also encouraged a similar mind-set in governments implementing adjustment policies, which, in the case of Zimbabwe at least, was nearly to have disastrous consequences (see below).

This failure relates to the main shortcoming of the UNICEF critique of structural adjustment: it focuses on the social and economic dimensions and excludes the political. Structural adjustment involved a tremendous reconfiguring of political power and responsibility.

The food security approach

The concept of 'food security' was propagated from within one of the central institutions of the neo-liberal hegemony: the World Bank. This is no aberration: the following discussion will elucidate why the 'food security approach' is less than the sum of its parts. It has reinforced the trends towards treating famine as a technical economic issue rather than a political one.

The stimulus to the 'food security approach' was a general awareness that fighting famine required a broader range of policy tools than those implicit in Amartya Sen's entitlement approach, together with a recognition that food policy was sufficiently politically sensitive to require special attention in economic policy. Food security touches on a wide range of policy issues ranging from structural adjustment and growth, through agricultural policies, marketing structures, national food buffer stocks, and food aid to emergency relief. In some of these areas, there have been important specific successes.

The food security approach cannot be called a 'theory'. This was deliberate: it was an attempt to keep the debate on famine prevention in the non-political arena of public policy. Flexibility rules: ' "Food security" is one of those terms – "rural development" and "farming systems research" are others – which authors feel obliged to define or redefine at frequent intervals' (Maxwell, 1990: 2). Simon Maxwell has written (ibid.: 6) that, 'It might be expected that the agency views would reflect different ideological positions, but in fact this is not the case. . . . Indeed this retreat from ideology into contingency theory [sic] is itself an important theme of the 1990s'. In fact, the 'retreat from ideology' is more apparent than real. Technicians can bend the food security approach to many ends, but only within the dominant neo-liberal paradigm. This obscures the contradiction between the neo-liberal enterprise and the historical fact that effective action against famine has always been achieved by interventionist social and economic programmes.

The food security approach makes solely technical recommendations. It is a regression from Sen's entitlement approach in two respects. One, and most importantly, there is no corresponding political theory of famine prevention, or even a recognition of the political requirements for fighting famine. Two, it is designed to make problems amenable to the policy-maker with whatever policy tools are available, rather than focusing on the basic problems themselves. The food security approach equates famine with extreme 'transitory food insecurity', yielding an exceptionally narrow and depoliticized definition of famine as 'epidemic undernutrition'. This contradicts the direction of field research on famine in Africa, which without exception emphasizes that famine is a broad social, economic and political phenomenon, with undernutrition as only one component among many, and rarely the most important component. (Concepts of health and livelihood security have since emerged in response to this shortcoming.)

Overall, the food security approach did not serve to legitimate good anti-famine practice. Some useful specific policies and programmes have been introduced, but within the context of wider political failures.

Governance and civil society

A third phase in neo-liberal doctrine in Africa became apparent at the end of the 1980s, when theorists began to move into more political waters. This reflected a growing readiness to criticize African governments' political records. It was also necessary to find a culprit for the failure of nearly a decade's attempts at adjustment in many countries. This shift was manifest in the World Bank's 1989 report *Sub-Saharan Africa: From Crisis to Sustainable Growth*. The Bank now spoke of a 'crisis of governance'. The use of the term 'governance' was an attempt to avoid making the political critique too explicit, and to enable a focus on certain specific technical aspects of government. The World Bank notion of governance was a legal and administrative order that facilitated private investment:

> Underlying the litany of Africa's development problems is a crisis of governance. Because countervailing power has been lacking, state officials in many countries have served their own interests without fear of being called to account. In self-defence individuals have built up personal networks of influence rather than hold the all-powerful state accountable for its systematic failures. In this way politics becomes personalised and patronage becomes essential to maintain power. The leadership assumes broad discretionary authority and loses its legitimacy. Information is controlled and voluntary associations are co-opted or disbanded. This environment cannot support a dynamic economy. (World Bank, 1989: 60–1)

Similar economic concerns underpinned its concept of 'civil society', which was envisaged as an entrepreneurial force waiting to be unleashed when the powers of the state were curtailed. 'Good governance' certainly provides a more humane gloss on the austerities of neo-liberalism. But critics have argued:

> Concepts like participation and mobilisation are ambiguous. They have a political-democratic side and a managerial one. The latter dominates the [1989] World Bank report. The emphasis is on

'releasing' and 'tapping' local energies and capacities. The concern is less with popular power, in a political sense, than with ensuring that development programmes are better attuned to local demands. . . . The primary concern is with development, not democracy. (Beckman, 1992: 91–2)

The World Bank's 1989 report appears to conflate the separate notions of the informal economic sector and 'civil society', overlooking, *inter alia*, the fact that in African countries the most vibrant elements of 'civil society' are to be found associated with the formal sector: trade unions, professional associations, academics and the like.

While the agenda of the international financial institutions (IFIs) was largely economic and managerial, the ideas they were pushing already had a life of their own. The Realpolitik of adjustment was centred on building internal coalitions that could protect economic reform (hence the importance of social funds to assist the 'new poor'). But notions of democracy, human rights and civil society had a wide currency throughout Africa, and those pressing for political liberalization saw the new discourse of 'governance' as providing potential tactical allies abroad. Some of the coalitions that emerged were, for the international financiers, unexpected. In Zambia, it was a trade unionist who rode the wave of democratization to victory.

Pressures for 'democratization' in Africa were enormously increased by the events of 1989 in Eastern Europe, culminating in the fall of Ceaucescu in Romania. In June and July 1990, the French and British Governments both made bold statements on democracy in Africa, explicitly tying continued aid to moves towards multi-party elections, civil liberties and respect for human rights. The World Bank's cautious and managerial use of words like 'governance' had been overtaken by Western leaders, who were far more political if rather less precise in their usage, introducing elements like multi-party elections.

The co-option of the concept of 'governance' by the donors presented several problems to the World Bank and the IMF (Gibbon, 1992b: 142–3). The first was a reduction in the autonomy of the IFIs *vis-à-vis* donor governments: they were becoming instruments of donors' own conditionality. Secondly, promoting political liberalism was a reversal of the IFIs' preference for authoritarian governments: at the very least, democracy was seen to 'slow things down'. Thirdly, political conditions are harder to define and monitor than economic ones. The donors were characteristically ambiguous in specifying exactly what the political conditionalities actually were, not least because they applied them inconsistently. Kenya, for example, was an exception to the British demand for multi-partyism for more than a year. Finally, the IFIs had a fear of 'conditionality overloading'. Imposing too many conditions might force default. Some of these fears were to prove well-founded. Encouraging democracy and then insisting that economic policy remained outside the domain of democratic decision-making was a recipe for tension, frustration and ultimately disillusionment.

The currency of 'governance' and 'democratization' in the early 1990s held out promise of protection from famine through respect for civil rights. This was over-optimistic. The principal beneficiaries of political liberalization were well-connected urban interest groups. For complex reasons that cannot be detailed here, most democracy movements and all human rights organizations failed to build a mass base of support, especially in rural areas. Their focus was too much on 'mobilizing shame'[1] among professional classes and the international community, and too little on mobilizing ordinary people in support of their own basic rights. Mobilization of people vulnerable to famine – such as poor farmers and pastoralists – around the issue of famine was conspicuously absent. (The case of Sudan, in Chapter 5, illustrates some of these themes.) The 'democracy wave' did not build new inclusive political contracts, and may indeed have intensified the urban bias of politics.

Implications
The single most consistent political impact of neo-liberalism in the 1980s and early 1990s was to introduce an unprecedented degree of involvement in African economic planning by the international financial institutions. In order to 'free' African economies, the IFIs had to institute more comprehensive negotiations, more extensive studies of policy, more intrusive monitoring: in short, more external controls. African governments became, simply through the routines of dealing with the IFIs, more externally accountable than ever before. Ironically, neo-liberalism justified a new interventionism. In turn, implementing the new economic policies required national governments to be resolute to the point of authoritarianism, even when newly elected by popular vote.

Accountability, adjustment and famine prevention in Zimbabwe

One casualty of neo-liberal economics and creeping authoritarianism was the famine-prevention system in Zimbabwe, which had been held up as a model, alongside Botswana, during most of the 1980s (Drèze, 1990b). In 1991/2 Zimbabwe suffered severe drought and very narrowly escaped unprecedented nationwide famine. Left-leaning commentators have put the blame squarely on the structural adjustment programme implemented from 1990 onwards under the guidance of the IMF and the World Bank. Apologists for the IFIs have argued that the policy was not incorrect and that the errors lay with the Zimbabwean Government's

---

[1]The phrase is from Aryeh Neier, former Director of Human Rights Watch.

implementation, plus a dose of bad luck in the shape of an exceptionally severe drought at exactly the wrong moment. This section argues that both the IFIs and the government contributed to undermining a commitment to fighting famine.

Liberation and democratic accountability
In contrast to the other case studies so far presented, the Government of Zimbabwe achieved power after a long liberation war. Food was a weapon in Rhodesian counter-insurgency, which involved forcible relocation of the rural populace in protected villages and 'Operation Turkey' which restricted rural food supplies and created widespread hunger on the eve of independence. According to nationalist mythology, the guerrilla struggle (especially the Zimbabwean African National Union, ZANU) relied on intimate inter-reliance between the liberation front and the people. Popular mobilization was achieved by articulating social and economic grievances such as land alienation and racial discrimination in employment, by condemning Rhodesian abuses during the war, and by the front's own respect for ordinary people. This would imply a strong political contract. But two factors complicate the picture. One is that the front used the support of traditional spirit mediums to gain legitimacy – an idiom of power as alien to the style of post-liberation government as to colonial and minority rule. Secondly, popular participation was never as widespread or as voluntary as was claimed, and the liberation front used a fair measure of coercion and violence. Structures for popular representation were weak, while internal party discipline subdued dissent.

Hence, at liberation in 1980, the new government of President Robert Mugabe achieved power with a strong commitment to several radical agendas, but weak structures for enforcing adherence to them. A massive improvement in health and education services was promised, and much of it delivered. Some of the structural inequities in the agricultural marketing system were removed, notably opening up the Grain Marketing Board (GMB) to communal (i.e. African) farmers: its registered producers increased from 30,000 to over 570,000 in the 1980s, while its storage capacity more than doubled. Land redistribution, one of the main hopes for the liberation, did not occur: one of the compromises conceded by ZANU in the Lancaster House agreement was not to confiscate white-owned lands. Another betrayal of hopes was the treatment of war veterans: few of them have been provided with the rehabilitation, employment or assistance they expected.

Just two years after liberation, the country suffered drought. Because Zimbabwe is structurally a grain-surplus country, the drought response was radically different from that of neighbouring Botswana: it was primarily aimed at ironing out variability in the food supply, rather than maintaining rural incomes. In 1982–3, this strategy succeeded well in most areas (Bratton, 1987; Drèze, 1990b). Rural distribution was organized by ZANU's local chairmen, and relief was given to all those earning less than the statutory minimum wage. One study (Leys, 1986: 270, 272) was impressed by the fairness of the distribution at village level. Between 1980 and 1984, infant and child death rates fell by about one-quarter (Jespersen, 1992: 44–5). In September 1984, the Ministry of Finance introduced a temporary Drought Relief Levy on income tax and corporation tax, aiming to finance any future relief measures without recourse to foreign aid. Over half of the target was raised, and was used for relief programmes in the (milder) drought of 1987.[2]

These successes were well publicized. Total official silence surrounded the famine in Matabeleland. Much of Matabeleland suffered harvest failures in 1982 and 1983, coinciding with a deepening political schism between ZANU and the Zimbabwean African People's Union (ZAPU) which descended into civil war. In 1983 the Fifth Brigade was deployed, killing at least 1,500 people and terrorizing the entire Ndebele community. By early 1984 with a third harvest failure, drought relief became the major source of food for much of the population. In its 1984 campaign, as well as killing at least a hundred people, the Fifth Brigade exploited this dependence. Later investigators found 'the use . . . of food as a weapon of coercion', (Lawyers Committee for Human Rights, 1986: 136–8) similar to the Rhodesians' Operation Turkey. A curfew and blockade were imposed across rural Matabeleland, lasting three months. All food supply channels were either blocked or closely controlled by soldiers, including: government granaries (the sole conduit for relief supplies); commercial food transport; gifts of food to relatives; and food sales from shops. When relief was distributed, recipients were not allowed to take any rations away, but had to eat their meals under army supervision. These measures, when combined with restrictions on movement, added up to a sentence of starvation. Many people were reportedly reduced to eating wild foods.

The Matabeleland famine has never been systematically investigated. One researcher concluded that investigating 'political entitlement' to food in Matabeleland 'might be politically unwise' (Leys, 1986: 271–2). But the political outlines are clear. The militarized use of food in Matabeleland was the counterpart of the free relief distributions via the ruling ZANU in other parts of the country; both were an extension of the power of party and state over the sustenance of rural Zimbabweans. (ZANU again used food in this way in the mid-1990s: there are well-documented allegations that the government manipulated drought relief for electoral advantage.[3])

The divide between ZANU and ZAPU was resolved in 1987 by an agreement on unity. This was an important break with the past which made a return to internal war unlikely. But the unity accord was won at

[2]'What is drought fund being used for?', *The Insider*, February 1992.
[3]'Politics of Food: No registration to vote, no food aid, no farm inputs', *The Financial Gazette*, 28 April 1994.

the cost of the demise of competitive politics. It assisted President Mugabe's efforts to create a one-party state and did not alter his tendency to regard dissent as a short step from treason. Meanwhile, other figures in government had their own reasons for holding on to power without accountability. In 1988, *The Chronicle* newspaper uncovered the 'Willowgate' scandal in which government ministers were buying cars from the Willowvale assembly plant in Harare and selling them at well above the officially controlled price. 'Willowgate' became the major public corruption scandal in Zimbabwe, and virtually the only one uncovered by the press, which has otherwise been remarkably docile. The government used its powers over *The Chronicle* to 'promote' the editor responsible, Geoffrey Nyarota, to the powerless post of public relations officer in Harare.

The array of violations of civil and political rights in the late 1980s indicated a political malaise at the heart of government, in the form of growing authoritarianism and corruption. The controls on the press and academic freedom had a direct impact on the quality of public debate about national food policy and structural adjustment. Declining standards of accountability also had a direct impact on famine relief. For example, the lack of expenditure from the National Drought Fund became a scandal as the drought intensified. The fund had contained Z\$52 million in 1988, which should have been available for relief programmes. By early 1992, it had made no allocations, and also had no audit reports available for the years 1989 and 1990.[4]

Food policy and structural adjustment
The agricultural reforms that followed liberation had a spectacular effect on communal farming: overall grain supply more than trebled (Zimbabwe Grain Marketing Board, 1991). This was labelled the 'Zimbabwean miracle' at the time. The surfeit of food made the government complacent, so that the persistent problem of rural undernutrition was neglected. National food surpluses did not solve the problem of hunger among those too poor to buy, and 40 per cent of communal farmers were in chronic deficit (Jackson *et al.*, 1987). The Grain Marketing Board, which was oriented to buying rurally and selling in urban areas, did not sell food at controlled prices in rural areas; its national-level success concealed a systematic failure to overcome rural poverty (Jayne and Chisvo, 1991).

Outside drought periods, the main technical problem for the GMB was trying to avoid being swamped by obligatory purchases and storing huge maize surpluses. This was expensive and by 1990/1 GMB losses reached Z\$68m. (Zimbabwe GMB, 1991). The rationale for some change was undeniable. The financial burden of GMB policy helped Zimbabwe's international donors to reach a consensus that the country should submit to a structural adjustment programme.

[4]"What is drought fund being used for?' *The Insider*, February 1992.

Food marketing reform began in 1989, predating the Economic and Social Action Plan (ESAP), which was formally adopted in January 1991 (Jones 1992). A range of reforms familiar from other such programmes was introduced, including the reduction of government expenditure on subsidies and services, the removal of price controls and the easing of import licensing and foreign-exchange controls, intended to improve incentives for exporters. Some of the reforms, such as proposals to abolish the national minimum producer price for maize, introduce school fees and lay off 10 per cent of government-employed nurses were very unpopular. A major component of the ESAP was the requirement that the GMB should not run at a loss (unlike similar institutions in Europe, the United States and Japan, which are all heavily subsidized). Consequently, the GMB was to export more when it had good stocks, and hold smaller stocks. At the same time, lower maize prices were introduced in order to encourage farmers to switch to other crops such as tobacco. By the 1990/1 season, the minimum producer price for maize was the lowest for twenty years. Rural grain marketing was slowly deregulated, with major donors such as USAID making the disbursement of grants conditional on very precise progress in this direction. On 12 September 1990 in a Policy Statement, the Minister of Lands, Agriculture and Rural Resettlement, Dr Witness Mangwende, stated hopefully: 'The large surpluses of maize are now coming under control'. Based on average production figures for the previous few years, this restructuring would not have jeopardized Zimbabwe's maize supply, and Mangwende was confident that 'this [stock] is still ample as a carryover stock into the 1991/92 season and is above our minimum requirements for food security needs'. Hence, starting in late 1990 there was a stock run-down of over 200,000 tonnes.

Though not secret, the decision to run down food stocks was not subjected to popular consultation, but was treated in an entirely technical manner and not publicly debated until the food crisis became evident. Senior government figures continued to make reassuring and misleading statements right up to the midst of the crisis. There can be little doubt that if the decision to reverse the food security policy had been exposed to public scrutiny, it would not have been allowed to pass. In fact, both food security and national economic policy were regarded as an exclusively technocratic preserve. The government consulted the Confederation of Zimbabwean Industries and the Zimbabwe National Chamber of Commerce, but there were no discussions with the churches, trade unions, small farmers or consumers (Thompson, 1993: 122).

In line with 'adjustment with a human face' thinking, a Programme of Action to Mitigate the Social Costs of Adjustment was launched. Its Social Development Fund (SDF) provided retraining and subsidies for some of the 'new poor'. But after eighteen months the SDF's impact was negligible: for example, a mere 8,000 people had received assistance with buying food (Stewart, 1995: 125). These programmes were also designed with minimal involvement from welfare organizations and NGOs. There was an assumption that the voluntary sector would simply provide for needs no longer met by state provision.

The lack of public debate on food policy was not entirely a domestic responsibility. The international donors also kept the implications of their adjustments out of the public realm, and quite deliberately so. The IFIs were not keen to have an open public debate, which could have led to the crystallization of an anti-reform coalition.

The ESAP undermined Zimbabwe's capacity to resist drought-induced food shortage at a vital moment. Advocates of ESAP have plausibly pleaded 'not guilty' to being implicated in the near-famine that ensued in 1991/2, on the grounds that ESAP is not incompatible with famine-prevention measures. In particular, the GMB reforms did not preclude maize imports at critical times, and the failure of the government to authorize such imports until the last possible moment was entirely a domestic political responsibility (see below). But this argument misses an important point: certain political consequences are inherent in ESAP. The entire 'adjustment' process reflects a reconfiguring of the lines of accountability: government officials were more and more concerned with meeting externally imposed deadlines and conditions. Even as the drought was unfolding, Western donors insisted on the implementation of policy reforms exactly according to a schedule worked out many months before. Thus the Zimbabwean dollar was devalued by 25 per cent in August 1991, at precisely the moment when the government should have been taking the first measures to finance emergency grain imports.

Emergency food imports
The government stubbornly refused to recognize the extent of the crisis and import food until almost too late. Whatever its motives, this displayed lack of concern for the well-being of ordinary Zimbabweans: the welfarist commitment of a decade earlier had faded, and there was little that citizens could do to revive it.

Matabeleland was already feeling the effects of drought in 1990. Journalists reported 'widespread hunger and malnutrition-related diseases among children'.[5] Relief measures were started, but the government did not alter its policy of exporting food or its agenda for reform. Early 1991 saw an indifferent harvest, following a large decrease in land under maize cultivation and poor rainfall. By the end of March GMB stocks had fallen to 643,000 tonnes and it began to warn that there might be a need to import food later in the year. A succession of warnings followed. In early June, a seminar of commercial farmers and

---

[5]Southern African Press Agency (SAPA) on 30 December 1990, quoted in BBC, *Summary of World Broadcasts*, ME/0959, 1 January 1991.

other experts in Harare predicted that reserves would be consumed by early 1992 and that Zimbabwe 'would join its neighbours in the food queue'.[6] Import needs of 180,000 tonnes were estimated. In July the Commercial Grain Producers' Association warned of a major maize crisis, reporting a 50 per cent drop in communal production and a 65 per cent fall on white commercial farms. The chief executive spoke of the need to import maize by 1992.[7] In August, the National Early Warning Unit of the GMB stated that maize stocks would be exhausted by March 1992. 'The closing stock of maize is anticipated to be zero if no import is planned and realised.'[8] This was the government's own systematic and formal early warning system, designed to prompt government action.

But the government did not respond. It merely (and reluctantly) halted exports of maize, and contradicted the warnings. Immediately after the June seminar issued its warning, the GMB Chairman, Cephas Msipa, said that the same grain producers had assured him that production would be sufficient to feed the nation.[9] Minister of Agriculture Mangwende called on citizens not to worry, saying 'It is too easy for anyone to start talking of maize shortages and import quantities.'[10] In September, Msipa issued his official report, in which financial returns remained a higher priority than food security needs:

> The expected large intake of maize which would have exacerbated the huge stocks resulted in an aggressive drive by management to export maize. Improved transport services enabled the Board to move 409,687 tonnes of maize exports with a net realisation of Z$115.8 million. . . . As it turned out, maize intake was only 780,000 tonnes against the initial estimate of 1.1 million tonnes. Regrettably, the looming drought forced my Board to suspend exports in order to reserve stocks for the domestic markets. (Zimbabwe GMB, 1991: 1)

The government raised producer prices to stimulate maize production for the 1991/2 season. It was gambling that a good early harvest in 1992 would bring food supplies back from the brink. This did not happen: the 1991/2 season was crippled by drought and production was less than half the previous low of 1984. No measures had been taken to authorize imports, and stocks were virtually exhausted.

Only in March 1992 did the government finally face up to the inevitable and declare a national disaster and set up a temporary drought response administration. By the time it made finance available for imports, the nearest available surpluses (in South Africa) had largely been bought up for relief distributions elsewhere in the region, and the government had to turn instead to the United States for food shipments.

[6]SAPA on 27 June, quoted in BBC, *Summary of World Broadcasts*, ME/W0187, 9 July 1991.
[7]SAPA on 9 July, quoted in BBC, *Summary of World Broadcasts*, ME/W0189, 23 July 1991.
[8]Quoted in, 'Maize stocks running out,' *The Chronicle*, Bulawayo, 14 August 1991.
[9]Quoted in, 'Zimbabwe won't import maize: Msipa,' *The Chronicle*, Bulawayo, 6 June 1991.
[10]SAPA on 27 June, quoted in BBC, *Summary of World Broadcasts*, ME/W0187, 9 July 1991.

Having responded belatedly, the government then mounted a nation-wide relief programme, much larger than that of 1983; at its height in November 1992, 5.6 million people were registered to receive emergency food rations, about three-quarters of the entire rural population. It did not reach its targets: about 23 per cent of those registered for rations did not receive them, and the ration was only 5 kg per person per month, one-third of the sustenance level (Thompson, 1993: 94).

Implications

The 'Zimbabwean miracle' can no longer be acclaimed as it was in the mid-1980s. But neither should internal political failings obscure the real achievements in famine prevention in most of the country during those years. There was a fragile political contract between the ZANU Government and the majority Shona community. The slide to the narrowly averted famine in 1991–2 illustrates how neo-liberal economic policies, imposed on a reluctant government, proved politically regressive and very nearly disastrous. The structural adjustment programme cannot be held solely or even predominantly responsible for the erosion of democratic accountability in Zimbabwe: President Mugabe is primarily responsible. But neither is it innocent.

More widely, the neo-liberal ascendancy has not been associated with the growth or entrenchment of democratic accountability. Structural adjustment was a response to real structural problems, but addressed economic symptoms (with uneven success) rather than political causes. Although its proponents were reluctant to acknowledge the fact, economic neo-liberalism was also a political project. Its political impact was to attack existing (mainly urban) political contracts, rather than building up alternatives. As such, it has not been beneficial overall for famine protection in Africa.

4

Retreat from Accountability: II

The Humanitarian International

International responsibility for the alleviation of suffering is one of the most noble of all human goals. Nobility of aim does not confer immunity from sociological analysis or ethical critique, however. To date most sociological study of humanitarian action implicitly accepts the axioms of the humanitarian international. Statements of the goals of non-governmental organizations, in particular, are commonly taken at face value. It is as though the sociological study of the church were undertaken by committed Christians only: criticism would be solely within the context of advancing the faith itself.

Much of history consists of the study of unintended consequences, and humanitarian action is replete with results that might surprise many of its protagonists. Relief agencies, like any institutions, are subject to their own requirements for survival and self-justification – requirements which may contradict higher ideals. Humanitarianism also masks many very mixed personal motives. The challenge of understanding humanitarianism (and indeed reforming it) is to identify the actual forces at work in the institutions that have taken on the humanitarian mandate. Two basic concepts will be used in organizing the argument of this chapter.

One is the 'humanitarian international' – the international elite of the staff of international relief agencies, academics, consultants, specialist journalists, lobbyists and also, to an increasing extent, 'conflict resolution' specialists and human rights workers. It is a sub-group of the larger aid and development industry. A generation ago, this group did not exist: governments, UN agencies and NGOs were staffed by different kinds of people who more often disputed common assumptions than shared them. Since 1980 there has been a marked convergence towards a common culture. One consequence of this is the ease with which individuals can move between different institutions. How can so many well-educated, cosmopolitan and to a fair degree well-intentioned people work within institutions with such noble goals, to such little effect? 'Actually existing humanitarianism'[1] is a disappointment.

The second concept is the distinction between 'soft' and 'hard' humanitarian interests. This is an elementary point but it is obscured with astonishing regularity in the writings of international humanitarians. 'Soft' humanitarian interests can be defined as the stated aims of humanitarian institutions: succouring the poor and vulnerable, protecting human rights, preventing war, etc. 'Hard' humanitarian interests are the institutional demands of the organizations themselves and their staff: for institutional expansion, career security, prestige, a sense of job satisfaction, etc. Clearly there is an overlap between the two: only relief organizations in good financial health can deliver the goods. But relief agencies have a powerful tendency to go much further and conflate their own interests with those of the people they avow to help.

The central contention of this and the following chapters is that the expansion of internationalized humanitarianism in the 1980s and 1990s reflects a retreat from accountability, akin to the dominance of neo-liberalism. This is no coincidence: the internationalization of social welfare is closely linked to the decline of state authority, which is central to the neo-liberal project. The humanitarian international may be the 'human face' of neo-liberalism, but it is a charitable face with little accountability. Moreover, both neo-liberalism and international humanitarianism are justifications for foreign institutions to intrude into the domestic politics of African countries. Usually, they have intruded when things were going badly wrong, but even when the intrusions have succeeded on their own terms, they have rarely supported progressive political contracts.

The evolution of humanitarian action

The history of voluntary humanitarian action is long and complicated, encompassing missionary societies and various traditions of religious alms-giving, trade unions and community mobilization, movements for political or social reform ranging from temperance societies to the campaign against the slave trade, pacifism and innumerable initiatives by idealists, cranks and charlatans. In recent decades the number of charitable organizations has increased at an apparently exponential rate (Smillie, 1995: 1), while some have become dominant 'brand names'. Writing the history of a single voluntary organization such as Oxfam is complicated enough (Black, 1992), let alone trying to make sense of the entire field. Here we shall be concerned solely with those agencies prominent in famine relief in Africa, including NGOs, the International

---

[1]The phrase echoes 'actually existing socialism', used by Ralph Bahro in the 1970s, cf. Leys, 1996: 177, fn.

Committee of the Red Cross (ICRC) and the UN specialized agencies, plus their governmental donors.

There are three important ancestors of contemporary humanitarian action. One is the use of international relief as an instrument of *Realpolitik*, famously encapsulated by Henry Kissinger's 1976 remark that 'disaster relief is becoming increasingly a major instrument of our foreign policy' (quoted in Kent, 1987: 81). When the United States launched the 'food for peace' programme in the 1950s, international aid served the twin purposes of disposing of surplus grain production from the American Mid-West and rewarding loyal allies in the Cold War. Over time, the institutions set up to administer food aid developed their own interests and coalitions with special interest groups such as farmers, so that they were in a position to contradict higher strategic policy. For example, continued US grain shipments to the Soviet Union in the early 1980s went against the Cold War logic of the time (Uvin, 1994).

The second ancestor is private charity for the relief of suffering. Religious orders provided for the hungry and destitute and occasional large-scale appeals were launched for famine relief. For example, US citizens sent relief to Ireland in 1847, British people subscribed to missionary famine relief funds for China in the 1870s and many Western countries sent aid to Russia in 1921–2. The Save the Children Fund, the Oxford Committee for Famine Relief (later Oxfam) and CARE were all founded as a response to war-created suffering in Europe. English law requires charities to be non-political – a demand that has posed recurring problems. For example, Oxfam was created in 1942 to provide relief for the famine in German-occupied Greece where the tight Allied blockade had cut off the country from its peacetime food supplies. The founders of Oxfam debated whether to challenge the British Government's policy of blockade, and chose not to. Instead they put forward proposals for 'controlled food relief' under the auspices of a neutral power, as had been implemented in Belgium during World War I. This was blocked by Churchill's intransigence: only in 1943 was Oxfam for the first time able to spend the money it had raised, channelling it through the Greek Red Cross committee in London to the ICRC (Black, 1992: 4–15).

The third ancestor is the ICRC itself, since its inception by Henri Dunant, horrified at the condition of untreated wounded soldiers at the battle of Solferino. His response was to seek to restrict the conduct of war by means of interstate protocols. The 1949 Geneva Conventions represent the apogee of these: though later Protocols have gone further in restricting the indiscriminate conduct of warfare, none have been so widely accepted nor so influential (Best, 1995). The ICRC and the Geneva Conventions have always been concerned with material relief, notably the medical care of the wounded on the battlefield. But the first large-scale relief operation in which the ICRC became involved was in Biafra in 1968. Until that point, the organization was overwhelmingly concerned with the protection of prisoners of war and facilitating assistance to them through national Red Cross or Red Crescent societies, and acting as guardian of the laws of war.

Overall, the quest for humanity in warfare has taken second place to the search for efficient delivery of relief supplies. In his account of the disaster relief 'network' (he prefers not to consider it a 'system') Randolph Kent quotes Senator Giovanni Ciraolo's words in 1921 as he tried to establish an International Assistance Union to co-ordinate disaster relief:

> Assistance to people stricken by calamities is, under present conditions, slow, poorly organized, and in a great degree, inefficient. The money allocated is badly distributed. Frequently the materials provided for purposes of relief are not adapted to the requirements of the people and the local climatic conditions. In many cases those who come to the assistance of the sufferers lack an expert knowledge of the technique of relief work. The offerings made by governments of the countries which are safe to those of affected nations are rather in the nature of charitable donations tending to embarrass the givers and humiliate the recipients. (quoted in Kent, 1987: 33)

Kent follows what has become the conventional approach in diagnosing persistent weaknesses in the 'network': a lack of preparedness, a shortage of accurate and timely information, failures of co-ordination between relief institutions, and inadequate technology. He charts the development of an ever more complex array of official disaster relief institutions, increasingly focused on the UN, and an NGO capacity. At first these evolved in parallel, but in about 1980 they began to converge. The irony of Senator Ciraolo's statement is manifest: 75 years later precisely the same problems remain as intractable as ever.

Institutional proliferation at the UN

In the aftermath of World War II, the UN set up specialized agencies with short-term mandates for relief and rehabilitation. Within a decade, most had either closed down (e.g. the UN Relief and Rehabilitation Agency) or changed name and mandate (the UN Children's Fund, UNICEF, and the UN High Commissioner for Refugees, UNHCR). The UN absolved itself of responsibility for disaster relief. Another decade later, the need to revive this capacity became evident. The first step was the simultaneous creation of the UN Disaster Relief Office (UNDRO) and the designation of the UNDP Resident Representative in any disaster-stricken country as the response co-ordinator. After 'almost two years of arduous discussions', this was agreed in December 1971 (Kent, 1987: 51–4). It is interesting in retrospect to see governments' loci of unease at the prospect of UNDRO: they feared loss of sovereignty to foreign institutions, especially where man-made disasters were concerned.

Hence UNDRO was given a minuscule programme budget of just $200,000 per annum and very little autonomy.

Contrary to the hopes of the UN and most member states, the creation of UNDRO marked the beginning, not the end, of the profusion of UN disaster institutions. Also in 1971, UNICEF created a special emergency co-ordination office, and the UN's Food and Agriculture Organization (FAO), the World Food Programme (WFP) and the World Health Organization (WHO) all followed suit in 1974 and 1975. A special Office of Sahelian Relief Operations was set up. This in turn contributed to a new branch of the disaster bureaucracy – the concern of the UN Environmental Programme with 'desertification' – formalized after the dire predictions made at the UN Conference on Desertification in 1977 (which glossed over the complexities of the scientific evidence to make grand generalizations more consonant with the interests of the environmentalist bureaucracies) (Swift, 1996: 79–81). In addition, most donor governments also set up special disaster units in the 1970s (Kent, 1987: 53). Following UNDRO's dismal performance in the 1970s, its role was reviewed and, after more prolonged argument, expanded. In 1980, after sharp disagreement with UNICEF on the Thai–Cambodia border, UNHCR set up an emergency office. In 1984, UNHCR enlarged its mandate when it reluctantly agreed to assist what it had hitherto called 'economic migrants' in Sudan from the Ethiopian famine, creating a new category of 'people of concern to UNHCR'. Initially a temporary *ad hoc* measure, this represented a fundamental switch in UNHCR's role from protection to assistance. At the same time, the UN Secretariat established a temporary office, the UN Emergency Office for Africa, with its most important sub-office in Ethiopia.

In the late 1980s, several *ad hoc* institutional initiatives were taken, notably the invention of the term 'complex emergency' as a way of dealing with the novel demands of relief operations in Mozambique, and the first negotiated agreement on access to a war zone (Operation Lifeline Sudan in April 1989). These were followed in 1991–2 with the concept of 'cross-mandate' operations, for example in eastern Ethiopia, where UNHCR, UNICEF and WFP assisted refugees, displaced people and impoverished residents without discrimination. The cross-mandate approach was further developed in the former Yugoslavia. At the end of 1991, the most ambitious attempt at institutional co-ordination to date was made, in the form of the appointment of a 'humanitarian Czar', an Under Secretary-General for Humanitarian Affairs, with his own Department of Humanitarian Affairs. Meanwhile a succession of Security Council resolutions have affirmed the UN's determination to provide relief, while merely making nods in the direction of enforcing human rights in wartime.

Each step was taken for specific reasons, with particular problems in mind. None was simply imposed by the international bureaucracy, rather they were negotiated between different governments and institutions.

Some were adopted reluctantly. But each step represented a transfer of power to international institutions. Two aspects of these initiatives stand out. One, each has been technical or bureaucratic: a pursuit of the Holy Grail of early warning and co-ordination. Two, each attempt has failed. The following chapters will document some of these failures.

The establishment of disaster institutions at the UN has contributed to the internationalization of responsibility for famines. This may seem a mundane statement but its implications are easy to overlook. Internationalizing responsibility means giving an indefinitely wide array of people (theoretically the whole population of the globe, practically the concerned citizens of aid-giving countries) a stake in disasters and disaster relief. UN institutions, international NGOs, foreign governments and any citizen of any country in the world become, by implication, stakeholders in any famine happening anywhere in the world. This process of internationalization is the key to the appropriation of power by international institutions and the retreat from domestic accountability in famine-vulnerable countries. Moreover, the 'responsibility' of UN agencies, NGOs and foreign governments is a vague and easily evaded moral responsibility – nothing more than an aspiration – rather than a practical obligation for which the 'responsible' institution can be called to account. Moral outrage plus technical proficiency does not equal accountability for results.

The technocratic ascendance
The UN institutional response is essentially technical and non-political. This has served the political interests of member states, the institutional needs of the UN and its agencies, and the professional needs of the new brand of 'experts' in the field – notably logisticians and statistician – nutritionists. A new technocratic discourse has been created which has had the effect of sealing off the new 'field' in a 'citadel of expertise' (Hewitt, 1983: 5) isolated from ordinary life, and above all from political life. This in turn reinforces the precept that 'disaster occurs because of the chance occurrence of natural extremes' and 'the geography of disaster is an archipelago of isolated misfortunes' (ibid.: 5, 12). Ironically, even the critical views on famine relief put forward, for instance in the independent journal *Disasters*, have served to legitimate the co-option of famines into a specialist discourse. *Disasters* may have let many more academics and practitioners breach the outer ramparts of the citadel, but it has not challenged the citadel's existence. Within the specialist institutions there are sharp differences of opinion and interest, which give the appearance of lively debate. But none of this debate questions whether famine relief, or any other form of emergency response, should be controlled by international 'experts', any more than warring barons ever contemplated the abolition of feudalism.

Nutritional surveillance is an example of the way in which certain technical demands have distorted the understanding of famine. Donors demand statistics on malnutrition, which entails nutritional surveys. Nutritionists disagree on the value of these surveys: they do not appear to measure risk of death, overall destitution in the community, or likelihood of mass migration. Interpreting the results of a nutritional survey requires a plethora of additional social, economic and epidemiological data, and even then remains contentious. Meanwhile, one of the most remarkable persistent technical shortcomings in the field is the reluctance of nutritional surveillance programmes to undertake mortality surveys as well. Mortality surveys indisputably measure something of interest: the numbers of people who are dying. Yet the exclusive preference for nutritional surveys has become so institutionalized that some nutritionists have even accorded measurement of undernutrition in children a more important role in diagnosing famine than excess deaths (Autier, 1988).

What does this reflect? First, the fact that nutritionists as a profession have become deeply enmeshed in famine and food policy (at considerable cost to the integrity of their discipline), whereas demographers have not. Second, the demand by senior bureaucrats and politicians for a simple and quantifiable measure of distress, however spurious its credentials. The consequence is the further mystification and bureaucratization of famine prevention and relief. Two disenchanted nutritionists write:

> The discipline of nutrition as it is currently applied is rapidly becoming irrelevant to the problems of famine-affected populations and refugees. . . . The role of the nutritionist . . . is frequently little more than to undertake anthropometric assessments and supervise supplementary feeding programmes. These temporary measures, and tunnel vision, have side-tracked nutritionists who have had minimal impact on the causes of malnutrition and thus have not succeeded in raising nutritional status in the longer term.
>
> We have been seduced by anthropometry, which is easy to measure, easy to manipulate and can be easily taken out of context to mean just about anything! This has stunted our analytical skills, and created a strait-jacketed approach to famine relief; high rates of malnutrition equal famine equal food distribution. (Young and Jaspars, 1995: 133)

The creation and entrenchment of this international technocracy have immense ramifications. One huge gap is the absence of any political approach to famine prevention. A second is the failure to address the accountability of the UN system itself. Accountability has been narrowed to a set of technical issues, notably financial probity. There are real issues of waste and corruption which the UN addresses only intermittently. In addition, there are the diplomatic–managerial procedures which are essential to the UN's existence as currently constituted. These include the managerial accountability of the specialized agencies to their boards (which include representatives of the main donor countries) and the accountability of the Secretariat itself to the General Assembly. Some of the innovations in disaster relief have been explicitly aimed at circumventing these procedures, which are seen as over-cumbersome and prone to meddling. No specialized agency wants to be subjected to the same tortuous negotiations that preceded the creation and reform of UNDRO, and so they prefer unilateral internal administrative reorganization.

Public or political accountability is a different matter. The UN technocracy is well defended against external scrutiny or exposure, let alone public access. There is no internal regulation or enforcement of professional standards. Institutional or technical disagreements are rarely resolved. Until very recently, evaluations of disaster responses at the UN have invariably been in-house investigations that have no binding power and are not made public. Some of them contain powerful insights or strong recommendations, but there is no mechanism for enforcing 'learning the lessons'. In fact, critical evaluations are used for the opposite purpose: they can be brought out later to defuse new criticisms with the riposte that the critic is not saying anything new. Repetition is a constant difficulty faced by critics of the UN specialized agencies: a critique repeated many times may be valid but is readily ignored because it has become boring. As well as concealed errors the agencies have (rarer) secret successes, but lack of accountability means that successful innovations are only occasionally recognized (and rarely replicated). Capable and committed staff are often not promoted: more commonly they leave and join NGOs. Without a commission of inquiry or another form of public accountability which allows independent evaluation of the record and verification of basic facts, the debate on the effectiveness of the UN agencies will continue to be marred by ignorance and driven by chauvinistic political agendas.

As the shortcomings of the UN-based relief system have become more evident, enthusiasm has increased among Western governments and their publics for supporting relief NGOs. Non-governmental organizations are elusive to the analyst, not least because they claim diversity and resent classification, and because of the meaninglessness of the name they prefer to use. When put under stress, however, famine relief NGOs tend to behave alike. The following analysis risks unfair generalization by identifying common pressures and tendencies among NGOs. But there is more to be gained by considering NGOs together, and as part of the humanitarian international, than by abandoning generalizations altogether.

Biafra: NGO totem and taboo

One episode in modern times stands out as a formative experience in contemporary humanitarianism: Biafra. An entire generation of NGO relief workers was moulded by Biafra, and several agencies were either born from the relief operation or forever changed by it. Biafra is totemic for contemporary relief; it was an unsurpassed effort in terms of logistical achievement and sheer physical courage. But Biafra is also a taboo: the ethical issues that it raises have still to be faced. In Nigeria, the Biafran war is rarely spoken of in public, as the wounds are still deep. It has a similar status in the humanitarian international.

The Biafran famine began in 1968. A year previously, political tensions between the Igbo-dominated Biafra State of south-eastern Nigeria and the Federal Government had erupted into war, with the Biafrans unilaterally declaring secession. The Biafrans gained almost no diplomatic support from either the West, the Eastern bloc or from African states deeply concerned about the precedent that secession would set, but came to gain enormous sympathy from the Western public. From the early months of the war, diplomatic isolation and military reverses made a Biafran victory all but impossible. As the Federal army made rapid gains and cut off all roads into the breakaway state, material hardship descended into famine. The only way in was by air.

The UN and official relief were wholly absent from the Biafran enclave. It was the first humanitarian effort dominated by NGOs. Aengus Finucane, who went on to found Concern, began his aid career in Biafra. He writes:

> The JCA [Joint Church Aid] airlift into Biafra has never been fully recognized for what it was. Recalling it now helps to put the belated and pathetic attempts to get assistance to Somalia in perspective. . . . As many as fifty flights a night flew into Uli. Not all were JCA flights, but, for example, on the night of November 19, 1969, JCA landed 376 tons of relief supplies at Uli! The nightly average in April 1969 was 70 metric tons (mts), in August, 150 mts, and in December, 250 mts. . . . Fuel, tires, and spare parts were also flown in during the hours of darkness and under fire. It was a marvelous ecumenical cooperative effort. (Finucane, 1993: 180)

These quantities were surpassed only by the Berlin airlift. One Biafra veteran, Bob Koepp, spent much of his subsequent career trying to exceed both with the Lutheran World Federation air bridge to Juba in Southern Sudan. Another veteran, Fred Cuny, became possibly the most influential US relief practitioner before he met his death in Chechnya in 1995. Two doctors in Biafra, John Seaman and John Rivers, went on to found the International Disasters Institute and the journal *Disasters*, and to develop influential models of emergency health care. Bernard Kouchner's humanitarian career and the ethos of Sans-Frontièrism also began in Biafra.

The famine first became news, almost wholly by accident, in June 1968, when the war was already decided in military terms. Both the Biafran leadership, including its capable propaganda secretariat, and the press had shown little interest in the 'famine story'. In fact the first journalist to take famine pictures never got them published because his paper considered them of no news value (Harrison and Palmer, 1986: 28). Shortly afterwards, an Irish priest, Father Kevin Doheny, took two journalists to a hospital and showed them severely malnourished children. Another British journalist in Biafra was Frederick Forsyth, who later wrote:

> Quite suddenly, we'd touched a nerve. Nobody in this country at that time had ever seen children looking like that. The last time the Brits had seen anything like that must have been the Belsen pictures. . . .
> The war itself would never have set the Thames on fire, but the pictures of starving children put Biafra onto the front page of every British newspaper and from there to newspapers all over the world. People who couldn't fathom the political complexities of the war could easily grasp the wrong in a picture of a child dying of starvation. (quoted in Harrison and Palmer, 1986: 33)

Newspapers claimed that 3,000 children were dying each day, and, combining this with coverage of Britain's continuing arms shipments to the Nigerian Government, accused the British Government of complicity in genocide by starvation. This 'tidal wave' of journalistic interest was brilliantly exploited and manipulated by the Biafran Government and its public relations firm, Markpress. Paddy Davies of the Biafran Propaganda Secretariat explained:[2]

> The watershed for Biafran propaganda was the use of images of starving, dying, hungry children. It completely obliterated what Biafra had done before then, and the outside world bought it. And so Biafra realised that this was an angle they could play on. It had tried the political emancipation of oppressed people, it had tried the religious angle, it had tried pogrom and genocide – these had limited successes – but the pictures of starving children and women, dying children, children with kwashiorkor stomachs touched everybody, it cut across the range of people's beliefs.

For the relief agencies, the impact of the first African famine to become world news was electric. Church agencies took the lead. They already had strong interests in Biafra, which has been described as 'the most intensely "missioned" part of Africa'.[3] Sectarian loyalty and anti-Islamic feelings contributed to the churches' commitment, as did latent anti-British sentiment among the Irish missionaries. Caritas and Africa Concern (later to become the Irish agency, Concern) were notably pro-Biafra and influential worldwide, including in the Vatican. The response of the church agencies can partly be explained by powerful

---

[2] Speaking on: *Biafra: Fighting a War without Guns*, Timewatch, BBC 2, 1995.
[3] de St Jorre, 1972: 249. The honour is shared with Rwanda, described as Africa's most Christian country, which was also to have a unique experience of international humanitarianism.

local pressures. This was not the case for relief agencies such as Oxfam, whose 'interests' in Biafra might be described as general–humanitarian and institutional. Their response was comparable, however. Immediately the press coverage began, Oxfam swung into action, breaking ranks with the other members of the Disasters Emergency Committee[4] and the ICRC, with whom it had previously made an agreement not to act unilaterally. It became operational in the field for only the second time in its history. Oxfam's public statements were partisan, for example one claim in March 1969: 'What Britain . . . must now face is that the price for a united Nigeria is likely to be millions of lives' (quoted in Black, 1992: 127). In Oxfam's official history, Maggie Black writes that 'they took on trust the Biafran claims of "genocide" and the "thousands dying daily" . . . they fell for it, hook, line and sinker' (ibid.: 121).

The churches had already done so. The first relief supplies were delivered by buying space on military supply flights. Later the church agencies chartered their own aircraft, but the military-relief integration continued. A single airstrip at Uli was used for both military and relief supplies; it was maintained by the relief agencies and the mixture of relief and military flights gave them a high degree of protection. The Biafran Government, dominated by hard-liners such as Colonel Odumegwu Ojukwu, refused to agree to any compromise proposals that would have separated out humanitarian supplies. For example, it never permitted the relief flights to come in by day and the military supplies by night, and never agreed to land corridors for relief convoys. Its argument was that the Federal Government was using starvation as a weapon and was only trying to gain a propaganda advantage. Certainly there were hard-liners in the Federal army who argued that a comprehensive blockade which included relief supplies would have helped bring the war to a rapid end, and they intermittently prevailed. Some Nigerian leaders stated publicly their position that starvation was a legitimate military tactic (see for example Allen, 1989: 31). International revulsion at the Federal blockade was instrumental in the inclusion of clauses prohibiting starvation as a method of warfare in the 1977 Additional Protocols to the Geneva Conventions.

But it was the Biafran leadership that was more determined to turn both relief and hunger to advantage. Colonel Ojukwu said in September 1968: 'Our aim all along has been to delay the enemy until the world conscience can effectively be aroused against genocide' (quoted in de St Jorre, 1972: 241–2). Relief agencies played a key role in meeting these twin strategic aims of prolonging and internationalizing the war. With foreign relief agencies present, the Federal Government could no longer treat the war as an internal matter, and the relief agencies and churches became the most effective propagandists for the Biafran cause. The

---

[4]A club of leading British relief NGOs formed to co-ordinate television fund-raising for disasters.

Biafrans never once called the bluff of the government, for example by accepting daylight flights for a period. Their largest and most regular supply of hard currency for the purchase of arms was the money exchanged (at favourable rates) for the relief programmes. The agencies also allowed relief resources to be used by the Biafran Government and army. Camps for Igbo civilians were preferentially fed at the cost of other ethnic groups.

The ICRC largely but not entirely avoided falling for the Biafran ploy. ICRC budgets rose from $500,000 a year worldwide to $1.4 million a month for Biafra alone in what it considered the gravest crisis since World War II. But, as its mandate specifies, the ICRC did not engage in any publicity. The Nigerian Government allowed ICRC relief into Biafra, fulfilling its commitments under the Geneva Conventions. But the Biafran Government objected to the conditions in Article 23 of the Fourth Convention which mandated Federal authorization and inspection of relief supplies. The ICRC negotiated a compromise which allowed it to fly to Biafra without Federal supervision but at its own risk. ICRC relief continued until June 1969 when the Federal Government shot down a Swedish Red Cross plane. This attack was sparked by the attempt of Count van Rosen, who had formerly flown for the churches' airlift, to set up a Biafran air force. The Nigerian Government then banned night-time flying, and terminated all ICRC activities on both sides. The ICRC complied, but only after an intense internal debate. In the end, the argument that the ICRC's worldwide responsibilities and adherence to principle should prevail over the needs of the Biafrans won out. The ICRC delegate protested strongly to the Nigerian Government, but did not speak out publicly, and the ICRC phased out its operations. The Joint Church Aid airlift continued.

The ICRC operation did not satisfy one of its French doctors, Bernard Kouchner. He later wrote: 'By keeping silent, we doctors were accomplices in the systematic massacre of a population' (quoted in Benthall, 1993: 125). Kouchner later broke his contract with the ICRC and spoke out publicly, comparing the ICRC silence to its failure to reveal the existence of the Nazi death camps. The agency Kouchner dreamed of, Médecins Sans Frontières, was founded in 1971 and from the outset adopted a very media-conscious, aggressive style.[5]

The Biafran line, repeated by Kouchner and other agencies, was that the Biafran people faced systematic massacre by Federal troops should the latter win the war. But there were no Federal massacres, and indeed by the time the relief operation began its massive expansion in September 1968, there was a large amount of evidence that there would

[5]Despite its name, MSF is highly respectful of (European) political boundaries, and has 5 national sections, each with a distinct organizational culture. Entering an MSF compound in the field is also to cross a major cultural boundary, as 'volunteers' are provided with many Euroatean comforts.

be no genocide. There had been none in the large tracts of Biafran
territory overrun by Federal troops by that time:

> Massacres did, of course, occur, and were perpetrated by both sides,
> usually in the heat of battle or during its immediate aftermath. There
> was, however, no constant 'genocidal' pattern or theme or even agent
> in these atrocities. . . . (de St Jorre, 1972: 285)

What influenced the aid agencies more were Federal army actions and
statements that affected their own security. Air raids against Uli were
indiscriminate, bloody and dangerous to relief workers, some of whom
were killed, but they cannot be properly described as genocidal. Direct
threats against relief workers were frequent, and one blood-curdling
promise by Colonel Adekunle against doctors in an ICRC hospital was
instrumental in Kouchner's decision to speak out.

The implications of the Biafran relief effort were clear almost as soon
as the war was over. While writers were ready to present the facts,
drawing the conclusions was more difficult. For example, writing in
1972, de St Jorre concludes: 'But the final assessment must be a positive
one' (ibid.: 252). It has taken 25 years for the ethical implications to be
faced more squarely. Ian Smillie writes:

> It was a historic feat rivalled in volume only by the Berlin airlift, and
> it is probably still unrivalled anywhere for bravery.
> The airlift and the broader relief effort was also something else. It
> was an act of unfortunate and profound folly. It prolonged the war by
> 18 months. . . . A great deal of post-war effort went into refuting the
> charge that the churches and NGOs prolonged the war. Because if it
> is true, they must also have prolonged the suffering, contributing to
> the deaths of 180,000 people or more. (Smillie, 1995: 104)

As in all African famines, figures for deaths are extremely unreliable
and range widely and no author has proposed a definitive figure (Aall,
1970). But this is not the point. Ian Smillie believes that the war was
prolonged by the humanitarians, and cites Biafran leaders such as N. U.
Akpan, the head of Biafra's civil service, who openly admits that 'the
efforts of the relief agencies did in fact help prolong the war' (Smillie,
1995: 104). Moreover, the cost of continued resistance was not only
many lives lost, but the transformation of Biafra's cause from political
independence to that of 'a ward of the international community' and an
object of pity (Stremlau, 1977: 238).

The 1970s: the NGO club

Biafra still retains the totemic status of a heroic lost cause, even a heroic
debacle. No sooner was the war over than many of the same NGOs and
relief workers relocated to Bangladesh, first for the September 1970
cyclone and then for the 1971–2 war of independence, which this time

the secessionists won. In Bangladesh NGO activity was on a larger but less spectacular scale than in Biafra. Although distrust and antagonism between the official and NGO relief networks persisted (a legacy of Biafra that was to last a decade), they showed that NGO humanitarianism was likely to be a permanent phenomenon. Bangladesh also led to the formation of fora for NGO co-ordination. One of the first began in 1972, when the League of Red Cross and Red Crescent societies combined with a group of larger NGOs to create the 'LORCS-Volag Steering Committee' (ungainly acronyms are another vibrant tradition that can be dated to this time).

The NGO relief network then decamped to Ethiopia and the West African Sahel, and then in 1979 set out on another headlong confront-ation with the UN: the relief programme in Cambodia after the defeat of the Khmer Rouge government by the Vietnamese. This was an extra-ordinary humanitarian operation, showing some of the most extreme tendencies of NGOs towards media-driven symbolic action, and some of the highest ideals of solidarity with suffering people shunned by the Great Powers in pursuit of their *Realpolitik*. The refusal of the Western powers to recognize the post-Khmer Rouge government, and the con-sequent absence of official agencies, gave unprecedented prominence to the NGOs operational inside the country.

As in Biafra there were considerable moral complexities. A fundamental issue raised but not resolved was the ethics of delivering relief to refugees and fugitives in Thailand (amounting to over $300 per head, compared with about $4 per head to Cambodians inside the country). This aid provisioned the defeated army of the Khmer Rouge and allowed it to remobilize. Excessive competition between relief agencies and the often very low standards of professionalism led some individuals to become extremely cynical. But there was no attempt at openly assessing the political impact of the relief programmes, let alone publicly learning the lessons. Some relief workers may have become sceptical, but their institutions did not.

Rural Cambodia made a rapid if modest recovery from the genocide and other extraordinary disruptions of the Khmer Rouge. Writers with such contrasting views as John Pilger and William Shawcross concur that aid agency predictions of 'two million dead by Christmas' exaggerated the scale of the famine and underestimated the resource-fulness of rural Cambodians (Pilger, 1989: 425, 431; Shawcross, 1984: 212–13, 371–3). The fund-raising machine developed its own momentum, regardless of realities in the country.

Relief NGOs came of age in the 1970s, gaining respectability and a measure of influence. The larger NGOs together formed an informal club. In retrospect, it was a decade of relative stability in the humani-tarian world, in which NGOs and official agencies shared a common agenda of trying to develop professional standards and mechanisms of co-ordination and regulation, under the authority of host governments.

The role of NGOs became increasingly recognized by donor governments. Most governments set up special fora for liaison with NGOs during the decade. The first major donor to do so was Canada (1968) and the last was Great Britain (1982) (Kent, 1987: 48). The UN remained aloof for longer, but NGOs were gradually ceded a role, starting with refugee operations. The 1981 International Conference on Assistance to Refugees in Africa (ICARA I) in Geneva was a breakthrough in this regard: it can be seen as a successful attempt by UNHCR to wrest back the initiative in refugee policy from African governments, which had held conferences in Arusha in 1979 and Khartoum in 1980 to press for increased refugee assistance. One of UNHCR's strategies was to enlist the NGOs as allies in its institutional aggrandizement, turning the nascent neo-liberal agenda of promoting non-governmental service contractors to its advantage. A key battleground was eastern Sudan, as examined in the following chapter. Between 1980 and 1985, the Sudan Government ceded near-total control over refugee programmes to foreign agencies. By this time, the idea was beginning to arise that the NGO network, in co-operation with the UN and funded by Western governments, might move from merely filling the gaps in official relief programmes run by national governments, to being the *primary* response to disasters. The outline of the modern humanitarian international was emerging.

1980–85: the beginnings of deregulation

The humanitarian international was transformed in the 1980s. The charitable 'market' developed rapidly. In this market, agencies (producers of a charitable product) compete to sell to consumers (donor institutions and the donating public). As donor governments began to channel emergency funds through NGOs, deliberately circumventing African governments, they radically changed the nature of institutional humanitarianism.

This section begins to map out the systemic flaws of the humanitarian international, which became evident in the 1980s. These include the lack of enforceable professional standards and the absence of formal barriers to entry. In the clubby world of the 1970s, these shortcomings had not appeared to matter, but with deregulation and government funding, the situation changed.

Relief NGOs are varied. There are differences in ethos and methods among them, for example between the operational NGOs (which have expatriate staff members 'on the ground') and non-operational NGOs (mainly church-based agencies that work through local 'partners'). Some refuse significant levels of government funding (for example Oxfam–US), others subsist almost entirely on official subcontracting. Like the UN agencies, international relief NGOs are committed to the principle of internationalizing responsibility for famine. Relief NGOs are less bureaucratic and technically ambitious than the official agencies and disavow legal mandates in favour of energy and flexibility, but their specific obligations to the poor are just as tenuous. The moral logic of charitable famine relief assumes an identity of interest between the NGOs and famine-vulnerable people.

There is a scarcity of industry standards and professional regulation in the NGO sector. There have been many gallant attempts and some successes by agencies with special skills. Most of these are a legacy of the 1970s. For example, John Seaman at the IDI and later at SCF–UK has helped establish minimum standards for refugee health care. Oxfam has developed good emergency water supply systems for refugee camps. The Centers for Disease Control have developed epidemiological monitoring systems. There has been an appreciable evolution in thinking about strategic planning for disaster-stricken areas, manifest in a growing literature that straddles the academic–NGO divide. Enforcement is the problem. All these technologies, methods and standards can only be subscribed to voluntarily. Among employees of the larger NGOs, a certain amount of peer pressure and a sense of professional pride remain, especially in the public health and nutritional sectors. There have been important successes: instances of impressive co-ordination, professional standards and a long-term commitment to operating in a country or region. These tend to have certain features in common: few NGOs are present (often just one); there is a strong regulating authority (usually a government but occasionally an institution such as UNHCR); most of the funds provided come from institutional donors rather than public appeals (related to a lack of media attention); and unusually capable individuals have taken a prominent role in guiding the programme. The demonstrable capacity for high-quality programmes makes the debacles all the more reprehensible. In the larger and more publicized disasters, standards have conspicuously failed to improve and have often deteriorated.

Specific NGO successes mask strategic failures. NGOs tend to focus their efforts on areas in which they have specialist skills, or which make for good publicity, such as feeding centres and orphanages. Crucial areas such as sanitation and public health are relatively neglected. The charitable market is unable to fill the full spectrum of relief needs.

Non-governmental and official agencies are alike in that they do not commission public evaluations or publicize their internal assessments. The demands of fund-raising and institutional survival make it imperative not to admit to failures. The competition is for funds, not successful famine prevention. Successful methods of fund-raising, however incompatible they may be with the stated goals of addressing the poor, are rarely if ever abandoned. For example, child sponsorship is generally felt by aid workers to be undignified and misleading, but it still remains a major fund-raising tool. Every few years, NGOs (re)adopt codes of practice that require disaster victims to be shown in a dignified light, but these are rarely adhered to for long.

NGOs spurn adopting professional standards or self-regulation. It might appear to be in the interests of the more reputable NGOs to negotiate a set of minimum standards with host governments and donors – in effect placing restrictions on entry to the select club of *bona fide* relief NGOs. But even the NGOs that pride themselves on having the highest standards refuse to do this. It may be an instinctive aversion to any form of regulation (though independence has already been ceded in more insidious ways, through accepting government funding), or a fear that their own emergency operations might not always meet the minimum standards. One result is that there are no formal barriers to entry to the relief NGO sector: literally anyone can start an NGO, obtain funds by public appeal or other means, and try their hand at running feeding centres, clinics or orphanages. (And they do.) The lack of regulation leaves the NGO sector open to manipulation. Donor governments are increasingly undertaking their own evaluations of NGO programmes that they support. But without agreed standards these evaluations become subjective, widen in scope to cover the entire agency rather than just the programme under consideration, and become a tool for the donor to exercise power over the NGO (Smillie, 1995: 158).

Public policy and lobbying is one area where NGOs have occasionally distinguished themselves, but most successes lie away from the field of disaster relief. In 1969–70, Oxfam and Christian Aid began to speak out more vigorously than before on the political and economic underpinnings of enduring poverty in the world. The UK Charity Commissioners considered this outside the remit of charitable action and warned the agencies, which were obliged to set up an independent non-charitable organization, the World Development Movement, instead. NGOs have also been vocal in campaigns on the environment, debt, fair trade, employment practices and the arms trade. But there has been no specific and politicized NGO campaign on the issue of famine. The closest there has been to an exception is MSF–France's outspoken attack on resettlement in Ethiopia, which followed that agency's expulsion from the country. More recently, some articles in the *Populations in Danger* publications series have been critical of aspects of international humanitarianism (Médecins Sans Frontières, 1992). However, this critique has yet to be manifest in substantive changes in MSF's practical approach to famine relief, which remains based on the despatch of European 'volunteers' to run health stations and feeding centres. More common are campaigns with innocuous titles such as 'Don't forget Africa'.

Even more than the UN-based system, the Western NGO network suffers from a lack of political triggers to action. UN agencies have mandates that require them to be present in all countries, so that UNICEF's absence from Somalia in 1991, for example, was scandalous.

Excepting church organizations with local constituencies, Western NGOs are under no such obligation; their presence is a privilege and not a duty. Those who suffer famine have very little leverage over foreign relief organizations, so that the impulse for action necessarily arises from elsewhere. The charitable market is driven by demand for a humanitarian 'product'. By far the most important stimulus to demand is the media.

The role of the international media

The press plays a key role in sustaining protection from famine in India. British journalists played a key role in exposing the famines in Biafra and Ethiopia and prompting an international relief response (Harrison and Palmer, 1986). Jane Perlez of the *New York Times* was extremely influential in prompting a US response to the 1992 famine in Somalia (see Chapter 8). Journalists have congratulated themselves that they provide the missing trigger in the international relief network's response to disasters.

The congratulation is not warranted. It is in fact highly questionable whether the international press does play a role in preventing famine. Certainly it plays a role – the major role, in fact – in prompting large-scale international relief response, but that is a very different matter. To *prevent* famine, the media would have to ensure that governments cannot create famine and that they respond before suffering reaches the stage where it is a dramatic news story. The international media are simply not set up to do this.

The predominant form of journalists' exposure to famines has been characterized as 'disaster tourism' (de Waal, 1987). This term was coined as a companion to Robert Chambers' 'rural development tourism' (Chambers, 1983), which was an attempt to explain why visitors to rural areas of poor countries so rarely appreciated the depths of poverty. Noting that 'what the eye does not see the heart does not grieve about', Chambers identified a set of biases in visitors' exposure, which meant that they saw better-off areas (aid projects, areas by the roadside) at better-off times of year, saw men rather than women, and did not question their hosts' optimistic assessments. In famine, these biases are thrown into reverse: the visitor (journalist, aid worker or dignitary) selectively sees the worst and assumes the worst from what he or she sees. Relief agency guides take visitors to the worst places (relief shelters) and are keen to stress the hunger and dependence of the people and the importance of relief. This leads to exaggerated, dire predictions and stereotypes of pathetic dependency.

Journalists know in advance what a 'famine story' looks like and search for the right elements. The overall plot has been characterized as a 'fairy story' (Benthall, 1993), consisting of a helpless victim in distress, a villain (until recently this role was usually played by the weather) and a saviour (preferably a white nurse). The story gives the comforting illusion that a solution is at hand, and that the reader or viewer is (or can be) part of it. Each component involves distortion and exaggeration. The journalist typically selects the worst cases of child malnutrition in the worst feeding shelters, giving the misleading impression that they are all like that. The role of the 'villain' is grossly simplified. The 'saviour', a foreign relief agency, is not subjected to any form of analysis. If there is a 'political contract' to be found, it is here, in the relationship between relief agency and media and the donating public. George Alagiah of BBC television, one of the most honest of correspondents, has written:

> Relief agencies depend upon us for publicity and we need them to tell us where the stories are. There's an unspoken understanding between us, a sort of code. We try not to ask the question too bluntly: 'Where will we find the most starving babies?' And they never answer explicitly. We get the pictures just the same. (Alagiah, 1992)

This intimate relationship between journalists and relief agencies is perhaps the crux of the problem. Journalists are usually dependent upon relief workers for many or all of the following: access to the country, local transport, access to feeding centres, accommodation, telecommunication, electricity, translators, recreation and social support, information, understanding of the situation and storyline, sound bites, and medical care. As the critique of disaster tourism has become more widespread, more established foreign correspondents have tried to maintain a distance from relief agencies, but few have succeeded and newer journalists consistently fall into the same trap. Part of it is fear: journalists are afraid of diseases and violent attack in unfamiliar places. Part is laziness: it is easier to find a story by talking to an agency information officer in English or French than by going out and investigating for oneself. Part is knowing that the editor wants an 'aid angle' anyway and will not appreciate a complicated inquiry into local politics.

Perhaps most importantly, most journalists do not see anything wrong with this intimacy. They tend to believe that relief workers are impartial and humanitarian and that aid work provides a solution to the problems they can see. The relief workers are usually not deliberately distorting the picture either: they are simply presenting their tasks and their views. Also, in a highly uncertain disaster, with many ambiguities and information black holes, a relief programme is an island of familiarity and certainty. Journalists are often emotionally affected by working in famine, both upset by what they see and uncomfortable with their own voyeurism, and seek solace and justification in implicitly supporting the work of relief agencies.

The consequences are profound. Some disaster stories in the news are little more than commercials for relief agencies, and many are refractions of the agencies' analyses and agendas in the form of news. Relief agency commercials follow the same 'fairy story' plot and use very similar images. One fund-raising consultant in 1969 advised his client, 'Show babies . . . all the time show babies and more babies' (quoted in Smillie, 1995: 137). The journalistic 'cult of the ordinary person' often leads to a focus on human tragedy to the exclusion of political analysis.[6] Meanwhile some relief charities have come to use mock 'news stories' in newspapers as commercials. Tensions arose between British agencies and broadcasters in 1989 when relief commercials were beginning to pre-empt and hence scoop news reports from Ethiopia. The genres are converging so that a single formula is repeatedly presented.

Voluntary relief agencies enjoy immunity from the rule of journalism whereby 'news' can be identified as the difference between what an institution says is the case and what is actually the case. From Biafra to Rwanda, aid agency claims have been taken on trust. Some journalists delve into the political roots of the crisis, usually for the broadsheet newspapers. Few if any analyse the competence and ethics of the aid response, and none call the aid agencies to account when their operations are over and the record can be analysed. An evaluation of a relief programme never makes the news. This is not to say that relief programmes escape criticism. But the criticism is equally formulaic: relief is not enough and not quick enough, and sometimes it is blatantly inappropriate. Blame for these failures usually attaches to host governments, large institutional donors and 'bureaucracy', and rarely if ever to NGOs (e.g. Gill, 1986).

In contrast to India, or to domestic disasters in Western countries, the consumers of Western media reporting of famine are wholly separate from the recipients of relief programmes. Western journalists do not need to worry if they present famine victims in false, offensive or degrading terms, because they know that the people portrayed will not complain and have no recourse mechanisms. Some reporters do maintain a remarkable level of human sensitivity, but this is both rare and fragile. The international media's lack of accountability to those vulnerable to famine is the fundamental obstacle to their playing a consistent role in famine prevention.

These tendencies are compounded by the technological and institutional development of the media. In Biafra, the news story was broken by print journalists who cabled their texts home. In 1973, Jonathan Dimbleby broke the story of the Ethiopian famine with a documentary screened some weeks after his return. In 1984, Michael

---

[6]Lindsey Hilsum, speaking at a workshop, 'The Fate of Information in the Disaster Zone', Oxford, 29 September 1995.

Buerk and Mohamed Amin covered the Ethiopian famine in a news story screened just days after it was shot. In 1994, correspondents reported live from Rwandese refugee camps by satellite link-up. In the meantime the specialist foreign correspondent had gone into steep decline, to be replaced by non-specialist high-technology units despatched from headquarters to provide brief saturation coverage of high-intensity stories. Overall, the time and resources devoted to foreign news coverage – especially from sub-Saharan Africa – has shrunk. In what remains, the sensational, visually gripping and 'live' drives out the balanced, forensic and considered.

There is no conspiracy at work. While the broad outcome can be known well in advance, the specific places and themes of the next media-hyped disaster cannot be predictably arranged (cf. Hitchens, 1993: 220). For spurring relief action, the international media are a blunt and unreliable instrument. For holding relief institutions accountable, they are practically no use at all. For those reasons, they are closely embraced by the humanitarian international.

Implications

Relief institutions are inherently political and, like governments, their accountability and pursuit of interest need to be analysed. One central theme of this book is that famine is caused by failures of political accountability – an analysis that also holds for relief institutions. A second theme is that both famine and famine relief can be used to entrench power and ideological hegemony. Again, this also holds for the humanitarian international, both in its own right and as a component of a neo-liberal international dispensation. With each big relief operation, the humanitarian international becomes more powerful and more privileged. The following chapters will examine the way in which this has happened, and its implications for freedom from famine.

5

Sudan ▌ Privatizing
1972–93 ▌ Famine

In the mid-1970s, the Sudanese state used its own human and material resources to weather the 'Sahelian' drought and respond to a large influx of Eritrean and Ethiopian refugees. Twenty years later Sudan has become chronically famine-prone and dependent on external assistance. This chapter charts a preliminary political economy of famine in Sudan over these two decades of decline (see also African Rights, 1997). Three features of the state recur. One reflects the quip, 'Sudan is not a state but a process'. The process in question is the spread of a set of exclusivist social values and political-economic structures associated with the northern Arab 'core' of Sudan. The values include Islam and various social *mores*, the structures include aggressive forms of trade and mechanized farming. The second feature is instability at the centre of power. A stable ruling coalition has yet to emerge, and politics has swung between authoritarianism and liberalism, secularism and adherence to political Islam. The third feature is external orientation: to foreign patrons and creditors, expatriate Sudanese and the Islamist financiers who control their remittances, and international aid institutions. What began as financial dependence has infected many aspects of Sudanese political life.

Revolution of dis-May

Before the 1969 'May Revolution', Sudan enjoyed a parliamentary system and respect for many civil and political liberties. The state was dominated by two major families (Mahdi and Mirghani), each with its sectarian following, in unstable coalition with each other and with secular professional and military elites. This political dispensation excluded many. The South was in rebellion against northern Arab–Muslim domination, and large sections of the northern populace were also marginalized and discontented. There was little populist rhetoric or

86

commitment to social welfare, partly because the nationalist movement had been both divided and elitist, and independence had been achieved through political and diplomatic intrigue rather than popular mobilization.

In the 1930s and 1940s the nationalists had used food shortages to embarrass the British administration *vis-à-vis* Egypt, and not for politicizing rural people. After independence, the colonial Famine Regulations were quietly abandoned, as the cotton boom and a rapid expansion of grain cultivation appeared to consign food crises to a bad memory. Two robust structures stood as guarantees against localized food shortages degenerating into famine (in the North at least). One was a civil service well-known for its professionalism, and which retained an ethos of safeguarding local food supplies. The second was the system of 'native administration' of village and sub-district chiefs, most of them members of either the Mahdist or Mirghani sects. Loyal supplication did not preclude these men from making representations on behalf of their people when scarcities threatened.

On 25 May 1969 a group of radical officers headed by Jaafar Nimeiri seized power, and promised a radical transformation of all aspects of Sudanese society. In his sixteen years in power, Nimeiri proved a master of political survival, allying himself successively with the communists, secular modernizers and Southern non-Muslims, the same conservative sectarians who had been overthrown in 1969, and finally the extremist Muslim Brothers. Sudan was indeed transformed, but not in the ways expected. One prominent critic dubbed it the 'Revolution of Dis-May' (Mansour Khalid, 1985).

Rejecting sectarianism, Nimeiri sought legitimacy by a promise of economic development. Sudan seemed ripe for rapid growth, especially after peace in the South in 1972. For the first time, there was both a broad coalition that included the South and marginalized Northerners (such as the Nuba) and a strong governmental commitment to welfare. The native administration was abolished and replaced with elected councils, an expanded civil service and a single party, the Sudan Socialist Union (SSU). These were the conditions under which Sudan faced the drought of 1972–4 and the refugee inflows of 1975–8. It coped with both in a manner that appears in retrospect as exemplary. For the drought, the SSU, local councils and Red Crescent Committees organized food distributions, food supplies for towns were transported from the surplus-producing East to the deficit-struck West, and labour migration to the cotton schemes was encouraged. No international relief was needed.

This was to prove an interlude, undermined by three factors. One was political instability, notably a succession of coup attempts that led President Nimeiri to declare 'national reconciliation' with his former sectarian adversaries and the Muslim Brothers in 1978. The second was the migration of most of Sudan's professional class to the Gulf states, where the oil boom provided lucrative employment. The third was the failure of Sudan's 'open door' strategy for foreign investors to lead to accelerated development. Money was borrowed recklessly, but much of it went into private consumption and greasing the wheels of Nimeiri's increasingly corrupt patrimonial system. When the debts fell due in 1977–8, Sudan could not pay. This economic crisis pushed Nimeiri to turn to the IMF, USAID and 'national reconciliation'. Earlier political alliances with secular professionals and the South were abandoned. His rule became characterized by an embrace of political Islam and deepening economic dependence.

The return of political Islam had profound consequences that were to become evident over time. Dr Hassan al Turabi, the most influential of the Sudanese Muslim Brothers, took the post of Attorney General, and embarked upon Islamizing the legal system. He also demanded that Islamic banks (which charge no interest and instead enter into a partnership with their clients) be allowed to operate, with tax privileges. The civil service, army and financial sector became dominated by Islamists. The social base of the regime narrowed: prominent secularists and regional leaders left one by one, and the South reverted to unrest and finally war. Nimeiri now sought legitimacy in political Islam, declaring Islamic law in September 1983 and proclaiming himself as Imam and demanding an oath of unconditional allegiance from all members of the civil service and judiciary. He claimed he was accountable solely to Allah: any enforceable commitment to popular welfare was jettisoned.

The finances of Sudan during these years were quite extraordinary (Brown, 1992: Ch. 4), and go a long way to explaining why the President appeared oblivious to domestic political accountability. Although the government was almost bankrupt (massively in deficit on tax revenue and foreign exchange and with a foreign debt mounting from $8 billion to $12 billion), the country was awash with hard currency remitted by the Sudanese expatriates in the Arab states. An estimated 350,000 expatriates earned about $5.5 billion a year, equal to fully three-quarters of Sudan's gross domestic product of $7.5 billion. The inflow of remittances, mostly through informal channels, did not appear in the official economic statistics, but was ten times greater than the next highest source of foreign exchange, cotton exports. Remittances financed a real estate boom in major cities, a lucrative market in consumer goods, and an explosion of the informal sector. They also allowed Sudanese capitalists to export about $10 billion in capital flight, which, when combined with accumulated savings abroad, more than outweighed the national debt: Sudan was actually a creditor country.

The political repercussions of this transformation were enormous. The government was able to abandon most of its internal tax base (and tried to, when an Islamic commercial code was introduced in 1984) and instead rely on the apparently magical liquidity of Islamist financiers.

Meanwhile, as sectarian and secular capitalists divested, the Islamic banks and Islamist merchants were investing, exploiting their tax privileges, political connections and access to hard currency. They virtually monopolized the new remittance-based economic sectors, and also bought up farms, transport companies, and former state assets that were being sold off. It is not a major exaggeration to say that Sudan was sold and bought in these years.

Sudan's renowned local government rapidly decayed in the late 1970s and early 1980s. Inflation eroded the value of government salaries, and many civil servants joined the mass migration of Sudanese professionals to the Gulf. Corruption became endemic and local government budgets dwindled. Experiments with regionalization fostered factionalism in local government and further lowered morale. The weakening of both 'native administration' and the civil service removed the main structures that had underpinned rural protection from famine.

The early 1980s were years of Cold War confrontation. In the 1970s Nimeiri had defected by stages from the Eastern to the Western camps and by 1980 Sudan was seen as a key piece of the anti-communist strategic map. (The anti-communist Muslim Brothers were attractive to the US Government at the time.) Though massively in debt to the Paris Club of Western creditors and the IMF, Nimeiri exploited his strategic advantages to the maximum. Sudan became the largest recipient of US foreign assistance in sub-Saharan Africa (over $1.4 billion in all), and the official debt was rescheduled no fewer than eight times. This slowed but did not prevent deepening economic crisis and Nimeiri's insatiable demand for foreign finance to stay afloat.

A routine became established in which the IMF recommended a package of economic reforms; the Sudan Government agreed; the IMF duly issued its 'seal of approval'; the Paris Club met and provided generous funds (supposedly on the basis that Sudan would honour its agreement and repay its debt); Khartoum made symbolic gestures towards reform and debt repayments, but in reality the money disappeared into the vortex of corruption around Nimeiri; the Ministry of Finance then ran out of money and came back to the donors to be bailed out; and the US State Department contacted the US Treasury and the IMF and began the process all over again. By 1984 Nimeiri's treasury was living from hand to mouth. At this point the donors began to balk at providing 'the extraordinary levels of foreign aid that [were] necessary to maintain some semblance of stability in an otherwise explosive environment' (Brown, 1988: 73). A further complication was that Sudan was now defaulting on its debt to the IMF itself. The IMF is constitutionally debarred from dealing with a defaulter, and getting round this required great ingenuity. (The US State Department took out a commercial bridging loan, repaid the IMF, and was then reimbursed by the Sudanese Ministry of Finance when the Paris Club aid tranche was unlocked.) The day-to-day ins and outs of these financial conjuring tricks and the accompanying negotiating manoeuvres not only took up a formidable amount of time and energy at high levels of government, but also reconfigured political accountability: Nimeiri was reporting to his financiers in Washington, DC. When the IMF and the State Department finally withheld their money and insisted on severe austerity measures, Nimeiri could not survive.

Two subplots in the Sudan–US relationship are particularly significant: each strengthened Nimeiri's external orientation and eroded his domestic accountability. One concerned the Falashas (Ethiopian Jews), who were evacuated through Sudan to Israel (Karadawi, 1991). The relative international importance of the Falashas is highlighted by the fact that $300m. was raised to finance 'Operation Moses' in 1984 and care for its 8,000 beneficiaries, compared with an overall expenditure of $30m. on the remaining 600,000 refugees in Eastern Sudan. By its nature the operation was clandestine; when it was revealed it helped to discredit Nimeiri. The second subplot was Chevron's investment of over $1 billion in drilling for large high-quality oil deposits in Southern Sudan. Nimeiri hoped that oil revenues would solve his demand for easy money. Southern anticipation of this contributed to the war, which began with attacks on Chevron's operations. Nimeiri tried various gambits, including forming militias and buying off fragments of the rebel forces, to buy enough time for the oil to flow – expected in 1986. (He failed.)

The reforms demanded by the IMF and the US Treasury included widespread privatization of nationalized corporations and the radical slimming down of the state budget. These were welcomed by the Islamist merchants and financiers as it gave them greater leeway to expand their investments. Another component, that was to have important ramifications for protection against famine, was the privatization of social welfare. Although there were clear precursors in the dominant role of international NGOs in the reconstruction of Southern Sudan after the 1972 peace agreement, the privatization of relief began in earnest with refugee programmes in Eastern Sudan. During the 1970s, a strong national institution (the Commission of Refugees) had placed an indigenous NGO (the Sudan Council of Churches) in the dominant role as implementing partner, in collaboration with the refugees' own organizations. After the 1980 Khartoum conference on refugees, this began to change. Donors increased their assistance for refugees in Sudan, but the funds were provided to UNHCR and foreign NGOs and the Sudan Government ceded control of the programmes. The number of NGOs working with refugees in Sudan rose from 7 in 1978 (most of them indigenous agencies) to 23 in 1981 and 57 in 1985 (Karadawi, 1988: 298).

The implications of the privatization of welfare provision, combined with growing international dependency, will be a recurring theme in the discussion of Sudan.

Nimeiri's famine 1983–5

In 1983, drought threatened hunger in north Kordofan, north Darfur and the Red Sea Hills: food production was 25 per cent of normal. The local governments made various attempts to distribute relief, but their budgets were extremely tight and the amounts distributed were meagre. Requests for assistance from the central government met with no response: Khartoum simply banked upon normal rains returning the situation to normal in 1984. The Governor of Darfur, Ahmed Diraige, made Nimeiri's inaction on the drought the spark for his resignation and departure into exile. In early 1984, the FAO estimated Darfur's relief needs at 39,000 tonnes. Khartoum cut the figure to 7,000 tonnes, and delivered even less. Nothing was sent to Kordofan. When the rains failed again in the summer of 1984, conditions became increasingly desperate. But, apart from the largely symbolic declaration of an emergency in Darfur, nothing was done. There was mass migration of destitute people to towns, including the capital. Children in rural areas began to die: it was the first 'famine that kills' for seventy years.

Officially, Nimeiri answered to Allah. In reality he was accountable to those with money or promises of money. The drought and famine were an embarrassment and a distraction. Nimeiri was struggling to persuade the United States that Sudan was stable, which meant denying that the troubles in the South amounted to war. (Mobilizing militias instead of the regular army was one result of this, and had profound consequences later on.) Admitting to famine might also have shaken US confidence. The famine also stood in the way of some important investments. Promising to make Sudan 'the breadbasket of the Arab world', the government had offered incentives to expand mechanized farming, mainly to Arab and Islamist investors. To have admitted that there was a food crisis would have jeopardized further 'bread-basket' investment. Meanwhile, the Faisal Islamic Bank became a major dealer in sorghum and reaped windfall profits from the sharp grain price rises in 1984/5. (Subsequently a judicial investigation was established into the bank's grain market speculation, but Hassan al Turabi's first action on becoming Attorney General again in 1988 was to close the file.)

Nimeiri's anti-famine strategy was simple: he denied that the problem existed (Article 19, 1990). In one of many similar statements, he said publicly: 'The situation with respect to food security and health is reassuring'.[1] On other occasions he blamed the refugees and contradicted reports from his own ministries that Sudan faced a food crisis. Only in January 1985, a full year after the drought became apparent, and under severe if belated pressure from the US State Department, did Nimeiri admit its reality. By then it was too late, and an entirely preventable tragedy cost an estimated 250,000 lives.

[1]BBC, *Summary of World Broadcasts*, ME/7792, 5 November 1984.

The famine helped crystallize a broad coalition of forces against Nimeiri. The coalition was led by a group of professionals, including lawyers, doctors and some civil servants. They had many reasons to oppose the government, but the famine provided a powerful rallying point. In November 1984 a group of leading doctors in the Ministry of Health published a report on famine conditions. This unilateral initiative was a test of the ability of civil groups to mobilize politically against Nimeiri. (It is interesting to note that, despite the prominence of health professionals in highlighting the famine, the political emphasis remained on food supply rather than health care – a testament to the narrow politicization of famine in Africa around the food issue.) Shortly afterwards the Ministry of Agriculture contradicted the President and released its estimate that 160,000 tonnes of food relief was needed for Kordofan and Darfur (*Africa Economic Digest*, 23 November 1984). One of the attractions of the famine issue was its international resonance: Ministry officials were in close contact with FAO and USAID, and the latter had already consigned food relief to Sudan in advance of an official request.

The famine also split the SSU and hence played a central role in bringing down the government. On 2 November, the Omdurman branch of the SSU asked the citizens to give help to the drought migrants encamped around the city. Many obliged: assisting the famine victims was simultaneously an act of charity and of protest. The Secretary General of the SSU, Mohamed al Tayeb, contradicted the Omdurman branch and ordered the expulsion of the migrants by force. He correctly feared that an urban-rural alliance would form against the government. Some migrants were removed on trucks, but most remained; and in any case the political momentum had been established. When the democratic forces organized the Popular Uprising in April 1985, many of the protesters were drought migrants. In the SSU's counter-protest, the Omdurman branch did not turn up: the poor pro-government showing was the turning point in the fall of the regime which occurred three days later.

The fall of Nimeiri was a triumph of the politicization of famine. Unfortunately the coalition was fragile and its use of the famine issue largely tactical. A robust anti-famine political contract did not emerge. The most blatant example of opportunism was the rebel Sudan People's Liberation Army (SPLA), which used its radio broadcasts to chastise the government for inaction over the famine, while the SPLA itself was helping to create famine in the South. Most of the political classes who mobilized against Nimeiri lost interest in the famine after the success of the uprising. The political agenda switched elsewhere, chiefly to peace in the South, elections and Islamic law. Only the drought migrants themselves had an enduring interest in anti-famine measures, and they did not remain politically mobilized. The failure of the anti-Nimeiri democratic forces to develop a strategic alliance against famine was to prove an important failing.

Dr Gizouli Dafallah, the representative of the doctors who had pressed Nimeiri on the famine issue in November 1984, became interim Prime Minister in April 1985. He promptly dealt with the problem by delegating all responsibility for relief to the international agencies. This was an important step in depoliticizing famine: it became the ideological property of international agencies rather than being owned by the democratic forces that organized the Popular Uprising. Famine prevention became an internationalized technical issue rather than a political one, reflected in the enormous amounts of money vested in a famine early warning system based on monitoring economic, climatic and agricultural data. This was not only a pragmatic political act but a manifestation of the neo-liberal agenda for eviscerating governmental responsibilities.

Sectarian famine, 1985–9

The post-Nimeiri political dispensation was dominated by the conservative sectarian parties, but not sufficiently so to guarantee strong or stable government. The Umma Party of Sadiq el Mahdi won the most seats in the 1986 elections and formed a coalition with the next largest party, the Democratic Unionist Party (DUP), closely associated with the Mirghani family. This coalition was threatened from the left by an array of regional and secular groups, including most of the alliance that organized the Popular Uprising, and from the right by the National Islamic Front (NIF, the party of the Muslim Brothers). The NIF won a small share of the popular vote, but, reflecting its mobilization among expatriate Sudanese and its powerful financial power base, it captured all but two of the 'graduate' seats in the new parliament and was the third largest party. Prime Minister Sadiq flirted with both wings of the opposition and then moved steadily closer to the NIF, bringing it into government in 1988. Throughout this period, Sudan enjoyed all the institutions of liberal democracy, at least in Khartoum and other urban centres. The press was uncensored and vigorous, and often highly critical of the government. Political parties, trade unions and professional associations were free to mobilize. There was no suspicion of fraud in the elections. The judiciary was independent and on several occasions overruled government decisions. It is arguable that this political liberalism was as much a reflection of the weakness of government as of a true spirit of tolerance; but the freedoms were genuine and were used by, among others, human rights activists.

The parliamentary period witnessed the most severe famine in Sudan's modern history. It was in the South and was caused by the war, or more precisely, how the war was fought. The military means of famine creation by both government and SPLA were elementary but devastating; they have been documented elsewhere (Keen, 1994; de Waal, 1993a) and will only be summarized here.

The main instrument was the militia, specifically the *Murahaliin* militia, drawn from the Baggara Arabs of southern Kordofan and southern Darfur, which raided the Dinka of northern Bahr el Ghazal. The *Murahaliin* emerged from the conjunction of local factors (such as impoverishment and unresolved inter-ethnic conflicts) with political and military decisions in government. Their raids were frequent, widespread and devastating. The raiders stole livestock, destroyed villages, poisoned wells and killed indiscriminately (Amnesty International, 1989). They were also implicated in enslaving captives. Displaced survivors fled to garrison towns, where they were forced to sell their cattle and other assets cheaply. They had to work for little or no pay; they were prohibited from moving outside the camps to gather firewood or straw; and they were often prevented from moving further north to places where work or charity might be available. Prohibiting movement and wage-earning amounted to a sentence of death by starvation.

Army commanders and local government officials also prevented relief assistance from reaching the displaced. In one instance, relief food donated by the European Community sat for more than two years in wagons in a railway siding in el Muglad, just a few hundred yards from a displaced camp where Dinka were starving. At a higher level, the government blocked a series of initiatives by local and international NGOs, the UN and the ICRC to send relief, and connived in the diversion of relief by the army.

The cumulative effect of the raiding, restrictions and relief failures was to starve people to death. In the summer of 1988, death rates in some displaced camps reached the unprecedented level of 1 per cent per day, far higher than any levels recorded before or since for famines in Africa. Perhaps 30,000 people died in the displaced camps of Western Sudan in that year.

More widely, localized famines were created by military tactics including raiding and requisitioning, scorched earth and sieges. The army and militias raided cattle and other movable goods and stole food on operations. Around garrisons the army prevented cultivation and cut down any cover, including standing crops, to give clear sight lines.

These military strategies should not be seen in isolation from the process of 'Sudanization'. Raiding cattle, depopulating villages and sweeping up their inhabitants into displaced camps were a violent form of expanding the political and economic power of the ruling elites. The *Murahaliin* were drawn from one of the main power bases of Sadiq's Umma Party, with powerful commercial and political connections. In 1982 the cross-over between military and commercial elites had been formalized in the creation of the Military Economic Board, which comprised seven military corporations with extensive ownership and privileges across economic sectors (Economist Intelligence Unit, 1983: 16). Merchant–officer partnerships making windfall profits from contrived scarcities in garrison towns were a feature of the war from the outset: a war economy developed, with vested interests in its continuation. The violence, the famine and the failure of relief represented a policy success for certain politicians, merchants and officers.

There is little evidence of a grand plan at the summit of power to use the famine as a genocidal weapon (though some politicians and militiamen undoubtedly contemplated such things). Rather, the moral, political and economic logic of the war as interpreted in Khartoum created a space where such near-genocidal motives and practices could flourish. The South was not only a war zone, it was a zone whose population had no political clout either nationally or internationally, and it was an ethics-free zone, where agents of the state could do what they liked with impunity. This abolition of restraint did not happen automatically, and was refracted through complex local politics: Khartoum still had clients and allies in the South, whom it had to mollify, and who had power bases in their own right. But in Khartoum, the famine was virtually invisible.

By contrast, the Sadiq Government was acutely sensitive to the demands of the Northern urban constituency over food prices. A wheat subsidy was targeted at urban consumers and was prohibitively costly to the exchequer (equivalent to 7 per cent of government revenue) (Maxwell *et al.* 1990). It was a legacy of colonial times, and its partial removal at IMF insistence in March 1985 had contributed to the downfall of Nimeiri. Sudan's donors, notably the IMF, insisted that the subsidy should be cut or abolished as the prerequisite for a firm agreement and further assistance. But, despite repeated negotiations in which all other austerity measures were agreed, Sadiq would not touch the bread subsidy. The slightest mention of cutting it brought crowds on to the streets. One donor representative explained, 'the current position may be 95 per cent of the way but the crucial 5 per cent is missing' (*Africa Economic Digest*, 14 August 1987), All government finance was hostage to this single issue. In Sudan, 'democracy' meant accountability to one limited constituency.

Two other strands of accountability remained familiar from Nimeiri's days: to international financial institutions and to a particular interpretation of political religion. Sudan's relations with its donors, particularly the US, resumed where they had left off in 1984. Both government and donors considered negotiations over official economic assistance, debt rescheduling and economic policy more important than the famine in the South. The game of keeping Sudan solvent needed ingenuity on both sides. The IMF invented a new policy instrument of 'shadow programmes' to maintain relations with a country with which it was officially debarred from working. It needed its debts repaid, and did not want Sudan to declare a formal default which would create a 'moral hazard' and might encourage much larger debtors such as Mexico to follow suit. The US rushed assistance through the small windows when Sudan was up-to-date on loan repayments; it wanted to keep the Sadiq regime afloat for the same strategic reasons as it had supported Nimeiri. Meanwhile the Sudan Government needed to display enough diplomacy and commitment to maintain the minimum of donor confidence. Financial and political decisions were structured around the visits of IMF delegations and the timing of debt-repayment schedules. As in 1983–5, the machinations of the international financial system were the heartbeat of the Ministry of Finance, which was in turn the key to the government's political survival.

The NIF remained the best funded and best organized political force in the country. Its absolutist Islamist agenda had called the bluff of the sectarian parties, which were ostensibly Islamist as well. Hassan al Turabi appeared to mesmerize Sadiq el Mahdi, and the political aims of the two men gradually converged. There were good financial reasons for this convergence, as the NIF's dominance in the financial sector persisted, and many sectarian-owned businesses were increasingly intertwined with Islamist finance. The price was furthering the Islamist agenda. The night after the disastrous 1988 floods in Khartoum, the Cabinet met in all-night session to debate the adoption of Islamic law.

The famine did not become a political scandal in Sudan. The Northern opposition showed no significant interest at any time. Northern journalists rarely covered the famine, which would have meant travelling to the war zone, which was risky (one journalist was killed by a landmine in 1987) and would have entailed challenging the security restrictions. One Southern journalist, Mike Kilongson, was arrested for reporting on the famine. But most importantly there was very little interest among their readership. Apart from the English language *Sudan Times* (edited by a Southerner), only the Communist *al Meidan* showed any interest, and that was largely confined to the political implications of the militias.

There were few Southern MPs in parliament, and they had to deal with many other pressing issues. Their obvious ally in this cause – the SPLA – proved to be an obstacle. The SPLA put military victory before political mobilization: the political philosophy of its leader, Dr John Garang, was to capture state power and then use it as an instrument for social transformation from above. In the meantime the SPLA made no attempt to deliver social reform or welfare. At its best its administration represented benevolent paternalism, at its worst it was violent and extractive. SPLA military tactics created food shortages in many areas (by requisitioning food, labour and livestock) and exacerbated them in others. It besieged garrison towns and reduced them to starvation. One of the reasons why so many victims of raids fled northwards or to garrison towns was that the SPLA made no provision for relief for civilians. It also consistently blocked relief supplies. This hobbled politicians in the North who could have rebuilt a broad anti-famine coalition. For instance, between February and July 1986 a group of

Southern indigenous NGOs (mostly church-related), Southern politicians and foreign relief workers pressed initiatives for relief to Southern civilians. The proposal was very similar to Operation Lifeline Sudan, which followed three years later. It was blocked by the SPLA and finally killed off by the SPLA shooting down a civil airliner at Malakal in August. (The UN then took up a similar relief initiative, under the name 'Operation Rainbow', but a combination of political incompetence on the part of UN personnel, obstruction by the increasingly hard-line Sadiq government, and lack of interest from Western donors killed off that proposal too.)

Large numbers of famine migrants around Khartoum began to become a political issue in 1987–8, and, as before, the government responded with proposals for forced removal, one rationale for this being that the displaced represented a security threat, a 'fifth column' of the SPLA. Although the removals were not carried out until several years later, the government did succeed in sowing political division between the displaced and the town-dwellers. Most mainstream Arabic newspapers echoed the government's fears; playing the 'security threat' card worked. For example, when a train from Bahr el Ghazal arrived in the capital in April 1988 with 3,000 famine migrants, and six children died at the railway station, none of the Arabic newspapers and journals mentioned the fact at all. At one moment it seemed that solidarity might emerge, when, following the August 1988 floods, there was criticism from all quarters over corruption and favouritism in the distribution of relief. But just as this was growing more vocal, the ruling coalition collapsed in a dispute over the issue of Sharia law, and the matter was taken no further. SPLA policy also began to change by 1988, when the loss of population from the South became a major obstacle to its military mobilization. But even the 1988 peace accords between the SPLA and the DUP made no mention of the famine or famine relief. The issue was raised only in the post-accord press conference.

The failure to politicize the famine passed the initiative to the Western donors, when they belatedly decided to act in late 1988. This came about through the lobbying of some international NGOs (notably Oxfam) and coverage in the Western press. The famine may not have discredited Sadiq at home, but it was devastating abroad – a potentiality overlooked by the Ministry of Finance in its dealings with the donors. By the end of 1988, pressure from the Netherlands and US Governments for a realignment of policy on Sudan was mounting. This finally emerged in the shape of Operation Lifeline Sudan (OLS), proposed, designed and implemented almost entirely by international relief agencies. It followed an apolitical technical design, a 'natural disaster' model together with practices drawn from the ICRC's methods of negotiated access. OLS's depoliticized nature was to constrain fundamentally what it could do as it gradually grew into a major institution in its own right (see Chapter 7).

Overall, political liberalism modulated but did not substantially alter the lines of accountability established in the last years of Nimeiri. The exclusivism of the government combined with the weakness of the opposition and external orientation to prevent democratic institutions from playing a vital role in protection from famine. The government was more sensitive to urban constituents, but that was all, and no urban–rural or North–South solidarity emerged to force its hand. In terms of the politicization of famine and the emergence of an anti-famine political contract, the 'democratic' period proved as regressive as its predecessor.

Islam, food and power

Brigadier (later General) Omer al Bashir seized power on behalf of the NIF in June 1989. The NIF's claim to legitimacy resides in its adoption of Islamic principle, and its goal is a theocratic rather than a democratic state. Shortly after the coup, General al Bashir promised a referendum on Islamic law, but this proposal was quickly dropped, partly because of the NIF argument that God's will is not subject to plebiscite. This represented both a rejection of social contract theories of political authority and an exclusion of those opposed to political Islam, particularly non-Muslims. The military-NIF Government was highly repressive from the outset. Newspapers were closed down, political parties and trade unions banned, and all forms of mass communication brought under government control. The apparatus of Nimeiri's police state was recreated in more extreme form.

Lines of popular accountability were fewer and more tenuous than before. The coup was the culmination of ten years of NIF financial dominance in Sudan, and in government the NIF was able to take that process to its logical conclusion. One component of the strategy was intensified privatization, which in effect meant selling off national assets at knock-down prices to NIF businessmen. Another component was an attempt to break Sudan's dependence on Western and conservative Arab donors. A precondition of this was greater self-reliance under the slogan 'we eat what we produce', and an unparalleled austerity programme, including cutting the urban wheat subsidy. This came at a high price: the National Economic Salvation Programme adopted in early 1990 made no mention of food security and included no provisions for a safety net to help the poor. Meanwhile, famine-creating military activities continued in parts of the South and intensified in the Nuba Mountains (African Rights, 1995b).

The NIF's radical agenda was almost blown off course at the outset of its rule by a major famine in 1990–1. This famine demonstrates two main themes: how lack of accountability creates vulnerability to famine, and how a determined and astute government can turn food relief into power.

Village in the Nuba Mountains, Sudan, burned by government troops (Julie Flint)

There was drought in the Western regions in 1989 and a poor national harvest (Africa Watch, 1990). Regional governments appealed for food relief, but Khartoum reduced the figures and the donors were complacent. For example, Darfur had asked for 66,000 tonnes; the World Food Programme assessed the needs at 3,500 tonnes; the European Community transported 1,000 tonnes and distributed none at all. The Islamic Development Bank, the government's chosen alternative for relief distributions, provided only 506 tonnes. Both donors and NGOs appeared to have forgotten all the lessons of the 1980s: they were gambling that an adequate harvest in 1990 and villagers' reliance on coping strategies would be enough to avert disaster (Young and Jaspars, 1995: 132). This did not pay off. The drought intensified and spread in 1990, and, most seriously, the grain-producing areas of the East faced a very poor harvest, which implied a 'food gap' in the months before the harvest began to be gathered in early 1991.

In August 1990, the famine suddenly widened to the central regions and Khartoum. Food prices rose by a factor of four between June and September, and frequently no grain at all was available in the market. The grain price hyper-inflation was totally without precedent, far more extreme than in the 1984/5 famine. Wage rates fell far behind the cost of basic provisions (Patel, 1994). The reason for this was panic. When President al Bashir announced his support for the Iraqi invasion of Kuwait, the Sudanese feared that remittances from the Gulf states and US food deliveries would be halted. Those with money rushed to convert it into food. In effect, middle-class people and traders bought up all the available food on the market, laying in stocks against the feared disaster. This panic-driven spiral then developed a momentum of its own, with speculators and others joining in the buying spree and in effect inflating the price of grain beyond what 'natural' market forces alone would have created. For those who depended on buying grain on a day-to-day basis, the result was immediate hunger.

A well-managed national food policy could have prevented this spiral by releasing grain on to the market. But the government had exported the reserves. After the 1984 famine, stringent controls on food exports had been introduced, regulated by the Agricultural Bank of Sudan. In March 1990 the NIF reversed this. Leading cadres were brought in to manage the strategic grain reserve, which was exported under the auspices of the Faisal and Baraka Islamic banks. A total of about 500,000 tonnes was sold to the European Community and Saudi Arabia for animal feed. By October, the main government silo contained just 9,500 tonnes, most of it unfit for human consumption.

The government's response to the August price hike was like that of its citizens: bewilderment and panic. Rather than the Agricultural Bank or the Relief and Rehabilitation Commission, the security services were put in charge of food security. The army was sent to markets in Khartoum to confiscate traders' stocks, a move that only undermined confidence. Traders responsible for 'smuggling' food were threatened with the death penalty. The movement of grain across regional boundaries was banned and the legal price of grain fixed at an unrealistically low level. None of these measures worked.

Unable to manage the situation with the resources available, and determined not to beg from international donors at the very start of its Islamist revolution, the government determined simply to ride out the crisis. Various regional governments made statements of food need; they were ignored. The national early warning system did its job, stating: 'immediate action is called for to avert the repetition of the 1985 catastrophe' (RRC, *Early Warning System Bulletin*, 15 October 1990: p. 1). Its bulletin included all the technical information a food security planner could ask for: updates on grain prices, livestock prices, wheat and wheat-flour supply, refugees, displaced population, and relief deliveries and stocks. Between early warning and the necessary political action there was a 'missing link' (Buchanan-Smith and Davies, 1995: Ch. 5). The official line from the central government was that no famine existed, nor was imminent. No declaration of famine was made, nor any appeal for assistance. The official view was naively and aggressively optimistic. For example, the Minister for Agriculture described accounts of an impending famine as 'unfounded rumours' circulated by 'some malicious circles to serve their own political objectives'.[2] A press release by the Sudan Embassy in London, dated 9 October, reads:

> The view of the government regarding aid is that relief work will be largely unnecessary in Sudan. . . . Those really interested in the welfare of the Sudanese people should support those efforts, instead of doling out meagre rations that only enhance dependency and loss of dignity. Those who are not should keep their peace and leave us alone.

Beneath the bluster, the NIF was developing a strategy of political triage: the limited grain supply was to be secured for politically vital constituencies. Khartoum was the priority. For the first time ever, sorghum, the staple of the poor, was rationed. The ration was distributed under the control of security and NIF appointees, through neighbourhood committees set up by a special Food Security Council for the capital. The committees later evolved into permanent Popular Committees, some of which were explicitly dedicated to the 'defence of the nation' and became one of the main instruments of surveillance and supervision in the cities. For the first few months there was barely enough food for the committees to retain their credibility, but nonetheless discontent was contained and the famine was turned into an opportunity for political control.

---

[2]'No imminent famine in Sudan', letter, *Daily Nation* (Nairobi), 15 October 1990; SUNA, 12 October 1990.

Displaced famine victims, Red Sea Hills, Sudan, 1991 (Panos: Sarah Errington)

The relocation of squatters and displaced people was another priority for the Food Security Council. Their number had risen to an estimated 1.8 million, almost all from the South and West. The government feared that food riots might make Khartoum ungovernable. The Food Security Council cut off water supplies to the shanty towns and in October about 30,000 people were forcibly removed and their houses demolished. It was not logistically feasible to remove all the displaced, but the show of force had the desired effect of intimidating them. The famine passed without serious disturbances and the relocations continued over the succeeding years (African Rights, 1995a).

Foreign NGOs planned to distribute food in rural areas: the government wanted to divert it to the towns. In one instance, after a food riot in Um Ruwaba town, NGO relief food intended for displaced Southerners was commandeered at gunpoint and distributed to the town's residents. The ban on the movement of food left 35,000 tonnes of USAID-donated food in warehouses. USAID suspected the government would redirect it from the Western provinces to Khartoum. This was the spark for a dispute with the US Government – the only serious political confrontation caused by the famine. On 2 October the US took firm measures: it turned down a request for $150 million of food aid (on concessionary sale terms), suspended all deliveries of food under the current food aid contract (worth another 55,000 tonnes), and diverted a ship carrying 45,000 tonnes of US (concessionary sale) food aid destined for Port Sudan. The effect was immediate: two days later, the government unblocked the internal movement of relief food, thus exempting international relief from its strategy of triage. It also made some concessions on food relief to the South. These adversarial negotiations over international relief contrasted with the lack of any internal politicization of the famine.

The 1990 food crisis dramatically demonstrated the Sudan Government's financial and technical dependence on unsympathetic Western donors. In the aftermath of the famine, the government put much energy into breaking this dependence and developing a form of humanitarian action tailored to its extremist Islamic philosophy. Together with ownership of mechanized farming and control of national grain reserves, Islamic relief NGOs made the third part of what was emerging as a comprehensive strategy for using food for power. 'Islamic' NGOs had been operating in Sudan since the late 1970s; after 1990 they were increasingly integrated into government-sponsored programmes of 'Islamic social planning' and the 'Comprehensive Call'. These agencies benefit from a range of tax privileges associated with the Islamization of the financial and fiscal systems, and also receive support directly from government institutions.

Western thinking on famine and relief is founded on the distinctions between charitable and commercial, humanitarian and military, religious and secular, governmental and non-governmental. The Sudanese Islamic agencies conflate all these categories. They can also act as trading companies, may assist in training or feeding soldiers, and are active in proselytization (including coercive conversion of non-Muslims). 'Peace camps' run by Islamic agencies are an integral part of the government's counter-insurgency strategy. Under Turabi's vision, an Islamic state is far more than a government: it is an entire, integrated community of believers (*umma*) (al Turabi, 1983: 241–2). Responsibility for implementing this programme rests with the *umma* and the institutions it sets up under the aegis of the *sharia*: Islamic humanitarianism is a central component of this comprehensive programme. In some of the war zones, Islamic agencies have become virtually indistinguishable from the government.

Even where no food was delivered, the government used the famine to promote its version of Islamic orthodoxy. For example, it ordered villages to organize the *istisga* rain prayer, 'to generate implicit public displays of the legitimacy of the regime' (Kevane and Gray, 1995: 282). The fatalistic attribution of drought and famine to the Almighty is the opposite of political mobilization against famine.

By September 1991, only about 200,000 tonnes of food aid – one fifth of the national deficit – had actually been distributed. No large-scale starvation was reported, and the government concluded that there had been no famine, as it had claimed all along. The donors and relief agencies were only marginally less sanguine, concluding that

> the major part of the impact of the food shortage was carried by the community who had, perforce, to resort to a range of traditional and non-traditional coping strategies, including reduced consumption, if the last can rightly be called a 'coping strategy'. (Patel, 1994: 317)

The government allowed no systematic measure of mortality, and in the absence of any hard data, it is easy to infer from the absence of mass starvation in relief shelters that no excess mortality existed. This would be wholly wrong. Certainly the 'megadeaths' predicted by some relief workers did not materialize, as they never in fact do. Famine deaths are more insidious and less spectacular. Examination of what scraps of evidence are available combined with extrapolation from nutritional surveys provides very strong indications that child death rates were at least twice the normal level in many parts of Western Sudan (Kelly and Buchanan-Smith, 1994). In Darfur, after the 1990 harvest, malnutrition did not decline; children approached the hungry season in an extremely vulnerable state (Young and Jaspars, 1995: 96). There was indeed a killing famine, but the Sudan Government was able to ride it out while entrenching itself in power.

Implications

Sudan has intermittently possessed both the technical capacity and the political will to prevent famine. Its calamitous failure to do so since the early 1980s has followed primarily from repeated political failures. A constant theme has been the decay of domestic political accountability, associated with financial dependence on remittances from expatriates in the Gulf and aid from Western donors, the growth of political extremism, and the development of a war economy based on the violent seizure of assets, including people.

There have been moments of hope. Notably, the Popular Uprising of 1985 briefly forged a broad anti-famine coalition, but could not sustain it. The liberal democracy that followed is a rebuke to any simplistic view that equates elections and a free press with freedom from famine; within an exclusivist political contract, liberal institutions can simply give legitimacy to political processes that create famine. The coalition that belatedly achieved the breakthrough of Operation Lifeline in 1989 also proved fragile.

The internationalization of responsibility for relief has played an ancillary role in Sudan's decay. There have been technical advances, but these have proved largely meaningless without political commitment to fight famine. The near-perfect operation of the famine early warning system in 1990 is a sad monument to irrelevance. There have also been policy successes for the humanitarian international; the coalition of NGOs and donors that helped push through Operation Lifeline Sudan is a case in point. But this success was not sustained: the agenda was too narrow and the engagement with Sudanese politics too superficial. A more consistent feature of foreign assistance is that it has helped sustain governments' authoritarian and militaristic tendencies. At key moments, humanitarian aid has been used to defuse the political implications of famine, finally assisting General Omer al Bashir to emerge politically strengthened from the 1990–91 disaster.

6

Northern
Ethiopia

Revolution,
War-Famine &
Two Models of Relief

The famine in northern Ethiopia which became world news in 1984 was an earthquake in the humanitarian world. The true story of that famine (more accurately dated 1983–5) has still not been acknowledged by most humanitarian agencies. Sensitivities are still raw more than a decade later. Only Biafra casts such a shadow over international humanitarianism in Africa.

Four elements of the story of the 1983–5 famine will be discussed in this chapter – a selection that leaves much unsaid. The first is the legacy of the 1973 famine in Wollo that contributed to the overthrow of Emperor Haile Selassie. This famine, and the fact that it was succeeded within a decade by another even worse disaster, throws light on the nature of political accountability in Ethiopia. The second is the manner in which the famine was created, specifically focusing on its epicentre in Tigray and northern Wollo. This is one of the great examples of how war fought in particular ways creates famine. Thirdly, the famine was a spectacular example of manipulated humanitarianism. After the famine became world news, a bargain was made whereby the Western humanitarians allowed Colonel Mengistu Haile Mariam to continue with famine-creating war strategies in return for access to some famine-stricken people. Lastly, the famine saw the development of a radically different form of humanitarian action, in the cross-border operations to areas held by the Eritrean People's Liberation Front (EPLF) and the Tigrayan People's Liberation Front (TPLF). Though successful, this model did not acquire political or theoretical legitimacy until after it had been disbanded.

Famine, revolution and legitimacy 1972–8

In 1973, Wollo province suffered a famine in which between 40,000 and 80,000 people are estimated to have died (Seaman and Holt, 1975). The famine struck two very different sections of the populace: Afar camel herders in the lowlands, and Oromo smallholder tenant farmers on the escarpment. Both groups were poor and marginalized, and had been subject to the depredations of the landowning class and the state, including widespread confiscation of land. Emperor Haile Selassie suppressed reports about the famine and refused to countenance relief. Only when the British journalist Jonathan Dimbleby screened a television documentary 'The Unknown Famine' did the truth become widely known. This contributed to the collapse of Haile Selassie's legitimacy and the 1974 revolution.

The revolutionary government promised to eradicate famine and enacted far-reaching reforms in 1974–5. But these proved futile and Ethiopia descended into famine again a decade later. The seeds of this failure should be sought in the ways political authority was negotiated during the revolution. In particular, while famine played a role, the famine-vulnerable people themselves were almost wholly absent from the political process.

The role of famine in the 1974 revolution
Numerous writers have recounted all or part of the story of the famine, how it developed and how it was concealed (See, *inter alia*, Mesfin Wolde Mariam, 1986; Nolan, 1974). All agree that it played a central role in undermining Haile Selassie's Government. The question is, how? The Emperor had ignored famines before (notably in Tigray in 1958 and Wollo in 1966) without political cost. The imperial government's reaction to a UNICEF report documenting the famine was:

> If we have to describe the situation in the way you have in order to generate international assistance, then we don't want that assistance. The embarrassment to the government isn't worth it. Is that perfectly clear? (quoted in Brietzke 1982: 127)

(UNICEF complied.) The Vice-Minister of Planning, who spoke these words, astutely identified 'political embarrassment' as the government's main fear: hunger itself was of secondary importance.

Famine-stricken peasants had never before successfully challenged a government. They carried out the peculiarly Ethiopian tradition of mass supplication, in the form of large marches to the towns or the court. This 'symbolic performance' doubled as a silent protest, and hence carried a political message (Dessalegn 1989: 15). The Emperor implicitly acknowledged this message when he changed the itinerary of his visit to Wollo in November 1972, to avoid meeting a crowd of 20,000 hungry supplicants from the villages, and when he ordered roadblocks to be set up to prevent two marches of destitute peasants reaching the capital.

There were no urban food riots: the early stages of the revolution were remarkably non-violent. (When the Dergue finally deposed Haile Selassie, they positioned just four tanks at strategic points in the capital.) Revolutionary actions came from students, town dwellers and junior army officers, who used the symbolism of famine as part of a new political idiom.

University and school students played an important role in setting a radical political agenda in the 1960s and 1970s. They combined practical action with political symbolism. For example, students responded to the 1970 cholera epidemic by assisting the Ministry of Health with preventive health education in rural areas. The initiative was stopped after government opposition (Balsvik, 1985: 310). The Wollo famine was an ideal instrument both for demonstrating the students' credentials as proponents of social justice and welfare and for discrediting the government. An exhibition of pictures of the famine was shown (and broken up by the police) (ibid.: 303), the Wollo Famine Relief Fund was established, and school students in Dessie protested over lack of relief (six students were shot in a demonstration against the arrest of the leaders of the first protest).

As the government reacted in a more repressive and violent manner, the famine became more and more of a political scandal. On the day when the Emperor was deposed, Ethiopian TV screened excerpts from Dimbleby's film, juxtaposed with footage of the ostentatious wedding of the daughter of a prominent aristocrat and provincial governor. A group of soldiers formed the Provisional Military Administrative Committee (popularly known as the Dergue) and took power, supported by some educated ideologues.

Revolutionary change and famine prevention

The students' outrage at the famine was genuine, and there is no doubt that many of the actions taken during the early days of the revolution came from a sincere commitment to radical change for the better. Most of the censorship of the press was lifted. A committee of inquiry was set up to examine the causes of the famine and the Relief and Rehabilitation Commission (RRC) was established. The most far-reaching measure was the land reform proclamation of March 1975, which abolished feudal land tenure. This also had pragmatic political motivations; it struck a fatal blow at the *ancien régime* and gained popular legitimacy for the Dergue in the rural south. It led directly to unprecedented well-being for millions of rural Ethiopians (albeit for a brief period). The revolutionary government was showing an unparalleled commitment to tackling the structural causes of famine, and was going well beyond standard relief measures.

On paper, Ethiopia was better equipped to prevent famine in 1975 than at any time in its history. The shortcoming was that while the *famine* played a role in the revolution, the *famine-vulnerable people* did not. There was no rural insurrection in Wollo or Tigray. Violence in the Afar lowlands was largely criminal in nature. After the land reform decree was announced (and in some places, even beforehand), tenant farmers in the south had seized their land and expelled the landlords: the decree was to some extent the recognition of a *fait accompli* in these areas. But the peasants were not developing a political programme, still less imposing it on political leaders. The land reform, the creation of the RRC and other progressive measures were the work of a small number of intellectuals. The reforms may have been popular, but they were imposed from above. Hence when the soldiers in power wanted to change course, only the ideals of a few urban intellectuals stood in the way. The revolution's gains came with no guarantees: it could not be considered a political contract.

All the radical groups contending for power in 1974–5 were guilty of, at the very least, political paternalism. The All-Ethiopia Socialist Movement (MEISON) joined the Dergue: its main political strategy was to capture the state and then impose revolutionary transformation. One MEISON leader, Haile Fida, was the architect of the land reform. He consulted with other intellectuals, including both ideologues and those who had carried out research in rural areas, before drawing up the decree. But there was no process of consultation that brought the peasants themselves into the process. (In fact many peasants in the north were deeply suspicious of the reform, regarding it as another government plot to deprive them of their land rights.) In 1978, when the Dergue turned on MEISON and destroyed it, including executing Haile Fida and purging the leadership of the Peasant Associations, any political guarantees of the progress marked by the land reform disappeared.

The Ethiopian People's Revolutionary Party (EPRP), MEISON's main rival, also aimed at creating a revolution by seizing state power, in this case through urban insurrection. It did not consider the peasants to have any revolutionary capability. When the EPRP set up a rural base in Tigray in 1975, it belatedly accepted the need for land reform, but then refused to consult the farmers and merely measured the land and imposed a more equitable reallocation (Young, 1994: 323–9).

At first, the main government institution mandated to prevent famine, the RRC, enjoyed more independence from the Dergue than any ministry. This did not stem from any democratic mandate or accountability to the people, however, but rather from its close relationship with foreign donors and the high calibre of some of its senior staff members.

Colonel Mengistu Haile Mariam himself embodied the revolution. At the outset, he was the manifestation of hatred for the former order – a non-commissioned officer who 'emerged out of the belly out of the Ethiopian masses' (Lefort, 1983: 276). At one time was rumoured that he had slave ancestry. He gunned his way to power, killing three heads of state and murdering his nearest rivals. During 1975–7, Ethiopians widely assumed that he was Oromo, given his alliance with the Oromo-led MEISON. Thereafter Mengistu's symbolic trajectory was up through the class system: he became representative of Amhara domination, and in his final years it was rumoured that he had aristocratic parentage. Mengistu even began comparing himself with the nineteenth-century Emperor Teodros, perhaps as a prelude to claiming Solomonic descent. Such opacity is the antithesis of any form of social contract.

Return to dictatorship

The symbolic order that sustained the imperial hegemony, with much lower levels of internal violence, was shattered by the Red Terror, which destroyed first the EPRP and then MEISON (and tens of thousands of young people) and with them the hope for a more just and peaceable future. Neither organization could mobilize the peasantry in its support. The Dergue ruled by force, gradually augmented by the deployment of old symbols of imperial rule (such as 'unity' and ethnic chauvinism).

Despite the submission of the cities in the Red Terror, a certain level of urban contentment had to be maintained, by keeping food prices reasonably stable. In addition, there was the imperative of regular food supplies to the ever-expanding army. Over the years after 1976 a series of measures were implemented that squeezed rural people extremely hard. The economic dispensation of the land reform was clawed back by the state, and extractive economic relations with the peasantry were re-established. These relations were state-oriented rather than feudal, but they had similar effect. The measures included heavy taxation, restrictions on trade, movement and employment, and concentration of investment in state farms. The Agricultural Marketing Corporation (AMC) became the central institution for extracting food from rural Ethiopia. Economists noted that, 'Although it has agents in all provinces the pattern of its operation is quite simple. It buys in five provinces to supply three cities . . . This is precisely the same pattern of distribution which prevailed before the revolution' (Griffin and Hay, 1985: 48).[1] In short, the flow of food supplies paralleled the Dergue's political concerns: feed the cities and the army, at the expense of the peasantry.

The disastrous consequences of the Dergue's economic policies have been documented elsewhere (see, *inter alia*, Alemayehu, 1987) and need only be restated in summary. The extraction of grain quotas at very low prices was a powerful disincentive to production and a cause of impoverishment. Some peasants had to delve into the reserves to meet their quotas (ibid.: 106); others even had to buy grain on the market to resell to the AMC (Dessalegn, 1987: 101). Drought-stricken Wollo continued to provide a quota to the AMC up to 1984. Taxation was extremely onerous (if unevenly collected), and included levies for the social programmes that were supposed to benefit villagers. Famine-stricken peasants in Wollo could not fail to see the irony of the enforced payment of a 'famine relief tax' to the government (ibid.). Restrictions

---

[1]The five provinces were: Arsi, Gojjam, Gondar, Shewa and Wollega; the three cities were Addis Ababa, Asmara and Dire Dawa.

on non-farm activities, notably petty trading and migrant labour, removed a large part of the income of rural households. These were enforced by strict systems of travel permits, but the collapse of labour opportunities on the commercial farms removed much of the reason for labour migration anyway. This meant that an estimated 500,000 farmers in northern Ethiopia who were also seasonal labourers lost a major component of their income (de Waal, 1990a).

Grain wholesaling became illegal in much of the country and most traders were forced out of the market. One Ethiopian economist noted 'it is unclear whether small scale grain trade is illegal or not' (Alemayehu, 1987: 52). In the ten years after the revolution, the number of grain dealers fell from an estimated 20,000–30,000 to just 4,942. The resettlement of people from the north to the south-west, and the villagization of the entire rural populace in the central and southern regions, though incompletely carried out, laid another set of burdens on Ethiopia's long-suffering cultivators.

These economic measures caused massive impoverishment and were partly to blame for the 1983–5 famine. But the chief instrument of food procurement, the AMC, had no operations in the worst-hit regions of Tigray and north Wollo. Clawing back the 1975 dispensation was not central to the economic processes that created famine: rather it was a manifestation of a return to a dictatorship based on the army and a modicum of urban contentment. Neither soldiers nor urban dwellers went hungry during the famines of the 1980s.

The Relief and Rehabilitation Commission

With the reversion to dictatorship came a changed role for the RRC. In its early years the RRC produced some of the finest ever analyses of poverty and famine in Ethiopia, and achieved impressive standards in its implementation of relief measures. A core of committed professional staff remained with it for years. But by the 1980s the RRC became seriously compromised as the Dergue sought to utilize it for other ends.

First, it was given a leading role in the government's programme of social transformation of rural Ethiopia. This began modestly with attempts to create a collectivized workforce in new villages, settlement schemes and state farms from urban vagrants and drought victims. But as the Dergue's military ambitions increased and its counter-insurgency strategies became more comprehensive, the RRC became the hand-maiden of the military. This reached its height when the RRC took responsibility for implementing the programme of forced resettlement.

A second role was as a procurement agent for foreign assistance. The RRC had early successes but then fell foul of Cold War geopolitics and deepening scepticism about its role. After 1985 it was again exceptionally successful in this regard, with the proviso that much of the food for the non-war regions was now channelled through international NGOs. Much of the RRC's food was used to supply militias, especially in Eritrea and Tigray. In other cases, the RRC pushed international agencies to set up relief programmes in surplus-producing regions, where the AMC continued to collect substantial quotas.

The RRC served an equally important propaganda role in distorting the nature of the 1980s famine. It portrayed the famine as a problem of drought and over-population, played down the existence of the war, and consistently claimed that all famine victims were being reached by it and the voluntary agencies working alongside it. Contrary to the simplistic view that news of the famine was somehow suppressed, the RRC never interrupted its flow of early warning information (which was the rationale for its procurement efforts).

War and the 1983–5 famine

The 1983–5 famine in Ethiopia is widely known but poorly understood. Even the most basic facts as to when it started and how many people were affected are disputed. There is a tendency to speak of 'the Ethiopian famine' as though it were a homogeneous national phenomenon, and to assimilate all experiences across the country into a single famine with a single explanation. This is misleading. But it meant that the RRC was able to claim that it had been predicting 'the famine' from 1981, and that 'the famine' affected over 4 million people in that year. In fact, many of the affected people were in the south-east, afflicted by a wholly different crisis, brought about by the Dergue's war against the Oromo Liberation Front. Many analyses based on the study of national statistics or case studies in southern Ethiopia spuriously claim to have validity for the north (Kumar, 1990; Webb and von Braun, 1994). The present analysis is concerned exclusively with the exceptionally severe famine centred on Tigray and northern Wollo in 1983–5, which also caused brief but intense suffering in Eritrea, Gondar and northern Shewa.

Outline of the famine

Ethiopian statistics in the early 1980s cannot be taken at face value. Subsequently, most figures for rainfall, food production, prices and famine-affected people, combined with anecdotal information, have been taken to indicate prolonged and widespread food shortage. But this hypothesis is not supported by a close scrutiny of the evidence.

As late as early 1984, no nationwide survey could have predicted severe or widespread famine. Consider the national situation after the main (*meher*) harvest in 1983: food production was estimated at well above average (the third highest on record), following the largest ever harvest in 1982. Grain prices were falling in two of the northern regions (Gondar and Gojjam). RRC estimates for those 'at risk' from famine were 3.9 million, up from 2.8 million in 1982 but lower than the 4.5 million figure for 1981.

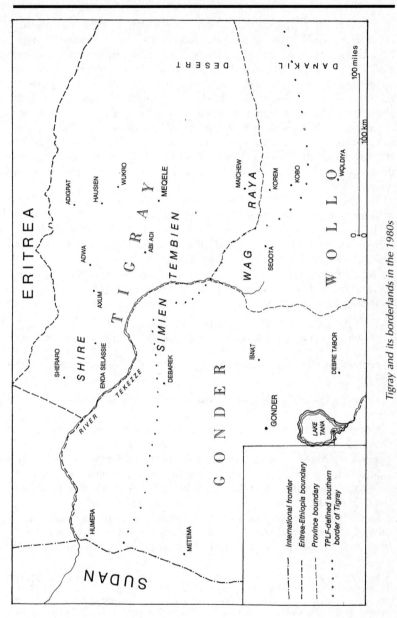

Tigray and its borderlands in the 1980s

Focusing on the northern regions, there is evidence for a persisting crisis in parts of Tigray, but no wider food crisis until the *meher* of 1984. Following two sharp droughts in the late 1970s, the years 1980 and 1981 were 'normal' and 'above normal' according to the RRC. In almost all areas, 1982 was a bumper year.[2] The exceptions were some parts of central and eastern Tigray (Smith, 1983: 15). But in February and March 1983, signs of famine began to appear, in the form of destitute migrants turning up at feeding centres. International NGOs appealed for aid. The RRC promptly revised its assessment and belatedly claimed a major shortfall in production (in effect retrospectively inventing a drought to disguise the destruction wrought by soldiers on an impoverished people).[3]

The main season of 1983 was less good, but far from disastrous.[4] Only in Tigray was there a serious shortfall (English *et al.*, 1984: 62). But once again, famine recurred. In May 1984, the RRC used the widespread failure of the short (*belg*) rains as a pretext for claiming catastrophic drought. *Belg* crops produce only a small proportion of the food produced in the north – about one quarter in the areas where the *belg* rains fall, and none at all in the majority of Tigray. But the RRC played up the 1984 *belg* failure:[5]

> The highlands of Wollo, Bale and Shewa are the major *belg* producing areas. *Belg* accounts for at least half of the annual production in most parts of these areas. There are also areas in most of the remaining regions which heavily depend on *belg*, particularly in Tigray . . .

Once again, it was fabricating an explanation of a crisis with a different provenance.

A more objective pointer to the contours of the famine is grain prices. These show a consistent story of high prices in eastern and central Tigray, spreading outwards after the 1984 harvest failure (see Table 6.1).

This general picture obscures a number of important local details, such as a brief price hike in Korem (Wollo/Tigray borderlands) in May 1983, and both rises and falls in different parts of Gondar.

Rainfall data confirm this picture. Localized droughts occurred in 1983, juxtaposed with above-average rainfall in some areas (Alemneh, 1990: 57, 84). Based on satellite observation of vegetation, the UN

---

[2]RRC, 'Report on a Reconnaissance Trip in Wollo Administrative Region, (August 11–September 4 1982)', November 1982; RRC, 'Meher Synoptic Report 1974/75 EC [Ethiopian Calendar] (1982) Crop Season', March 1983; RRC, 'A Report on a Reconnaissance Trip to Gondar Administrative Region (October 6–November 6, 1982)', Addis Ababa, November 1982; RRC, 'Food Supply Status and Forecast by Administrative Region', March 1982, and 'Food Supply Status and Forecast No. 1', December 1982; Baulch, 1987.
[3]RRC, 'Food Supply Status and Forecast No. 2 (Oct–Dec [1982])', April 1983.
[4]RRC, 'Food Supply Status and Forecast', March 1984 (based on data from late 1983); RRC, 'Meher Synoptic Report 1976/76 EC (1983) Crop Season', January 1984.
[5]RRC, 'The *Belg* Rain Failure and Its Effect on Food Production, Special Report', May 1984.

Table 6.1. Average grain prices in Northern Ethiopia (birr per quintal, 100 kg)

	E. Tigray	N. Wollo	N. Gondar
Nov/Dec 1981	100	50	40
Nov/Dec 1982	165	65	55
Nov/Dec 1983	225	90	45
Nov/Dec 1984	300	160	70
Jun/Jul 1985	380	235	165

Sources: de Waal, 1990b: 44; Cutler, 1988; Baulch, 1987: 199.

Disasters Relief Office maintained that conditions on the ground were improving throughout 1983 and early 1984, leading one staff member of Oxfam to comment that the satellite merely observed 'green starvation' (Kent, 1987).

It was not until the *meher* of 1984 that there was widespread and severe drought (which ironically lent credence to the RRC's earlier distortions and inventions). The drought affected much of eastern and southern Ethiopia, while a food crisis struck Wolaita in the south-central highlands. None of these crises was as prolonged or severe as the famine in the north, but all were conflated in government statistics and agency statements, giving the false impression that the entire country was suffering from famine, and that it was essentially the *same* famine.

The 1984 drought was made the culprit for a famine that had begun earlier. It proved an excellent scapegoat, as its effects were visually and statistically dramatic. Production in Wollo was only 28 per cent of the 1983 level. (But in Gondar it was 86 per cent, and no figures are available for Tigray.) It was the results of this drought that observers saw when they visited the region in late 1984 – dry fields, withered crops, waterless wells. The fact is, however, that a visitor can only see a single year of drought, and that is not enough to cause famine. Those who wish to explain the famine in meteorological terms are impelled to fall back on either convoluted arguments or blatant untruths. 'It was only in 1984 that the sequence of droughts from 1977 to 1980 began having its true effect,' write Webb and von Braun (1994: 2). 'There have scarcely been any real rains in the drought-prone areas since the 1972–4 catastrophe', wrote the RRC (1985: 231).

The causes of the famine

Drought and harvest failure contributed to the famine but did not cause it. The economic and agricultural policies of the government also contributed, but were not central. The principal cause of the famine was the counter-insurgency campaign of the Ethiopian army and air force in Tigray and north Wollo during 1980–85. The zone of severe famine coincided with the war zone, and the phases of the developing famine corresponded with the major military actions.

People on the move, the Ethiopian Highlands (Panos: Barbara Cheney)

War creates famine in many ways: the destruction caused by battle and scorched earth tactics, the requisitioning of food by armies, blockades of food and people in sieges, the imposition of restrictions on movement and trade, forcible relocation of the civilian population and enforced rationing of food (de Waal, 1993b; Macrae and Zwi, 1994). Some counter-insurgency doctrines are tantamount to manuals for the creation of famine (Trinquier, 1964). The Ethiopian Government had used many of these methods in Eritrea in the 1960s and in Harerghe and Bale in 1979–84, but reserved their most protracted and severe implementation for Tigray. They undermined the rural economy, not merely by the destruction of harvests and assets such as oxen, but by making impossible the trading and migration that sustained a peasantry already on the edge of survival (Africa Watch, 1991: Ch. 8).

There were five components to the comprehensive strategy: military offensives aimed at the TPLF strongholds (which were largely in the surplus-producing western lowlands); the bombing of markets in rebel-held areas; restrictions on movement and trade; the forced relocation of population; and finally the manipulation of relief programmes. Famine was used as a weapon (although it is probably true that the architects of the famine were unaware quite how devastating the weapon would be). It was a war crime. In December 1984, Acting Foreign Minister Tibebu Bekele told the US Chargé d'Affaires, 'probably with more candour than he intended', that 'food is a major element in our strategy against the secessionists' (Korn, 1986: 137). This section briefly examines the components of the military strategy and their impact.

Three major offensives were launched into Tigray and its borderlands between 1980 and 1985, in addition to many smaller attacks, and three even larger offensives in Eritrea. The 'Sixth Offensive'[6] was launched in August 1980 in central Tigray and lasted seven months. The army destroyed grain stores, burned crops and pastures, killed livestock, burned houses, enforced the collection of taxes and contributions including 'arrears', and displaced about 80,000 farmers.

The 'Seventh Offensive' began in earnest in February 1983 and was aimed at Shire in western Tigray, a major surplus-producing area. More than 100,000 residents and 375,000 migrant labourers were forced to flee. These labour migrants were probably more numerous and poorer than would have been the case a few years earlier, but they were still following an identifiably 'normal' coping strategy, which would have at least prevented the descent into mass famine. The offensive made this impossible. Some of the human debris from the assault turned up at Korem and Ibnat shelters and forced the international agencies to cry 'famine' and the RRC to revise its picture of the 1982 *meher* crop and invent a drought.

---

[6]The numbering of offensives is based on Africa Watch, 1991. Eritrea suffered a parallel sequence of offensives; its 'Sixth Offensive' was in 1982.

Further army sweeps continued in mid-1983 in southern Tigray and at the end of the year in northern Gondar. The first exacerbated the effects of the poor rainfall, while the second disrupted food supplies from one of the region's main granaries.

The 'Eighth Offensive' began in February 1985 and continued for three months. One front was in central Tigray and a second in the west, which not only disrupted the one relatively self-sufficient district in Tigray, but also blocked the relief food pipeline from Sudan. (One of the aims of the offensive was to convince USAID that a cross-border relief operation from Sudan would not be viable.) A third series of attacks was in north Gondar and north Wollo, and involved the forcible closure of the relief camp at Ibnat, with the aim of ensuring that no food from the rations distributed there could be passed on to the TPLF.

The second major component of the Tigray campaign was aerial bombardment, which began in earnest in 1980, with profound economic consequences. Bombing created terror and forced people to hide and conduct their activities at night. In particular, the main target of the bombing in Tigray was the network of rural markets in TPLF-controlled areas. Medebai, a market near Axum which lies on the important Shire–Eritrea trade route, was bombed more than a hundred times during the 1980s. Hausien, the most important market in northeast Tigray, was bombed equally often until it was completely destroyed in June 1988. Welel, an important market which links Tembien, Raya and Wag, was also frequently bombed. Hundreds of people were killed in these attacks. As a result, markets were held at night. Conducting business in the darkness is more difficult, hazardous and slow. Many traders were forced out of business and markets contracted or were closed down altogether.

Another target of the bombing was means of transport, forcing all lorries off the road. Pack animal transport is between three and ten times as expensive as vehicle haulage. In areas of greatest TPLF control, such as Shire, the bombing even forced people to cultivate at night.

The third component of the strategy was restriction of commerce and migration in contested areas (which ranged well south of the battle-lines). The government was determined to halt food supplies to the TPLF and the civilians under its control, which it did by a host of arbitrary measures, national and local. Permits were difficult and expensive to obtain, soldiers could confiscate goods with impunity and unauthorized travellers were liable to arrest or worse. Petty trade (particularly by women) became almost impossible. The sequence of the intensification of restrictions on trade and migration does much to explain the pattern of grain price rises.

Checkpoints outside government-held towns were present through-out. Further restrictions were imposed by the networks of garrisons left in the wake of the big offensives of 1980, 1983 and 1985. These stifled the flows of grain from western to central and eastern Tigray. More

Graffiti in Ethiopia (Panos: Neil Cooper)

controls were imposed on the southern margins of the war zone and slowly marched northwards. Restrictions on movement followed a similar pattern, starting in central Tigray in 1980, extending to southern Tigray in 1982 and to Wollo and Gondar thereafter. Migration itself was never expressly forbidden, but migrants were required to obtain so many permits and passes and pass through so many checkpoints that any form of movement in government-controlled areas became expensive and hazardous.

By preventing free movement, the government tore at the economic ties that sustained the rural economy. Grain could no longer move from the surplus-producing areas of Raya (southern Tigray), northern Gondar and central Wollo to the deficit areas. The price of grain shot up far beyond the level that would have prevailed otherwise. In 1982, prices in government-held Enda Selassie were more than three times those in nearby rural markets (Firebrace and Smith, 1982: 37 fn). Prices in Mekele and eastern Tigray were even higher. Meanwhile, the loss of markets undermined the demand for labour in the surplus-producing areas. Counter-insurgency restrictions on the grain trade were instrumental in starting the famine, and played a key role in maintaining it.

The fourth element in the government's war was the forced relocation of people out of Tigray and northern Wollo to south-western Ethiopia. If carried through, it would have deprived Tigray and northern Wollo of a large section of the adult population. In contrast to most of the rest of the counter-insurgency campaign, the resettlement programme created much international controversy (Jean, 1986; Clay and Holcombe, 1985). Though it cannot be said to have caused the famine (it began only in October 1984), resettlement was an illusory solution that killed a minimum of 50,000 people and compounded the problem (Africa Watch, 1991: 224–7).

The final component of the strategy was the manipulation of relief. This included its denial to non-government-controlled areas and the abuse of relief under government control, and will be discussed below. Although this had less overall impact in creating famine than the strategies outlined above, it was the most blatant instance of manipulation of food as a weapon.

Hence, the famine was caused principally by the Ethiopian army and air force. In 1984–5 it appeared as though the very existence of the Tigrayan people was in jeopardy. In August 1985, the Dergue turned its military attention to Eritrea, with a huge offensive – as large as the 1982 'Red Star' campaign – and considerable battlefield success. It seemed that the famine strategy of the government was on the brink of success. But the government had underestimated the 'stubborn, enduring strength' (Knuttson and Selinus, 1970: 41) of the Tigrayan peasantry, and the capacity of the TPLF to mobilize resistance (see below).

The wider famine

The widespread 1984 drought was superimposed on the government's counter-productive agricultural policies and the ripples from the severe famine in the war zone. This combination of events turned the dearth into something far more serious, much to villagers' puzzlement. The names given to the 1984 famine in Shewa, which followed a single bad season, translate as 'we were unprepared' and 'I slipped on it' (McCann, 1987). Similarly, a woman from Lalibela is quoted as deriding the survival skills of people to the south: 'That was not a real famine! *Theirs* was easy; they simply became unnerved; the troubles afflicted *us* for three years' (quoted in Pankhurst, 1990: 97).

Much has been written about 'the Ethiopian famine' based on research in the non-war zones. Scholars have identified many genuine technological, economic and institutional constraints on rural development. But it is of limited relevance to the north. A fine example is a recent book by Patrick Webb and Joachim von Braun (1994), which totally neglects the role of the war except with reference to its impact on government finances. Webb and von Braun go further: they appear to believe that excluding politics and war from their analysis ensures their objectivity, and dismiss as biased those (including the present author) who have documented the political and military causes of the famine. In Mengistu's Ethiopia, this amounts to exonerating those responsible for the famine. This at least had a (reprehensible) rationale when Mengistu remained in power, but to repeat the error three years after his defeat smacks of serious lack of scholarly responsibility.

BandAid humanitarianism

Until early 1984, international donors were justifiably sceptical about the Ethiopian Government's appeals for relief. There was evidence of both diversion of food aid and the strategic abuse of relief to support counter-insurgency efforts in the south-east. This scepticism prevailed into mid-1984 when the need was real, and in the face of mounting pressure from international NGOs. In October 1984 the famine suddenly became international news. Some of the elements leading up to this sudden exposure have been analysed (Harrison and Palmer, 1986), including the Ethiopian Government's relaxation of censorship and travel restrictions following the September 1984 Tenth Anniversary celebrations, the mass influx of people to feeding centres after the failure of the 1984 *meher* rains, and a fortuitous combination of circumstances surrounding journalists' itineraries. In retrospect, several other elements stand out.

One is the close relationship between journalists and relief agencies, which at the time was quite unapologetic. Peter Gill, then of Thames Television wrote:

When Ethiopia's famine hit the headlines, it did so because of the relationship between private relief agencies and the television companies. Michael Buerk's visit in July was accomplished through Oxfam. In news coverage in October and beyond, the relief agencies provided most of the reference points – up-to-date information, places to visit, interviewees in the field and at home, and a means of response for concerned viewers. Our own *TV Eye* film 'Bitter Harvest', made for Thames Television and transmitted on 25 October, had its origins in Oxfam's decision to purchase large quantities of grain for Ethiopia. Oxfam helped us secure visas, and although we were happy to pay all the bills, we depended on Oxfam and Save the Children in Ethiopia for transport in the famine area. (Gill, 1986: 93)

Later, after the critique of journalistic coverage along the paradigm of 'disaster tourism', journalists became more coy about admitting this close symbiosis, but Gill's comments remained equally valid.

A second point is the language and imagery used, especially in the news broadcasts. The famous 23 October BBC broadcast from Korem opens with the following words, spoken by Michael Buerk over the misty atmospherics of the late Mohamed Amin's shots of daybreak:

Dawn, and as the sun breaks through the piercing chill of night on the plain outside Korem, it lights up a Biblical famine, now, in the twentieth century. This place, say workers here, is the closest thing to Hell on earth. Thousands of wasted people are coming here for help. Many find only death. They flood in every day from villages hundreds of miles away, felled by hunger, driven to the point of desperation. Death is all around.

Religious imagery and metaphors of hostile nature pervade the broadcast. It is an appeal to an idea of famine as something simple, huge and apocalyptic and above all beyond human agency. It is as though Buerk and Amin had stumbled across a forgotten world, and then realized to their surprise and shock that it was real and contemporary. The power of the broadcast undoubtedly helped provoke the unprecedented international reaction, but it also suited Mengistu extremely well.

Thirdly, it is interesting to chart the way in which the famine progressed from its niche as a news item and a campaign by relief agencies into an unprecedented international media event with political repercussions in leading Western democracies. BandAid played a key role in this: while not the first, it was the definitive media-charitable event. The timing was crucial: Christmas is the fund-raising season for relief agencies and a time of particular sensitivity in the public conscience. The BandAid agency was relatively sensitive in how it spent its money, but its true legacy is in the domestic politics of aid in Western countries. It had the effect of intensifying competition among NGOs, with a greater scramble for media exposure and endorsement from stars: another stage in humanitarian deregulation. Meanwhile, for

Western governments, the political priority became to avoid embarrassment at the hands of figures like Bob Geldof. Aid became a strategic alibi.

The big lie

The Ethiopian Government cannot have expected such a response in the last two months of 1984. At first it was bewildered and instinctively sought to restrict what the foreign media and relief agencies were doing. But the Dergue soon turned the international relief presence to its economic, diplomatic and military advantage. The key event in this was the creation of the UN Emergency Office for Ethiopia (UNEOE), headed for the first year by the Finnish diplomat Kurt Jansson.

The ostensible reasons for setting up the UNEOE were to co-ordinate international relief efforts with the Ethiopian Government and to centralize the flow of information. Why was a new institution needed for this? For ten years, the RRC and the Christian Relief and Development Association (CRDA, a co-ordinating body for local and international NGOs) had regulated relief work and ancillary tasks such as early warning. This relationship often worked well, though within strict political limits. The creation of UNEOE did not expand that political space. For example, it did not make it possible for relief agencies to work on both sides of the front line or ensure that abuses and diversions were halted. Instead, UNEOE created a higher-level political dispensation for humanitarianism, to reassure both Colonel Mengistu and the UN system itself:

> UNEOE's main function was to act as a 'screening device', giving the appearance of competent action in response to famine but not compromising its actual position in Addis Ababa by unduly antagonizing the host government . . . it would have been as embarrassing for the donors who had entrusted resources to the Ethiopian government as it was for the government itself to have aid misallocation exposed. (Cutler, 1988: 408)

The appearance of a broader and more effective response was created: this is still the 'official' UN view (Jansson *et al.*, 1987). The Ethiopian Government intensified its creation of famine and its manipulation of humanitarianism, and UNEOE was happy to act as its mouthpiece. Journalists and diplomats frequently turned to it as an authoritative voice on issues to do with the diversion of food, forcible resettlement, and other abuses. Rather than investigating the abuses, UNEOE consistently concealed disturbing evidence, including evidence produced by its own monitors. In the same month as it was set up, the government launched the 'silent offensive' in Eritrea – so named because it was not given any publicity, unlike its predecessors – and began its resettlement programme. The Eighth Offensive in Tigray followed in February 1985. UNEOE did not mention the offensives, even when they involved direct attacks on relief programmes in the areas held by the EPLF and the TPLF. Information about diversion of food to the army and militia in Eritrea was suppressed. One of the more remarkable public relations efforts undertaken by UNEOE concerned resettlement: it consistently played down reports of forcible resettlement, tried to rebut independent research into the programme and even appealed for aid to the resettlement sites (Africa Watch, 1991: 216–17).

The one international agency to withdraw from Ethiopia in protest at government policies was MSF–France – leaving just before the government issued an expulsion order. It later published a damning indictment (Jean, 1986). After its departure, other agencies tried to discredit MSF–France, arguing that its young volunteers had proved incompetent. Professional ineptitude has never been a cause for an agency's expulsion, but it is probable that MSF was guilty of political naiveté; its field staff were unaware of the implications of reporting on what they had seen, and had they been more experienced they would have followed their colleagues in other agencies and remained silent.

The nature of the compact between the Western humanitarians, the media and the Ethiopian Government prevented any systematic evaluation of the famine. No-one can say how many people died to within half a million, and when the present author proposed trying to investigate the issue in 1987, the UN refused to co-operate. This lack of accountability was essential if the 'Ethiopian famine' was to remain a 'product' that could sell in the fast deregulating charitable market. In short, the Ethiopian Government's relief effort and international humanitarian operations under government regulation were founded on a big lie.

Militarized relief

Perhaps the most remarkable distortion of the famine surrounded the government's policy of starving rural Tigray. In July 1985, in the aftermath of the Eighth Offensive and just before the launch of the largest-ever offensive in Eritrea, Kurt Jansson made a four-day visit to garrison towns in Tigray in the company of senior government officials. At this time, relief programmes on the government side were reaching at most 15 per cent of the Tigrayan population, and the only serious option for access was cross-border from Sudan. Between April and August 1985, Tigray received only 5.6 per cent of the food relief distributed through government channels, despite having between 21 and 33 per cent of the needy population, according to different estimates.

However, Jansson preferred to maintain the fiction that the majority of the needy people were being reached. His report stated that a total of 1,126,468 people, 75 per cent of those in need, were receiving rations of between 5 and 15 kg per month (Jansson et al., 1987: 51). In August, when the report was issued, the RRC distributed a mere 569 tonnes, and World Vision (the principal private agency in the region) was well short of its target figure of 180,000 recipients. Subsequent evidence revealed that the majority of the relief food in Tigray was being consigned to the militia (each militiaman received 90 kg., plus the rations given to his family),[7] a fact that Jansson implicitly admitted later:

> The fact was that the small peasant militia helping to provide protection against guerrilla attacks could not be considered wrong since they would have received food aid whether or not they served in the local militia. What was objectionable was that their rations were often higher than for the rest of the recipients. When I raised this matter with the authorities it was explained that peasants were reluctant to do this job and an incentive was needed; the food ration was their wage. (ibid.: 56)

Such are the command of logic and adherence to ethics of the individual chosen to represent the world's conscience before the famine-stricken people of Ethiopia.

Jansson's July visit to the north had wider repercussions. It compelled the US Government to become a fully active member of the cover-up in the north, something it had hitherto hesitated about. Days beforehand, the US Congress had required the President to determine whether the Ethiopian Government was using starvation as a weapon of war. If the answer was yes, the US would have been obliged to take drastic steps against the Ethiopian Government, and would have destroyed the credibility of government relief efforts. Jansson's report was part of concerted pressure on the US to find the Ethiopian Government 'not guilty'. A month later the Presidential Determination duly equivocated. It accused the government of policies that 'have no doubt caused vast and unnecessary suffering including starvation', but said that there was no evidence that the government was 'at this time conducting a deliberate policy of starvation'.[8] The careful use of 'at this time' allowed Mengistu to escape the implications of his earlier policies. Even so, the determination was certainly too generous (Africa Watch, 1991: 369). The full version of the report remains classified.

At no time during the 1980s did any UN agency consign food to the cross-border operation. Most references to the Eritrean Relief Association (ERA), the Relief Society of Tigray (REST) and their sponsors were derogatory or false. In 1985, Ethiopia received about 1.25 million tonnes of food relief, of which a mere 90,000 tonnes was distributed cross-border in non-government-held areas of Eritrea and Tigray, where between a third and a half of the famine-stricken population lived. The proportion gradually shifted to become less favourable to the government, but never approached equivalence relative to need. Only after the EPLF captured the port of Massawa in 1990 did the UN slowly move

---

[7]The militia were locally known as the 'wheat militia'.
[8]Presidential Determination No. 85–20, 'Determination with Respect to Ethopia', 7 September 1985.

towards recognizing that the rebel fronts might be acceptable intermediaries for negotiation.

The compact between UNEOE and the Ethiopian Government also meant that relief food came to be used for counter-insurgency purposes. Western donors pushed for the 'Food for the North' (FFN) initiative in early 1985 when it became clear that virtually no relief aid was travelling into the severe famine zone. The FFN was delayed by the Dergue until the military moment was apposite; the army needed to capture enough territory to prevent an embarrassing revelation that they could not provide access to most of the famine area.

The FFN initiative meant that private agencies moved in behind the army during the huge 1985 offensives. Feeding centres were set up in Barentu and Areza (Eritrea), Abi Adi (Tigray) and Sekota (north Wollo). One was due to be established in Sheraro (Tigray) but the town was recaptured by the TPLF before World Vision could arrive. Food relief fed soldiers. It helped keep the roads open and protect the garrisons, as much by the privileged diplomatic status accorded to foreign relief programmes as by the material resources provided. One of the government's aims was to make the donors identify the army's successes with the efficacy of foreign relief programmes. In this they met with some success. When a TPLF-led force (re)captured Sekota in 1986 an outcry by aid workers and diplomats duly followed. After Abi Adi was captured by the TPLF in March 1988, the director of USAID commented, perhaps more revealingly than he intended, 'It's going to hurt us hard' (*International Herald Tribune*, 10 March 1988). The outcry against the EPLF for attacking joint military-relief convoys in late 1987 was even harsher. The entire war was seen through a relief lens. After the EPLF's decisive victory at Afabet in March 1988, which turned the tide of the war and in which a government force of 15,000 men and over 50 tanks was destroyed, a London newspaper headline ran 'Stepped up guerrilla raids threaten food deliveries' (*The Times*, 31 March 1988).

For the peasants, the reality was that the removal of the Ethiopian army and the destruction and restrictions it inflicted was at least as important to survival as any food aid provided. Few humanitarians appreciated this. They made operationality a priority over principle, with the result that relief operations were ripe for manipulation.

The depoliticization of the famine had profound repercussions throughout Ethiopia. The conflation of the war-famine in the north with distress in other areas helped the government attract generous relief, which helped support the gargantuan programmes of social engineering in the south.

A culprit had to be found for the famine, and a convenient one for both government and donors was at hand: the natural environment. The outlines of this explanation are familiar: drought, overpopulation and unsustainable land-use practices mean that Ethiopia cannot sustain its population without radical measures, particularly in population control and environmental management (Constable, 1984). 'Saving' the natural environment was a suitably non-political way in which Western donors, especially the US, could channel aid to communist Ethiopia. An ambitious environmental reclamation programme followed the famine. It was deeply flawed: farmers had better understandings of the local ecology than the planners, and the 'conservation measures lowered production, income and food security' as well as failing to 'preserve' the natural environment (Hoben, 1996: 203–4).

Overall, official aid flows to Ethiopia rose from $221m. in 1982 to peak at $784m. in 1985. They remained above $640m. before the 1987 drought caused another increase, to $984m. in 1988 (OECD, 1990: 120–1). (This latter drought, which elicited the fastest and most generous contributions ever to government-side relief efforts, was confined almost wholly to non-government-held Tigray.) The 'defence' budget, which excludes the security forces, averaged about $450m. in these years (IISS, 1989: 127). There is no doubt that this relief programme supported President Mengistu militarily and politically. In Tigray, very few rural people and very many soldiers were fed by the relief. The humanitarian effort prolonged the war, and with it, human suffering.

Political contract and secret humanitarianism in Tigray

In the non-government-held areas of Tigray, the famine was politicized in a radically different manner. This was possible because of the nature of the political mobilization attempted by the TPLF, and the limitations imposed upon humanitarian assistance by the Ethiopian Government. Ironically, by doing all it could to prohibit relief in the rebel-held zones, the Dergue forced international relief agencies to adopt an innovative model of assistance that meshed very closely with the mechanisms for socio-political mobilization employed by the TPLF, and therefore strengthened the front.

The TPLF–peasant political contract
The key to fighting famine in TPLF-held Tigray was not REST, though that proved very important, but the political relationship established between the TPLF itself and the people at the very outset of the war. The TPLF was founded in 1975 by a small group of students and teachers with a similar social and political profile to that of the EPRP. Unlike their rivals, the TPLF believed from the outset that the peasantry provided the key to a successful revolution. A small and impoverished group, the first TPLF cadres relied on the peasants for everything: food, shelter, intelligence, recruits. In turn, their practical social, economic and political programmes were worked out with the close involvement of the rural people. The TPLF's first land reform, at Sobia, was a slow

and consultative process (Young, 1994: 330). It was, in short, the foundation of a social contract in which the TPLF committed itself to acting in the interests of the peasants. The contract was enforceable because, without rural support, the TPLF would have been quickly crushed by either of its militarily stronger rivals, the EPRP or the conservative Ethiopian Democratic Union (EDU), or the Dergue itself.

The TPLF tried to mobilize in refugee camps in Sudan, and quickly discovered how difficult this was. The leadership learned from the EPLF, which had in turn studied the problems faced earlier by the Eritrean Liberation Front and the Palestinians, who had found that refugees tended towards either apathy or extremism. The TPLF became determined to discourage refugee flows.

The Relief Society of Tigray was set up in 1978 on the model of ERA, which had been established three years earlier (and which will not be discussed here). Like ERA, REST was a quasi-autonomous relief administration, presenting itself to the outside world as an independent NGO. It had separate offices, staff and bank accounts from the TPLF, and its literature and appeals were all scrupulously humanitarian. To the people of Tigray, REST was virtually indistinguishable from the civil administration of the front. At a local level, relief food was distributed through the same *baito*s (village councils) that were also responsible for implementing land reform, administering justice, collecting taxes and contributions, and selecting members for the defence militias. There were no parallel relief structures, and the headquarters staff of REST in the field in 1988 remained remarkably few for such a huge operation: eleven people. The fact that REST allocations were subject to the same processes of popular participation as all the other social programmes of the TPLF was one of its strengths.

By the time the famine began to deepen in 1983, the TPLF was the only opposition force in the region. REST was well established but very small; the front faced the famine without any confidence that it would receive external support. During 1983–5, the TPLF leadership made a number of political decisions that renewed its commitment to the political contract established in the 1970s. The decisions were reached only after a long and sometimes bitter debate, in which the balance of power within the front shifted decisively. Among the winners were Meles Zenawi (subsequently president), Abaye Tsehaye and Siye Abreha; the most prominent losers were Berihu Aregawi and Ghidey Zeratsion, both of whom later fled into exile. The debate had ideological, political, military and socio-economic dimensions. One of the resolutions on the military side was that the TPLF would not move towards a conventional war (in contrast to the EPLF), and would therefore refuse to defend any towns that it had captured; instead it would concentrate on a guerrilla war and mobilizing the people.

The shifts in social and economic policy – small but important – were most significant in the fight against famine. A policy of trying to control market prices was abandoned, and a liberal policy of issuing trade licences was instituted. Employment of wage labourers was encouraged. Moneylending was allowed. This was justified ideologically on the grounds that the incipient petit bourgeoisie (traders and richer peasants) was a strategic ally in the struggle until the achievement of the national democratic revolution. It was also based on the indisputable fact that Tigrayan peasants relied heavily on seasonal trading, migrant labour, and borrowing; they demanded that 'liberation' should mean that they could engage in these activities, which were forbidden by the Dergue. Simple economic realities were important. When the TPLF tried to regulate prices in Sheraro market in 1983, the traders boycotted the move and the front backed down. When the TPLF experimented with co-operative farms, it rapidly found them uneconomic.

A previous section has shown how sharp increases in grain prices in 1982–5 were closely associated with the government's restrictions on the grain trade. The trade liberalization of the TPLF was instrumental in bringing down prices, as the front gradually came to control more territory (especially the main roads), and the marketing infrastructure was re-established (de Waal, 1990b).

War against famine

In mid-1984, the TPLF made its strategic priority the struggle against famine. This immediately included the evacuation of over 200,000 people to Sudan, the employment of large numbers of internally displaced people in harvesting gum Arabic and incense, giving protection to grain merchants and endeavouring to secure access routes for REST's cross-border relief programmes. The evacuation to Sudan, born of desperation, did not have the expected consequences. It brought the unknown dimension of the famine to international attention, but at considerable human cost. Many people died of disease in the refugee camps. The TPLF forfeited some political control to the international relief agencies (to the extent that the refugees even had to stage a hunger strike to be allowed to return home) (Hendrie, 1991). Most significantly, the evacuation brought home the impossibility of fighting a guerrilla war in depopulated areas. The refugees began to return home in March 1985 and the camps slowly emptied. In the 1987 drought, the TPLF conducted a survey to determine whether another migration to Sudan should be organized, and the great majority of villagers indicated that they preferred to remain in Tigray. The evacuation was not repeated: the TPLF's strategy concentrated on maintaining people in their home areas.

In essence, Meles Zenawi tried to link the physical survival of the Tigrayan peasantry in the face of famine to the political fortunes of the TPLF. It was one of the great strategic political inspirations of modern Ethiopia. As the Dergue's war intensified, more and more peasants saw their survival and freedom from famine as inextricably linked to the military overthrow of the regime. The resettlement programme was the *coup de grâce*: it appeared to prove the genocidal intent of the government. In Tigrayan villages, supporting the TPLF became a long-term famine survival strategy. This was evident even in central Wollo, where Dessalegn Rahmato wrote: 'for obvious reasons, I shall leave out of our account resistance and rebellion as a form of survival strategy' (Dessalegn, 1987: 7) As a weapon of war, famine was double-edged: it ultimately defeated Mengistu himself.

In these circumstances, the question of what material support the cross-border operation provided to the TPLF is complex. There is no doubt that the assistance helped. As Mark Duffield puts it, 'relief assistance can never be neutral in relation to the ongoing conflict: it has an impact. The fact of keeping people alive in an internal war is a political act and deserves to be recognised as such' (Duffield and Prendergast, 1994: 162). How did the relief programme assist? There was an instance in which REST used exchange-rate differentials to accrue a substantial hard currency balance (which was later returned to the donors, explaining that a 'mistake' had occurred). However, the TPLF was not a conventional army diverting relief grain, rather it was a political front mobilizing a classic 'people's war'.

From about 1987, the cross-border flow of resources to REST was such that, rather than the people supporting the front with resources, the front (through REST) was becoming a net contributor to the welfare of the people. Having already established efficient institutions and a strong political contract, the relief did not corrupt the TPLF, but rather enhanced its legitimacy and enabled it to direct more of its own resources to the war front. The strategic aim of fighting famine could now be delegated to REST, while the capture of the towns and main roads in 1988–9 re-established a regional grain trade and brought prices down to their lowest since the revolution. The TPLF ultimately won its war against famine.

There is no doubt that the humanitarian assistance helped the TPLF (ibid.: 163–4). At no stage, however, did the amount of relief channelled to the non-government side begin to equal the amount handled by the Ethiopian Government, and it was never enough to meet overall need. But measuring the amounts is not the issue, as if military victory depended on the balance of aid through the cross-border operation as against the official programme. The front used its aid far better: it mobilized people in a war against tyranny, while Mengistu used relief to reinforce oppression.

An unacknowledged model
Externally, these political dynamics were not made explicit to the donors. On the contrary, an elaborate charade was played whereby the superficial requirements of neutral humanitarianism and NGO-ism were established to protect the operation from the perils of publicity. The first cross-border relief was provided through a consortium known

as the Emergency Relief Desk (ERD), which was a conduit for European church-based agencies to fund ERA and REST while maintaining a formal distance. ERD was an innovative way of providing clandestine assistance, and had the handicaps of its pioneering role: its members could not go public and claim the credit for what they were doing.

At the height of the 1984–5 famine, USAID approached CARE to discuss the possibility of a major cross-border operation. It declined, as did UNICEF when approached by ERA. One factor appears to be that they knew that the Ethiopian Government would not permit them to operate on both sides, and they would thus lose programmes in government-held areas and, more importantly, publicity. They knew that operations in the rebel-held areas could never achieve the same level of publicity, because journalists could not make quick, comfortable and safe visits.

Later, the Eritrean Inter-Agency Consortium (EIAC) and the Tigray Transport and Agriculture Consortium (TTAC) were set up. These consortia were more ambitious than ERD. First, their programmes were formally 'owned' by ERA and REST. Secondly, they brought in a wider array of international agencies, some of whom established their own programmes in the field under the co-ordination of ERA and REST.

The cross-border operation as a whole was handicapped by the lack of publicity given to its fundamental nature. Even today some writers refer to 'corridors of tranquillity' used to bring food to the front-held areas (Webb and von Braun, 1994: 35), apparently unaware of the fact that the cross-border routes were systematically bombed till the last days of the war, and the government conceded the supply of eastern Tigray with a 'cross-line' operation from the government side only in the final months. The operations of ERA and REST and their relations with the consortia remain a subject of mystique and admiration among those who participated, and of ignorance and suspicion among many who did not. This shortcoming meant that after the defeat of Mengistu, the ERA–REST model of relief was almost wholly abandoned. The consortia were wound up, while their members began to operate in their own right as NGOs. ERA became a government department and REST was registered as a national NGO, though both continued to base most of their programmes on community participation. The model was surrendered in the face of the institutional interests of relief agencies, both international and national, for a place in the public eye. The interests of the new governments in Eritrea and Ethiopia no longer demanded such consortia. Only in 1994, with the independent review of ERD by Mark Duffield (Duffield and Prendergast, 1994), did the cross-border operation receive belated legitimation as an alternative model of relief. Meanwhile, the suggestion that fighting against the Dergue was itself a famine-survival strategy has yet to be widely adopted in studies of the political economy of Ethiopia.

Implications

The famines of the 1970s and 1980s in Ethiopia are replete with ironies, which are explicable only by attention to the existence or not of an anti-famine political contract. The highly intellectual, elitist and institutionalized response to the 1973 famine proved fragile and was quickly unravelled. One of the most tragic famines of modern times – that of 1983–5 in Tigray and north Wollo – must be considered a major policy success for the then government of Ethiopia, at least in the short term. One of the most written-about famines is one of the least understood. The TPLF, which conquered the famine, has not been able to take the credit, because of the way the discourse about fighting famine is removed from the discourse of the politics of war.

The final irony is that the innovative and successful model of humanitarianism in Tigray has proved to be a *sui generis* deviation that was abandoned as soon as possible. Arguably, the successes of REST could not have been replicated in war-famines elsewhere, which have been characterized more by warlordism than by well organized liberation fronts. But the attempt was not even made. By contrast, an amended 'conventional' model, symbolized by BandAid's fund-raising and UNEOE's operations, has become the model for subsequent international humanitarian action.

7

The End of the Cold War

A New Humanitarian Dispensation

In retrospect, the period between Biafra and BandAid stands out as one of relative stability in the international relief network (cf. Seaman, 1995a). It was a time of vigorous NGOs operating within a framework imposed by overarching geo-politics, strong states and weak UN institutions. There was optimism that the weaknesses of the system would be overcome with time, effort and goodwill. This clubby world began to fall apart in the mid-1980s, and by the end of the decade whatever informal regulations had existed among humanitarian agencies were being rapidly dismantled. Chaotic operations such as the one on the Thai border in 1980 came to be seen not as aberrations but as omens for the deregulated future. The tendencies towards intense competition, political naiveté and the promotion of salvation fantasies through the media, all present in the mid-1980s, became more pronounced. There have also been some energetic attempts to stem the tide and develop codes for good conduct, better evaluations and closer co-ordination, but successes have been limited. The twin themes of this chapter are the growing excesses of a humanitarianism freed from its earlier constraints, and the expanding arsenal available to the humanitarians. The implications for anti-famine political contracts will also be examined.

At the end of the Cold War, leading international humanitarians began to sense that a historic opportunity lay within their grasp. The geo-political straitjacket was at last being removed and it seemed that the humanitarians could set their own agenda for the first time. Over the previous decade, the more thoughtful of the aid workers found themselves becoming amateur political scientists as they realized the shortcomings of material relief. Equitable development had always been on the humanitarian agenda, concerns now broadened to human rights, conflict resolution and the principle of state sovereignty itself.

The end of the Cold War created a vacuum in Western strategic interest in Africa. Major Western commercial interest in most African countries had already vanished. Into this vacuum rushed humani-

133

tarianism and its twin, liberal human rights, as alternative guiding lights
for Euro-American foreign policy. But while humanitarian agencies
were trying to influence policy, governments were also using humanitarian aid, albeit in different ways. Andrew Natsios, formerly director of
the US Office of Foreign Disaster Assistance, explained:

> diplomats now use disaster response as a preventative measure to
> stave off chaos in an unravelling society, as a confidence-building
> measure during political negotiations, to protect democratic and
> economic reforms, to implement peace accords which the U.S. has
> mediated, to mitigate the effects of economic sanctions on the poor,
> where sanctions serve geopolitical ends, and to encourage a political
> settlement as a carrot to contending factions. (quoted in Refugee
> Policy Group, 1994: 94–5)

It is doubtful whether humanitarian aid can actually help achieve this
miscellany of worthy goals. Sending relief is a weapon of first resort:
popular at home, usually unobjectionable abroad, and an excuse for not
looking more deeply into underlying political problems. At worst,
supporting humanitarianism is a smokescreen for political inaction.
Quite often, Western political leaders seem actually to believe their
anodyne public statements that humanitarianism works. The personal
factor should not be overlooked: all save the most hard-bitten politicians occasionally like to do something that is, at least *prima facie*, an
act of simple goodwill.

Humanitarianism – or rather, the actions of Western relief agencies –
has become a major determinant of Euro-American policy towards
Africa. The humanitarians have become hugely powerful: their information, even their presence, influences the perceptions and concerns of
Western diplomats. Their intermittent ability to dominate the headlines
and embarrass their home governments into action gives them leverage.
Some have tried to use this leverage to tackle what they see as the root
causes of humanitarian crises. For others it is a chance for undreamed-
of institutional expansion. The combination of the two has proved
particularly potent.

Actually existing humanitarianism

Charitable action needs only vague principles: it is driven by an emotive
concern for the poor. It is notable that Western charities avoid specific
commitments to human rights principles, preferring vaguer slogans
such as 'H stands for Hunger, Oxfam stands for justice'. To fight famine,
especially in war zones, it has become apparent that more specific
guidelines are needed. Rather than engage directly with the laws of war,
relief agencies have produced a profusion of statements of 'humanitarian principles' – a remarkable effort of applied moral philosophy.

The record shows that while humanitarian agencies are good at drawing up principles, they are rather poor at enforcing them. One reason is confusion over what humanitarian principles are for. An example is the 'Code of Conduct' adopted by a wide range of relief agencies led by the Federation of Red Cross and Red Crescent Societies in 1994, after several years of discussion. This begins:

1. The humanitarian imperative comes first.

The right to receive humanitarian assistance, and to offer it, is a fundamental humanitarian principle. . . .
    The prime motivation of our response to disaster is to alleviate human suffering amongst those least able to withstand the stress caused by disaster.
    When we give humanitarian aid it is not a partisan or political act and should not be viewed as such. (Federation of International Red Cross and Red Crescent Societies, 1995)

The statement continues in similar vein, with commitments to 'involve programme beneficiaries in the management of relief aid', 'hold ourselves accountable to both those we seek to assist and those from whom we accept resources', and 'in our information, publicity and advertising activities, we shall recognise disaster victims as dignified humans, not hopeless objects'. It a clear representation of abstract humanitarian principles, Unfortunately that is not what it is called: it is heralded as a 'Code of Conduct'. This implies that it can be resorted to by relief workers on the ground when confronted with a difficult choice, for example whether to tolerate a certain rate of diversion of relief food by local militiamen or whether to open a clinic even though the staff and equipment available are such that it is unlikely that it can meet minimum standards of care and hygiene. In fact, not only have relief organizations not followed this Code, but it would have been impossible for them to do so, simply because it is cast at such a level of abstraction. There are no specifications of professional standards (though these are planned for a later code) and no provisions for sanctions or enforcement: adherence is entirely voluntary. A relief organization's chief sanction is withdrawal, and without an enforceable agreement among the signatories on when and how to withdraw, the document is practically unusable.

Formal principles are routinely – and inevitably – violated. Instead, it is more useful to identify some *de facto* principles or tendencies in the humanitarian international, at least in its contemporary state in Africa. Three are identified here. All agencies, whether NGOs, UN agencies or others, are subject to these tendencies, though in different measure (non-operational NGOs are probably the least susceptible): they cut across typologies of NGOs developed by David Korten (1990), Ian Smillie (1995), John Saxby (1996) and others.

The regressive empowerment of aid
The tendency for aid to assist governments rather more than it assists the poor people who are ostensibly its target is widely acknowledged. Amounts of aid that are too small to have an appreciable impact on development can nonetheless significantly increase the resources available to governments. In Tanzania, official aid has amounted to 18.1 per cent of (recorded) GNP, 106.8 per cent of tax receipts and 152.8 per cent of export earnings (Bauer, 1991: 49–51). Foreign aid often facilitates inappropriate economic policy; an illuminating parallel is with the way oil revenues can bolster authoritarian governments. Aid flows alter the economic underpinnings of the political process in favour of those in power. Aid has a centralizing tendency, increasing the power of the branches of government that procure and dispense aid *vis-à-vis* those that rely on treasury allocations or local taxation. It directs the energies of politicians and civil servants towards external sources of money and influence rather than towards internal problems, changing mind-sets and the direction of day-to-day accountability. It creates opportunities for corruption. One of the slogans of popular enfranchisement in Europe was 'no taxation without representation'; aid-dependent governments can dispense with domestic taxation and thereby lessen pressures for representation, or continue in power after domestic revenue-gathering structures have collapsed. The geo-strategic rationale for US foreign aid during the Cold War was precisely in order to ensure clients' loyalty, and to enable them to override domestic political pressures and when necessary crush internal opposition by force. Broadly, this worked. The democratic record of the six largest recipients of US bilateral assistance in sub-Saharan Africa (1962–88) is not encouraging: Sudan, Zaire, Kenya, Somalia, Liberia and Ethiopia (Clough, 1992: 78).

Significantly modified, the argument is valid for emergency relief. The simplest case is relief provided directly to governments for them to distribute, in which case the benefits are evident. Although precise figures are unavailable, it is fair to estimate that food relief in government-held Tigray and Eritrea in 1985–6 provided perhaps 5 per cent of the diet of the famine-stricken rural population, 20 per cent of the diet of townspeople and 100 per cent of the diet of militiamen. External relief usually benefits disproportionately government institutions, village distribution committees and the like. The failure of most attempts to 'target' aid to the poorest stems from this reality: at all political levels there are obstacles to aid reaching the poorest without some taxation or diversion. The relief programme in Sudan in 1984–5 is a revealing case: at all points in Western Sudan, the 'neediness' of the recipient was inversely related to the amount of relief that person received (Keen, 1991). Within the army, for example, a private soldier received 10 kg in the first ration, and a captain 45 kg.

The situation is more complicated if relief is distributed by foreign agencies. A tightly regulated NGO programme can be identical to a government distribution, and in most cases (such as the Sudanese example above) NGO programmes use local intermediaries. Even the most independent programme brings financial benefits to the exchequer in terms of hard currency. Often, the creation of parallel structures by relief agencies has been seen to undermine the ability of host governments to deliver services. This is a variant on the theme of empowering the powerful, not a refutation of it: it is the more accountable and welfare-oriented sections of government that generally suffer, and the more authoritarian and security-oriented sections that gain in power when government capacity is undermined. The strategy followed by Mobutu Sese Seko in Zaire is an extreme instance: he deliberately set out to destroy any institutions other than the Presidency and its security networks (with almost $900m. of US aid). Perhaps the most common subversive impact of foreign-run relief programmes is that they invite favourable comparison with the government's own efforts, thus undermining the legitimacy of government.

Aid empowers the powerful, and also creates new political or economic groupings around it. Any established aid programme creates a local constituency to defend it. As programmes become entrenched, they tend to become more conservative, and as the donor agency invests more, it becomes less willing to change the programme or withdraw.

Aid *can* be politically progressive. Discreet assistance to anti-apartheid organizations in South Africa empowered democratically minded people more than the ruling authorities. Aid to ERA and REST during the war weakened the Ethiopian Government, while it also strengthened the rebel fronts *vis-à-vis* the people. In both these cases there were deep political commitments that pre-dated the arrival of aid, and remained more important than the aid relationship. It is also possible to be in political solidarity with retrogressive anti-government organizations. A notable example is the Hutu extremist opposition to the post-1994 government of Rwanda, which continues to garner sympathy and support from some religious and humanitarian organizations (see Chapter 9).

Aid institutions themselves present a curious model of political authority. Anxious to project a particular moral image, aid agencies are often unaware of exactly how they are perceived in recipient countries. In many African languages, the same word is used for (commercial) 'companies' and (aid) 'agencies' (often to the chagrin of aid workers). An agency with collegial internal relationships and inclusive processes of consultation may appear patronizing or domineering to the recipients of its largesse. Throughout Africa, aid agencies are surrounded by a mystique of power, wealth and opportunity. This problem is compounded by the indeterminacy of aid negotiations. A representative of an aid agency cannot be totally frank about what resources are on offer and what promises can be kept, because he or she does not know. The representative can only make promises to try to obtain resources, not definite contracts to deliver. The value of these promises cannot be calculated. Often there are disappointments, occasionally expectations are exceeded. The overall effect is to create both external orientation and indeterminacy among local people, and project a sense of mystery and inscrutability on to the aid agency. This mystique is the opposite of the transparency that underpins democracy, it is more akin to the transcendental or religious legitimation of pre-democratic political authority. A politician who derives legitimacy by standing beside an aid worker is retreating from accountability.

The aid relationship is therefore fundamentally different from a political contract. The benevolent ethos of aid should not obscure the practical and ideological ways in which it erodes the basis of political contracts. This problem can be overcome, but successes are rare, are achieved with difficulty, and depend upon a strong pre-existing political contract.

The humanitarian Gresham's Law

The 'humanitarian Gresham's Law' is derived from the decoupling of aid agencies' hard and soft interests (their institutional interests versus their stated aims).[1] It states: in a situation of unregulated private humanitarian activity, 'debased' humanitarianism will drive out the 'authentic' version. Or, to answer a question incisively posed by Bill Yates, 'Is Oxfam primarily a service to the Victorian charity ethic in Britain, or is it a service to the marginalized populations of the world?' (Black, 1992: 195). The humanitarian Gresham's Law implies that aid institutions will tend towards the former. MSF-France is explicit about the fact that it is primarily a service to a certain ethos of voluntarism.

The terminology needs to be deployed with care: it might be taken to imply that a 'pure' humanitarianism exists and that it could be (re)asserted if current conditions were to change. This is not the case: *all* international humanitarian action is subject to some irremediable constraints. Nor should it imply that some agencies are genuine and some fake: all agencies are caught within the same tendencies, and different programmes succumb to different degrees. An agency with a highly 'authentic' operation in one country may have a 'debased' one in a neighbouring one. The terminology is adopted to indicate merely that some forms are more likely to see high professional and ethical standards than others.

The humanitarian Gresham's Law works this way. The agency most determined to get the highest media profile obtains the most funds from donors (both the public and donor governments). In doing so, it prioritizes the requirements of fund-raising: it follows the TV cameras,

---

[1]Gresham's Law is the rule whereby, with no regulation, debased coinage drives pure coinage out of circulation. For example, if a 'silver' florin which is 50% base metal and 50% silver is accepted as tender, then all florins with more than 50% silver will be driven out of circulation; they will be melted down and recast as debased florins.

employs pretty young women to appear in front of the cameras, engages in picturesque and emotive programmes (food and medicine, best of all for children), it abandons scruples about when to go in and when to leave, and it forsakes co-operation with its peers for advertising its brand name. Agencies that are more thoughtful – a category that includes most non-operational agencies (mainly church-related agencies that work through local partners/clients), consortia, and a handful of the older secular agencies – fail to obtain the same level of public attention, and suffer for it. They may be able to obtain a certain level of support from institutional donors and the more discerning public for their more 'authentic' programmes, but the greater pressure is in the opposite direction.

The most common quantifiable measurements of agencies' effectiveness used in the media consist of the proportion of income spent on administration, the overall quantities of relief delivered, the number of 'volunteers' dispatched and the speed of response. Most important is simply the sheer amount of attention in the media and the volume and tenor of the agency's own advertising material. Other things being equal, the agency which is more media-aware will prosper at the expense of the less media-aware. In aid projects, media-friendliness does not correlate positively with effectiveness. Within a single agency, fundraisers and those adept at grabbing media attention will prosper at the expense of those who grapple with the problem of making aid a genuine service to its target group. In short, 'hard' interests prevail at the expense of 'soft'.

This tendency is unconstrained where it matters most, in the most severe disasters. In the 'development' arena, there is a healthy trend towards Western donors supporting indigenous organizations directly, and bypassing Western NGOs as intermediaries. But this means that Western NGOs are more reliant on disaster relief money for basic income. In turn, the agencies are more reliant on prominent media coverage in these disasters.

In principle, the supply of funds to 'debased' humanitarian agencies could be influenced by a sustained programme of public education by the more 'authentic' humanitarians. Some agencies – notably non-operational ones – have long been committed to 'development education', but the funds devoted to this are small, and none has the courage to launch an emergency appeal based on a more subtle message. Possibly they have learned the lesson of Oxfam, which tried to do exactly this in response to the 1973 drought in Maharashtra when the field director for India, John Staley, refused to mount a standard appeal. Instead, Oxfam issued 'a modulated message about long-term prevention and building on local capacities . . . [and] no-one took the slightest notice' (Black, 1992: 195).

This problem has been recognized by some aid workers, and some agencies have instituted sophisticated internal evaluations of programmes, and drawn up codes of good practice. These efforts are a struggle against the trend. The more 'authentic' agencies are very reluctant to criticize their more 'debased' competitors, perhaps for fear that any critique of aid would drag them down as well (just as airlines do not advertise each others' safety records because this would deter all passengers). Partly because of the strength of the voluntary ethos, 'authentic' agencies have also not proposed any system of regulation and independent evaluation. There are some good reasons for this: a regulatory office could become over-bureaucratic or the tool of chauvinistic political interests. It would change the basic philosophy of NGO action (see below). Nonetheless, if the experienced agencies do not adopt a regulatory system that works, they will either have one imposed upon them by institutional donors, or become increasingly 'debased' themselves.

The results of the debasing tendency are evident across the spectrum of relief agencies. The ICRC, forced to compete with MSF, has been obliged to abandon its famous discretion and publicize its activities. If the ICRC threatens to withdraw because its hallowed principles have been broken, another agency may jump in to take its place, and the principle becomes worthless. Another case is the non-operational NGOs. It is probably true that these agencies spend their money better than operational agencies, not least because of the lower expenditure on expatriate salaries and expenses. But their programmes are not visible to TV crews or visiting dignitaries, and they are increasingly under pressure to become operational in order to safeguard their income. A classic case is the abandonment of the cross-border consortia to Eritrea and Tigray after the end of the war, when most of the agencies that had contributed to the consortia were able, for the first time, to become operational under their own names in Ethiopia. The decline of consortia in general is a wider manifestation of this.

The humanitarian Gresham's Law militates against co-operation among agencies, except in a few areas where hard and soft interests converge to make tactical co-ordination essential. One thing that all agencies agree on is the right of 'humanitarian access', and they will unite whenever this is threatened, for example by the attempt of a host government to regulate their activities or by critical press coverage. Another important overlap is in the size of agencies' budgets. If humanitarianism is a good thing, it follows that more is better. Only financially healthy relief agencies can actually deliver the goods. Most NGOs also value their independence from governmental donors, but the logic of the 'big is beautiful' argument in relief operations, by appealing to both 'hard' and 'soft' interests, usually wins out. A former director of ActionAid writes: 'The record of the [NGO] sector shows the risks and negative aspects of growth are outweighed by the benefits' (Hodson, 1992: 128). Maximizing impact is stated as the paramount objective of most NGOs.

From the early 1980s, more and more NGOs have taken more and more government money for relief programmes and become what David Korten calls 'public service contractors'. At first the significance of this passed almost unnoticed, perhaps because emergency work was considered a distraction from the main task of 'development', and emergencies occasioned a partial suspension of critical faculties as well as a readiness to bend the normal operating rules. For example, Oxfam put a ceiling on the proportion of income it could receive from governments for 'development' work, but made an exception for relief. Three-quarters of UK food aid is now handled by NGOs, and the major US relief agencies – CARE, Catholic Relief Services and World Vision – regularly undertake major food aid programmes funded in large part or even wholly by USAID. The creation and rapid expansion of the European Commission Humanitarian Office has led to some European agency programmes being wholly reliant on EU funding. Even Christian Aid, a non-operational agency explicitly dedicated to a high level of quality control in its grant-giving, has taken high levels of government money, chiefly for its emergency programmes. The proportion of its income from the British Government rose from zero in 1975 to 35 per cent by 1989/90 (Ondine Smerdon pers. comm.).

The donors are making no compromise by engaging NGOs: for twenty years the neo-liberal paradigm has been to contract out public services to the independent sector. When they first made a strategic alliance with governmental donors, NGOs recognized that they might forfeit some independence in policy-making. Most NGOs would claim that they have gained from the deal: their programmes are much bigger and more secure, and they still criticize governments over (for example) slowness in sending troops to Rwanda, unwillingness to ban land mines, and cuts in aid budgets. Most private agencies have not become agents of government. But there have been more subtle changes. Cases of NGOs taking consistent stands against official relief policy in specific countries are extremely rare. The cool and even hostile relations between NGOs and donor governments' embassies that characterized the situation in Ethiopia in 1983–4, let alone Biafra and Cambodia, are now consigned to the past. The criticism of the French military intervention in Rwanda by MSF-France was merely a hiccup in an otherwise cosy relationship. NGOs may have gained influence at the margin in ministries of development co-operation, but they have lost the capacity to set themselves against the entire system.

The move to subcontracting for official aid is an important shift. More formal systems of competitive tendering are developing in ministries of development co-operation. Private companies, local NGOs and governmental agencies are likely to become major bidders in the relief market in the near future, a move that would increase the pressure for a formal system of regulation. International NGOs often claim to be more efficient service providers than their rivals, especially at reaching the poorest. The evidence for this is not strong (Robinson, 1992; Edwards and Hulme, 1995a; Fowler and Biekart, 1996). Rigorous regulation will create serious challenges for Western NGOs: will they become a 'third force' of non-commercial service subcontractors, or return to being a 'first force' that mobilizes citizens' moral outrage and sympathy (Edwards and Hulme, 1995b: 225)?

Understandably, most large NGOs prefer not to have to make such a stark choice. Instead, they manage on an *ad hoc* basis, while anxiously examining what principles might make institutional sense. (Interminable institutional reorganization is one symptom of this lack of confidence.) The idea has been put forward that it is the very ambiguity of NGOs' position that is their strength: their adaptiveness and qualities of 'partnership' with local organizations and communities, rather than their adoption of the 'right' model of work (ibid.: 224–7). In theory, being *both* a 'third' and a 'first force' should strengthen both. Debate at headquarters and public action should help bring vitality to field programmes, while field experience brings credibility to lobbying and advocacy, and substance to research. For some single-issue organizations with strong leadership, this formula has worked well. Examples include the advocacy of children's charities on child labour and prostitution and the involvement of mines clearance organizations in the campaign to ban land mines. A key reason for this success is that the agencies concerned can make a substantial contribution to achieving these goals in full: child labour can be outlawed and land mines banned. (Enforcing such prohibitions will require a different kind of organization.)

For generalist organizations, including the mainstream relief NGOs, the formula does not work. Taking on a much broader cause, such as the conquest of poverty, injustice or famine across the world, is a wholly different matter. Claiming that 'such-and-such an agency is on the side of the poor and oppressed' is mere rhetoric. Humanitarian agencies simply cannot make a comparable contribution to conquering famine. In the meantime, the ambiguity is an obstacle to fighting famine.

A vigorous debate within an agency is *ipso facto* a good thing, but it does not necessarily lead to the required results. For a start, an agency busy talking to itself may find it difficult to listen and respond to what its 'recipients' want. The issues are being problematized inside a Western institution, not in public, and even less in disaster-vulnerable countries. Secondly, the absence of a clear philosophy gives more leeway to fund-raising departments and 'can-do' emergency officers – the principal engines of 'debasement'. Most importantly, such an ambiguous status reinforces the indeterminacy of aid negotiations and the opacity of the humanitarian language (see below), and in general the mystique and lack of accountability of the humanitarian business.

The humanitarian Gresham's Law militates against supporting local political contracts. In their role as subcontracted service providers, foreign NGOs *could* work within such contracts, provided the regulatory framework were subject to some form of popular accountability. Radical independent agencies can also support progressive political contracts. But in their current unclear situation, subject to powerful pressures to adopt a high media profile, it is extremely difficult for international NGOs to play a progressive political role in recipient countries.

The humanitarian code language[2]

Relief agencies that try to be operational in famines, especially war-famines, are trapped. To reveal the truth about where their resources go would endanger their 'hard' interests *vis-à-vis* donors; to insist on following the principles enshrined in a code of conduct would entail withdrawing on the first day in the field. Agencies habitually get around this trap by deception (simply lying about what is happening), by functional ignorance (assuming that all has gone correctly unless they are formally told otherwise) or by creating a dynamic situation in which they are constantly searching for 'improvements' that will find the elusive magic formula of effective relief. The last option is simply the most sophisticated form of self-deception.

There is in fact a tendency towards systemic duplicity. The language that relief agencies use to their peers, donors and constituents is a systematic distortion of the realities of their work on the ground. The actual language of humanitarian action remains either unspoken or relegated to a somewhat distasteful substructure of 'fieldcraft'. This is the language of pragmatic deals, compromises and turning a blind eye. This is a code – in the sense of a cipher. Many terms in the official humanitarian language have a coded meaning that signifies something quite different and even opposite. 'Partner' means 'client' – there is no genuine sharing of power. 'Participation' means 'collaboration'. The complexities of the term 'neutral' are commonly ignored, and as a result the concept is misused (Plattner, 1996). 'NGO' means almost nothing at all.[3] One of the difficulties faced by local NGOs and the local staff of international agencies is that in order to rise in the system they must become fluent at speaking in this humanitarian code. The key requirement for their advancement in the system is realizing that terms in the humanitarian language do not possess a profound inner meaning (understood at headquarters), but are means to of preserving institutions in the face of an intractable reality.

The opacity of this humanitarian code does not make for good relief work. Before local staff and 'beneficiaries' reach the same state of enlightenment, they are locked with foreign staff in a situation of mutual distrust. Local staff or public officials who do recognize the code

[2]This section owes much to work done by Michael Medley.
[3]The term was first widely used when 'non-governmental organizations' were accredited as observers to the UN Economic and Social Council in 1950.

for what it is often have more insight than expatriates who have internalized too many precepts of the humanitarian international. Another conflict may then emerge, in which local staff quit, try to press for reform or decide to turn the system to their personal benefit. In addition, the duplicity of the humanitarian language makes frank evaluation impossible. Another response to failure is to assume that it stems from the agency's inability to exercise sufficient control itself. The agency sends more expatriate (i.e. trusted) staff to monitor or evaluate, or the field director him- or herself takes on more powers. Frustrated altruism is displaced into personal aggrandizement, camouflaged as an ever more sincere concern for the needy.

There are counter-examples in which international agency and local political authorities have shared the same concerns and have not been forced into a dishonest relationship. These occur when relief is given in a spirit of political solidarity, and in political and economic circumstances where there is no need for unauthorized diversion or manipulation. Agencies that have discarded superficial claims to 'neutrality' and are prepared to endorse the political agendas of their local political counterparts can eliminate most of the humanitarian duplicity, though they may have to pretend otherwise if they are to obtain funds from donors concerned with apolitical humanitarianism. On occasion, good personal relationships between relief agency staff and local authorities have also allowed a frankness at an individual level that can mitigate some of the systemic distrust. Even an acknowledgement that relief work requires speaking two different moral languages is a considerable advance in establishing an effective programme.

Much agency practice makes it hard for a good long-term understanding to determine a relief programme. The humanitarian Gresham's Law means that nuances are jettisoned in the rush to meet a perceived charitable imperative. One striking result is the habitual inflation of estimates of expected deaths. 'One million dead by Christmas' (or some variant thereof) has been heard every few years since 1968, and has never been remotely close to the truth.[4] For a variety of reasons – not including massive relief programmes – these predictions are usually an order of magnitude (or more) too large. Such exaggerations contribute to clumsy and inappropriate relief operations, but justify emotive fundraising appeals. Accurate estimates, detailed understanding of the dynamics of the crisis and good personal relationships usually come later, by which time the damage has been done. The international NGO system is arguably the best international disasters information network in the world, but it only operates in the aftermath of disasters. Before the disaster strikes, widely available information rarely drives action (DeMars, 1995).

[4]The list includes Biafra 1968, the Sahel 1973, Cambodia 1979, Ethiopia 1984, Sudan 1985, Ethiopia 1987, Sudan 1990 (and most years since), Somalia November 1992, Rwandese refugees 1994, and eastern Zaire 1996.

As critiques of humanitarianism become more common and more accepted, some thoughtful agency staff are becoming more questioning. There is a noticeable decline in the self-confidence that until recently marked established aid organizations. There is a higher degree of internal self-criticism than ever before. At the time of writing, however, few if any of the internal critics have succeeded in breaking the code. It is not coincidental that the debate is largely framed in terms of 'whither NGOs?' but not 'where do we find solutions for famine?' The institutional blinkers have yet to fall away.

Political contract requires frank negotiation, and the pushing aside of mystique. This cannot be achieved while the language of humanitarianism remains so foggy and oblique.

Implications

The regressive empowerment of aid and the opacity of relief organizations mean that the aid process is almost always opposed to the very principles to which the humanitarian international aspires: rights, empowerment of the poor, democracy and accountability. This is not to say that aid cannot help achieve these things, merely that for it to do so successfully demands an exceptional ability to overcome all these tendencies at once. This requires a political situation in which the desired qualities of democracy and empowerment are already present to be built upon: where an agency can be simultaneously a 'first force' (mobilizing citizens in a progressive cause) and a 'third force' (service contractor). These conditions rarely prevail in situations where people are vulnerable to famine, and are very exceptional indeed in wartime (the clandestine humanitarianism in wartime Eritrea and Tigray is the outstanding exception). Humanitarianism is also increasingly dishonest in a systemic way, dependent upon erroneous views of the problems it claims to tackle and false claims about its success.

Negotiated access and humanitarianism in war

The humanitarian arsenal expanded in the late 1980s. The principle of 'negotiated access' was one of the most important, pioneered with Operation Lifeline Sudan (OLS) in 1989 and preserved in the face of repeated objections by the new military government since 1990. Negotiated access was extended to Angola with the launch of the Special Relief Programme for Angola (SRPA) in 1990. 'Peace corridors' were established and the UN stated its hope that the operation would add to the momentum towards peace: in fact it became a bargaining chip complicating the peace negotiations and never became effective until the 1991 ceasefire was in place (Duffield, 1994b). The SRPA took one of the OLS principles a stage further and specified the expansion of NGO activity as one of its aims. In 1990 'negotiated access' was also extended to Ethiopia, with the Joint Relief Partnership cross-line operation into Tigray and a WFP operation from the EPLF-held port of Massawa into government-held Asmara.

Where there is protracted war, relief assistance rapidly becomes integrated into the dynamic of violence. The diversion or taxation of relief supplies becomes a major way for belligerents to provision themselves, and, in time, the very command structures and military strategies themselves will come to reflect the availability of external aid and the means whereby it is delivered. Relief agencies have increasingly accommodated to violence, in the context of assistance programmes that are integrated into the cycles of violence in internal conflict (Duffield, 1994a).

The integration of relief into violence is no mere accident, it is inherent in the current structure of the humanitarian international. An additional tendency of actually existing humanitarianism may be called the 'irreducible residue of naiveté'. It refers to the way in which humanitarian institutions can never be as politically adept as politicians whose overriding concern is power. This is a version of the truism that, in international relations, the drunk driver has right of way: a democratic and law-abiding country cannot confront a dictatorship by using comparable unscrupulousness, because in doing so it would cease to be democratic and law-abiding. Similarly, UN peacekeeping forces cannot win battles against adversaries who do not publish their rules of engagement and travel in white-painted vehicles.

Relief agencies facing cynical politicians and generals are subject to their own forms of irreducible naiveté (in addition to the quite reducible naiveté that comes from often employing young and incompetent staff in positions of responsibility). The commitment to being operational in the field is the most enduring and transparent principle followed by NGOs, and it leaves them vulnerable to manipulation. Safeguards against diversion or strategic abuse were weakened by the deregulation of humanitarianism. One safeguard (now lost) was the near-monopoly over humanitarian action in war held by the ICRC, combined with the provisions of the Geneva Conventions and the ICRC's own rules of procedure. A second safeguard is the rule of law in the host country, but in many African countries this has broken down, or relief agencies have put themselves above the domestic law. The alternative is the adoption and enforcement of a code of practice by agencies. This is exceptionally difficult to achieve.

Take an example in which a local militia commander is systematically diverting food relief to feed his militiamen, who otherwise have only a meagre income. It is almost certainly preferable for the NGO to consign a certain proportion of relief formally to the commander and obtain his signed receipts. The remainder can then be delivered to the target group. Compared with the existing extortion and semi-secret diversion, the situation would be improved in four ways. One, it would remove the duplicity from the current arrangement, making the commander into an honest man (in one respect, at least). Two, it would allow an evaluation of the programme by the agency involved, making relief personnel into honest people. Three, some of the physical dangers of criminalizing a 'normal' activity would be prevented (for example, the risk of an over-zealous aid worker getting martyred trying to stop the diversion). Four, the moral elasticity of tolerating ever more severe diversions could be avoided: a breach of contract by the commander would result in a termination of the programme.

Under current circumstances, this course of action is possible only in very unusual situations. First, no donor or agency would be likely to countenance such a measure of honesty. The laws that govern foreign assistance mean that it is illegal in most countries to acknowledge that diversion is tolerated. Secondly, the practice has to be enforceable among the agencies themselves. To create a *de facto* law requires all relief agencies to co-operate. The modest and brief successes in this illustrate why it cannot offer a general remedy. In early 1992, the handful of relief agencies operating in Mogadishu formed a cartel to establish rates of pay for hired guards. This worked well for some months until more agencies arrived, wealthy and in a rush to begin programmes. These agencies immediately offered higher rates for guards.

In Southern Sudan, UNICEF has a paramount position through the structure of OLS (Southern Sector), whereby it provides logistical support and a legal basis for NGO operations. Even so, it cannot enforce co-operation. In 1992, when four expatriates, three of them aid workers, were killed by the Sudan People's Liberation Army, UNICEF tried but failed to enforce a relief boycott until the murders were investigated. In 1994, one NGO decided to pursue a case of diversion by an SPLA commander through the local courts, rather than following the usual procedure of negotiating a compromise. This was possible only because the agency held a local monopoly and because its field officer exercised unusual patience and diplomatic skill. But, despite their stated commitments to 'civil society', no other agency was prepared to follow this lead. Moreover, the accused commander played a simple waiting game, knowing that the case would be dropped when the field officer responsible was transferred.

Relief agencies will remain vulnerable to manipulation by those more ruthless and politically adept than themselves. Their central naiveté is to believe that protracted humanitarian action can be effective in the absence of enforceable principle. One result is moral elasticity. Agencies regularly adopt working principles but then abandon them. For example they may say they will tolerate only so much extortion – but then, when the intolerable occurs, they proceed to tolerate it. This inexorably draws them into an ever deeper accommodation with violence, and the role of quartermaster to armies. Relief staff agonize over the ethics of this in private, but the programmes still remain ethically unchallenged in public, and continue. This, in turn, bestows *de facto* immunity upon various means of provisioning armies.

Operation Lifeline Sudan

One of the longest running and most complex humanitarian operations in wartime is Operation Lifeline Sudan. It emerged from the famine of 1985–9 in Southern Sudan, and was designed almost entirely by international agencies using an *ad hoc* amalgam of ICRC principles (negotiated access) and depoliticized disaster relief. The history of OLS is complicated. In its first stages it benefited from the ceasefire in the war and the government's preoccupation with other political priorities. When the war re-started under General Omer al Bashir in November 1989, OLS almost foundered immediately in the face of renewed government determination to return to the old military strategy of blocking all relief. Under pressure from the donors, the government backed down and conceded a renewed OLS in March 1990. The pay-off was that it gained some aspects of formal control over the operation. There was a shift in assistance towards rehabilitation, and away from merely food aid. Several times in the following two and a half years OLS nearly came to a halt again: many times monthly flight permissions were not forthcoming until literally the last moment, and in late 1992 only seven non-government-held locations were permitted for UN flights. Within days of the authorization of Operation Restore Hope in Somalia by the UN Security Council, the Sudan Government became much more co-operative and OLS was given a new lease of life: many more locations were permitted, and the operation expanded into areas such as building-up the capacity of indigenous organizations, supporting conflict resolution and developing humanitarian principles.

Operation Lifeline Sudan has become institutionalized, part of the military, political and economic landscape in Southern Sudan. Since its relaunch in 1990, both the government and the SPLA have shifted from using starvation as a military tactic to the strategic manipulation of aid, both to provision their forces and to protect key garrisons. The structure of the aid programmes has come to have an important influence over the structure of the military command.

On the government side, the relief operation has made possible the maintenance of garrisons that would almost certainly have fallen otherwise. The main case is Juba, which was repeatedly saved by relief airlifts in 1990 and 1991. The Lutheran World Federation has run an extended airlift to Juba. Smaller garrisons have also been sustained: UN and NGO operations have been crucial in the viability of the outpost at Terakeka, and a WFP airdrop to Kapoeta when it was under assault by the SPLA in September 1994 provided the garrison with supplies it could have obtained no other way.

The Sudan Government has outmanoeuvred the UN, insisting on recognition of its sovereignty as a precondition for any UN programmes in the country, in both the war and non-war areas. The UN has consistently compromised and been willing to supply relief without guarantees that it will not be diverted to the army or used to feed civilians abducted during counter-insurgency operations. Operationality has again triumphed over principle. The level of monitoring and evaluation has been extremely poor, and was criticized in the 1996 official review of OLS. The review noted:

> [T]he principle of neutrality is frequently violated both by the government's insistence on ownership of the OLS operation, and by the fact that this ownership has not been sufficiently challenged by the UN. . . . [T]he UN's acceptance of the primacy of sovereignty is seen by some to be a pragmatic position which ensures continued access in the south. (Karim, Duffield *et al.*, 1996: 90)

The most extreme manifestation of this is in the Nuba Mountains, where the Sudan Government has prohibited any form of negotiated access to the SPLA-held and contested areas. While keeping out OLS – and hence any of the principles of neutrality and accountability it may bring in its train – the government has succeeded in persuading UN agencies and some NGOs to operate in the areas it holds, under its own tight regulation. This has led to UNDP supporting the peace camps and implicitly facilitating and legitimizing the near-genocidal campaign against the Nuba.[5]

The position of the SPLA with regard to relief is more complex. Until May 1991, the SPLA's rear base was in Ethiopia. Its political organization was modelled on the Dergue, which was its patron, supplying arms, training, a radio station, and security facilities. Several huge refugee camps in Gambella region received large amounts of international relief supplies, the distribution of which was not monitored. Colonel John Garang was quartermaster for the movement courtesy of UNHCR and Ethiopian security – a pattern familiar from Mengistu himself and the UN Emergency Office in Ethiopia. This arrangement in turn meant that the SPLA had little need to develop reciprocal relations with the inhabitants of the areas under its control; its guarantors were weapons and external patronage. Only in 1988 was the need to provide services to maintain civilians in the 'liberated' areas belatedly recognized. One of the chief roles of the Sudan Relief and Rehabilitation Association (SRRA) was facilitating a flow of relief that could also help provision the SPLA itself. The SRRA was superficially similar to ERA and REST, but lacked the managerial capacity and was operating in a wholly different political context. Even its sympathizers bemoaned its

---

[5] 'The Official Review of Operation Lifeline Sudan Condemns, UN Agencies' Complicity in Sudan Government Policies in the Nuba Mountains', *NAFIR: The Newsletter of the Nuba Mountains, Sudan* 2(3) October: 7.

'close attachment to the military aspects of the SPLA. . . . Unfortunately, military considerations have regularly hampered the SRRA's ability to provide relief' (Malwal, 1991: 8). International donors were never prepared to entrust significant resources to the SRRA, which soon became no more than a co-ordinator for the operations of international agencies on the ground.

The defeat of Mengistu in May 1991 removed the SPLA's source of supplies, and about 300,000 refugees suddenly returned to Southern Sudan. The absence of internal political mobilization immediately became apparent. Several regional commands were left militarily vulnerable and without provisions, and the bitterness from years of internal repression surfaced. The SPLA split, with two commanders in Upper Nile, Riek Machar and Lam Akol, forming the 'Nasir Faction'. The viability of the split was enhanced by the fact that there were, briefly, large camps of returnees from Ethiopia in Nasir, which were attracting international relief and could provide an independent source of sustenance for the forces.

Meanwhile, the fact that OLS and foreign relief agencies were delivering relief directly to numerous locations across the South meant that the opportunities for large-scale diversion at source no longer existed. To the extent that aid could now be used to provision the SPLA, it was in the hands of local commanders, who duly used the opportunities they had. One of Garang's major sources of centralizing power was removed. Combined with the absence of centralized arms supplies from abroad and the lack of political mobilization, this contributed to a process of military fragmentation. In one instance, William Nyuon, the then breakaway commander controlling Lafon, appears to have deliberately maintained a camp of displaced people in a state of malnutrition in order to attract international relief supplies, which were then used to provision his forces.

By 1994, the diversion of relief supplies by all the SPLA factions and the Sudan Government had become so systematic that some experienced relief workers canvassed the proposal that a certain proportion of all supplies be formally consigned to the military. This possibility has been discussed above – and, for the reasons outlined, it was never seriously considered. Publicly, OLS continues to maintain the fiction that it does not supply soldiers. The final result is that relief is inextricably bound up in the political economy of war in Southern Sudan. Relief is provisioning both civilians and soldiers, is influencing political mobilization and military strategy, and is one of the prime foci of international diplomacy.

Humanitarian law and humanitarianism

There is one notable omission from the enlarged humanitarian arsenal: strengthening the law of war itself. While the UN Security Council has been increasingly concerned with the protection of humanitarian actions, the core of international humanitarian law – the protection of individual human rights in wartime – has been neglected.

The use of starvation as a weapon of war has a long history. The Lieber Code, which was hailed as determining legality in the American Civil War, notoriously permitted starvation in Article 17: 'War is not carried on by arms alone. It is lawful to starve the hostile belligerent, armed or unarmed, so that it leads to the speedier subjection of the enemy.' (cited in Allen, 1989: 33). Scholars have interpreted this provision more strictly than commanders such as General Sherman, arguing that it does not give a *carte blanche* for wantonly creating famine (ibid. Provost, 1991: 49–50). It is notable that no subsequent formulation of the laws of war gives such licence. The 1907 Hague Conventions were imprecise on the issue but Article 23 prohibited destruction of 'the enemy's property' unless 'imperatively demanded by the necessities of war'. When Field Marshal Reichenau, commanding the German Army in Russia in 1941, ordered 'To supply local inhabitants and prisoners of war with food is an act of unnecessary humanity' (Moskoff, 1990: 44), he was paradoxically affirming the illegality of starvation at the same time as proposing to inflict it.

The 1949 Geneva Conventions went much further in placing obligations on armed forces and occupying powers with respect to the provision of food to the civilian population. The Additional Protocols of 1977, formulated in the aftermath of Biafra, East Pakistan and Vietnam, were much more precise in prohibiting the use of starvation as a weapon of war. Article 54 of Protocol I is remarkably strong:

Protection of objects indispensable to the survival of the civilian population.

1. Starvation of civilians as a method of warfare is prohibited.

2. It is prohibited to attack, destroy, remove or render useless, for that purpose, objects indispensable to the survival of the civilian population, such as foodstuffs, agricultural areas for the production of foodstuffs, crops, livestock, drinking water installations and supplies and irrigation works, for the specific purpose of denying them for their sustenance value to the civilian population or to the adverse Party, whatever the motive, whether in order to starve out civilians, to cause them to move away, or for any other motive.

'Starvation' is used in its active, transitive sense: death by lack of food does not need to ensue for 'starvation' to have occurred, or more precisely, been inflicted. Two other elements in the Article are especially worthy of note. One is that any action that contributes to the process of starvation is prohibited, *whatever the motive*. Secondly, it should be noted that no exemption is made if the food and other items in question can be used by enemy combatants as well as civilians. It is solely when the siege or destruction of items can be demonstrated to affect combatants exclusively that it can be considered legal.

The only evident weakness in this formulation is the failure to specify a prohibition on the *prevention of activities* (such as trade or labour migration) indispensable to the survival of the population. Such a provision would be important in situations when preventing move-ment, trade and wage-earning is instrumental in starving populations.

Protocol I relates to international armed conflicts. The formulation in Protocol II (Article 14), which relates to internal conflicts, is much weaker. There are crucial omissions, including the words 'whatever the motive', so that only military actions with the *primary aim* of starving civilians are expressly forbidden.

The main challenge to using the law to deter famine crimes is enforce-ment. To date, no-one has ever been brought to court charged with the war crime of starvation or a similar charge. The trials of the members of the former Ethiopian Government for war crimes provided an opportunity, but the Ethiopian Special Prosecutor's Office considered the legal basis for the charges too unreliable. Instead, it investigated whether charges should be brought against those responsible for the resettlement programme. A case can be made for their criminal responsibility, but it required detailed inquiry and complex legal argument that were not a priority, given that the prosecutions were already expensive and behind schedule. There are no signs of this initiative being replicated elsewhere, for instance at an international tribunal.

One reason for the lack of enthusiasm is that prosecution is seen as a *post hoc* response which does nothing for the victims when they need it most. This is not a valid objection. First, it is not suggested that criminalizing famine should be the *only* response. Second, if the same argument were applied to criminal justice, there would be no courts. Taking a more long-term view of war famines, the priority is to create effective deterrents, of which criminal liability is the most obvious and potentially the most effective option.

Humanitarian law is concerned with conflict, starting at the point at which conventional human rights law stops. During the 1980s, the main thrust among legal scholars and activists was to broaden human rights law into areas related to conflict, such as arbitrary executions, 'disappearances' and states of emergency. There was a succession of initiatives and statements of principle by organizations such as the International Commission of Jurists (1985) and the International Law Association, (1984) aimed at developing legal restraints on armed force used in internal conflicts. In the early 1990s there were attempts to extend this effort to internally displaced persons (Deng, 1993).

Despite their shortcomings, the laws of war and human rights law provide a strong legal foundation for protecting civilians from famine caused by war. Pursuit of strengthening the law of war itself and its enforcement would be a logical strategy for the humanitarian international. However, it has not happened. Humanitarian activity and the efforts of legal scholars have been pursued almost entirely in separate spheres. The only significant overlap has concerned the 'right' of humanitarian intervention (see below). For the most part, humanitarian practitioners have either found the legal initiatives unhelpful or have been unaware of them, and instead have developed their own principles in isolation. Whatever the reasons for this, it has suited relief agencies well, because humanitarian law is also rigorous in the conditions it applies to the providers of humanitarian aid. Many relief operations from Biafra onwards have been conducted in violation of some of the principles laid down in the Geneva Conventions – notably, there have often been inadequate safeguards against the diversion or abuse of aid. Meanwhile, human rights lawyers have generally responded to war famines by studying their legal texts ever more intensely, rather than by undertaking empirical investigations of war, famine and relief. Some human rights lawyers have advised humanitarian agencies, but this has taken the form of putting legal expertise at the service of the humanitarian enterprise, rather than trying to redirect that enterprise. The minimal dialogue between the two efforts has contributed to the shortcomings of both.

A notable divergence between human rights law and *de facto* humanitarian principle can be seen in the case of sanctions. Powerful countries, led by the United States, have imposed sanctions through the UN on errant weaker countries such as Iraq, Haiti and Serbia. In each of these cases, humanitarian concern has been secondary to strategic political goals, such as overthrowing a government or forcing it to sue for peace. The logic of sanctions – that inflicting human suffering is a legitimate way of bringing about desired political change – is the converse of the logic of privileging humanitarian activities in wartime. It is striking that, although a number of relief agencies have criticized sanctions, they have not done so with the volubility or sense of urgency with which they advocate immediate action in crises such as Somalia, Bosnia or Rwanda (while, in South Africa, many supported them). In the case of Iraq, a UNICEF investigation into the human cost of the sanctions was suppressed and only later released independently in truncated form.[6] At the UN, the Security Council resolutions have prioritized the Iraqi Government's compliance with military, political and financial demands, making its humanitarian obligations less onerous and less binding. Since its creation in 1992, the Department of Humanitarian Affairs has not been able to change this set of priorities. This is an indication that the power of the humanitarian international stems from its unwillingness to mount any serious challenge to the Euro-American political order. Actually existing humanitarianism is not universalist: it is a servant – albeit an unevenly supervised one – of that same political order.

[6]Hoskins, n.d. See also Center for Economic and Social Rights, 1996.

The humanitarian ascendancy

The most formidable addition to the humanitarian arsenal was 'humanitarian intervention'. This has a curious legal foundation – in the notion of the 'right' of humanitarian access. Articles 23 and 59–63 of the Fourth Geneva Convention of 1949 laid down, for the first time, the obligations of belligerents towards humanitarian relief. They required a belligerent government to provide and accept relief for civilians in territories under its control, and to allow free passage of relief to territories not under its control. The draughtsmen also foresaw the possibility of the strategic abuse of humanitarian relief and placed stringent conditions on the provider. According to Article 23, a belligerent need only agree to free passage of relief to civilians under the control of an adversary if it 'is satisfied that there are no reasons for fearing':

(a) that the consignments may be diverted from their destination,

(b) that the control may not be effective, or

(c) that a definite advantage may accrue to the military efforts or economy of the enemy through the substitution of the above-mentioned consignments for goods which would otherwise be provided or produced by the enemy or through the release of such material, services or facilities as would otherwise be required for the production of such goods.

Inter alia, this article arguably gives a legal justification to the Nigerian Federal Government's embargo on relief to Biafra.[7]

The Geneva Conventions also stress that the provision of external relief does not remove the obligation from the occupying power to carry out any of its responsibilities for the welfare of the civilian population. There is also no specific mention of humanitarian organizations other than the ICRC and Red Cross and Red Crescent Societies; the present wide spectrum of relief NGOs did not exist in the 1940s.

The 1977 Additional Protocols mark both a strengthening and a subtle shift in emphasis. Article 70 of Protocol I restates the duty to accept impartial relief, while Article 71 specifies that relief personnel should be 'respected and protected'. The 1949 formulation had given relief workers the same rights as neutral civilians, but these rights did not necessarily extend to carrying out relief work. This omission was now rectified: not only must relief workers 'not be knowingly attacked, they also must not be unnecessarily prevented from discharging their proper functions' (Allen, 1989: 75–6). At the same time, the require-

---

[7]Jurists may argue *ad infinitum* about the precise legal standing of the Geneva Conventions, for example with respect to internal conflicts, UN forces and humanitarian organizations, but there can be no doubt that they express the *spirit* of international humanitarian law. The argument of non-applicability is made solely by those who want to abuse this spirit.

ments that relief personnel should not exceed the terms of their mission, and should take account of the security requirements of the governing authority, were also specified.

How does the 'right' or 'duty' of humanitarian intervention using military force derive from these modest legal provisions? It appears to be through a conflation of two separate points. From the outset, the UN has been empowered to use force to terminate serious breaches of international law, which encompasses humanitarian law. Stopping a belligerent from, for example, committing genocide by despatching troops falls squarely within this capacity of the right to wage war (*jus ad bellum*). However, sending troops to ensure respect for humanitarian law within a conflict is a conflation of the laws of war (*jus in bello*) and the right to wage war. One consequence of this legal distinction is that the ICRC, concerned exclusively with the laws of war, considers that it cannot take a position on humanitarian intervention beyond pointing out the dangers involved (Sandoz, 1993). It also implies that the legal grounds for armed intervention to protect relief deliveries are slender.

The law determining military humanitarian intervention has in fact been made at the UN Security Council in a more or less *ad hoc* manner. Two strands of international crisis propelled it on to the Security Council's agenda. One was the revived concept of a UN protectorate, implemented by the UN Transitional Authority in Cambodia (UNTAC). This was a negotiated temporary take-over of some of the basic functions of a state to cover the transition to normalcy. It was both an *ad hoc* deal arising from the *Realpolitik* of Cambodia refracted through some Cold War peculiarities, and a possible precedent in law.

The second was the unilateral forcible intervention in a state's territory, violating sovereignty under the authority of the UN Security Council, avowedly in pursuit of humanitarian aims. This was first implemented with the creation of the 'safe haven' in northern Iraq in 1991. In this case the decision was made rapidly in response to public outcry after media coverage of the attempted exodus of the Iraqi Kurds to Turkey. It took more than a year and the deepening crises in Bosnia and Somalia before the UN and the US State Department began to consider it as a legal precedent of some utility. The institutional interests of the UN and some voluntary agencies were instrumental in creating this new model of essentially relief agency-determined military action (see Chapter 9). Somalia in 1992–3 was a fusion of the model of UN-authorized unilateral intervention with a slightly watered-down UN protectorate. Another variant was later manifested in Haiti, in the form of a semi-negotiated intervention with the avowed aim of restoring democracy.

The idea of 'humanitarian intervention' has excited both lawyers and humanitarian practitioners, and has been an arena for unique co-operation between them. For each group, the concept appears as the vanguard of a fundamental principle that will change the world. In the case of lawyers, it is the enforcement of human rights law or the laws of war, and in the case of humanitarians, the triumph of compassion over political obstacles such as sovereignty. These hopes have not been fulfilled. Neither have the human rights and humanitarian projects united under the banner of 'humanitarian intervention'.

Both the shortcomings and the growing hegemony of the humanitarian international in marginal areas of the world can be seen clearly in the history of the UN Department of Humanitarian Affairs (DHA). The DHA was heralded in 1991 and created in 1992. It was the latest in a long line of institutional initiatives at the UN aimed at creating better preparedness, rapid response and co-ordination, and in particular at resolving the vexed issue of conflict of mandates among the specialized agencies, so that assistance and protection could be provided across mandates. The DHA was headed by an Under-Secretary General, a 'humanitarian czar' with the highest rank of any UN official ever to be concerned specifically with humanitarian issues. The appointment of the Swedish diplomat, Jan Eliasson, who had a strong reputation for taking human rights issues seriously, was an encouraging sign.

Both in its mandate and its execution, the DHA failed to address two fundamental issues. One is public accountability. Characteristically, the UN response to a critique of its failures has been to introduce another level of bureaucracy and another set of powers, in the hope that these powers would override lesser ones and enforce the rapid action and co-ordination. It did not have that effect: the UN's specialized agencies guarded their autonomy and the DHA in effect became another competitor rather than a co-ordinator. There was no attempt to enforce the learning of lessons or to expose incompetence and corruption. The DHA did not even spend its early months assessing and evaluating, instead, it plunged straight into operational issues, notably in Sudan and Somalia.

The second issue was human rights, and by extension, the protection of civilians in conflict. The need to give legal protection to internally displaced people, comparable to the rights enshrined in the 1951 Refugee Convention, was one of the main motives for the creation of the DHA. This is an extremely sensitive area, trespassing on national sovereignty and also infringing the mandates of the specialized agencies. In September 1990, the Dag Hammarskjöld and Ford Foundations commissioned two UN veterans, Erskine Childers and Brian Urquhart, to undertake a study into reinvigorating the institution. They recommended the creation of a Department of Humanitarian Affairs and Human Rights, headed by a Deputy Secretary General. They wrote of the 'substantial connection' between the humanitarian emergencies of mass migration and human rights, 'not only in the broadest sense that such movements place the rights of human beings in jeopardy, but in numerous specific provisions of the UN International Bill of Rights relating to them'. (Childers and Urquhart, 1991: 28). The substance of the integration of human rights and humanitarian action was more slender than this might suggest: it was confined to crises of mass displacement alone.

However, no sooner had this modest integration been proposed than the UN backed away from it. The General Assembly Resolution of December 1991[8] that established the DHA conspicuously failed to specify human rights. It began weakly: 'Humanitarian assistance is of cardinal importance for the victims of natural disasters and other emergencies', and specified a new department with responsibilities for disaster prevention, preparedness, a stand-by capacity, making consolidated appeals, co-ordination, co-operation and leadership, and the continuum from relief to rehabilitation and development. In short, it avoided all the fundamental issues, even in the weakened form proposed by Childers and Urquhart. It was a classic case of the UN member states protecting their sovereignty.

Within the confines of an ostensibly non-political approach to problems in politically marginal areas of the world, it is conceivable that the DHA could have achieved some modest technical progress. It did not. Its subsequent failings can be laid largely at the door of the UN itself. Jan Eliasson took a narrow interpretation of his mandate and – in typical pursuit of immediate fixes – did not pursue the issue of human rights at all. One of the earliest meetings he attended was a 'humanitarian summit' in Addis Ababa. Dealing with the Sudan Government, Ambassador Eliasson found himself in the familiar position of a UN negotiator, of trading increased access to landing sites in SPLA-controlled territory in return for UN acquiescence in the government's programme of relocation of the displaced around Khartoum. Thereafter the DHA fell victim to bureaucratic mandate wars within the UN system and the determination of the Secretary General, Boutros Boutros Ghali, not to delegate any powers to it.

Meeting with the present author in February 1992, just three days before taking up his post at the DHA, Jan Eliasson promised immediate action on Somalia. 'I think we will jump the gun on this one', he said. Somalia was to prove the stillbirth of the DHA and the new humanitarian order that it promised. It is the concern of the following chapter.

Implications

The humanitarian debates of the late 1980s and early 1990s are a striking case of a discourse that legitimated the extension of a particular form of political action to areas formerly out of bounds. The results were dramatically successful: an enlarged humanitarian arsenal, and the

---

[8]UN General Assembly, 46th Session, Agenda item 143, A/46/182, 'Strengthening of the Co-ordination of Humanitarian Assistance of the United Nations,' 19 December 1991.

assertion of new legal and ethical principles that justified unprecedented actions by international institutions. The new humanitarian
discourse was hugely persuasive in Europe and North America; it also
persuaded many Africans. Its language of basic rights and humanitarian
principles obscured the total lack of any engagement with the local
political processes that can actually resolve the problems of famine. It
was becoming harder, not easier, for the humanitarian international to
recognize and support anti-famine political contracts.

8

Somalia
1991–92

Famine & Relief
after the Demise
of the State

International humanitarian operations in Somalia have been intensively analysed. A recent (and incomplete) bibliography of humanitarian action in Somalia runs to 155 pages (Clarke, 1995). There are dozens of articles and a growing array of books dealing with the US-led intervention of 1992–4. Some are passably good (Refugee Policy Group, 1994), others are better passed over. All are largely devoted to the aid operation or to military, political or diplomatic aspects of the intervention, and draw upon the views and experience of expatriate aid workers.

Far less has been written about the famine itself: what were its causes and its dynamics, and what indeed were its basic outlines? Some accounts of the famine are written almost as though it emerged out of a dark age in mid-1992. One of the better-informed accounts includes the statement that the 'famine had its origins in the collapse of the state and the general disintegration of law and order that contributed to an economy of sustained plunder' (Menkhaus, 1994: 148). In one form or another, attribution of the famine to 'anarchy' is almost ubiquitous in journalistic, policy-related and academic writing. This chapter will present an outline response to the challenge of charting the famine with more subtlety. Still less has been written about the political processes in Somalia in 1991–2 (as opposed to chronicling major military and political events). This chapter will show why, even after the demise of the state, famine reflects the nature of political accountability.

Like all famines, the Somali famine of 1991–2 was highly selective. It primarily struck two groups: the inhabitants of the riverine areas and displaced people. This pattern was evident as early as July 1991, when nutritional surveys by the ICRC found near-normal levels of nutrition among pastoralists and most townspeople, but alarmingly high rates of undernutrition among farmers along the Jubba and Shebelle river valleys. Worst hit of all were those displaced by the fighting and living in encampments in and around towns and villages. But some pockets

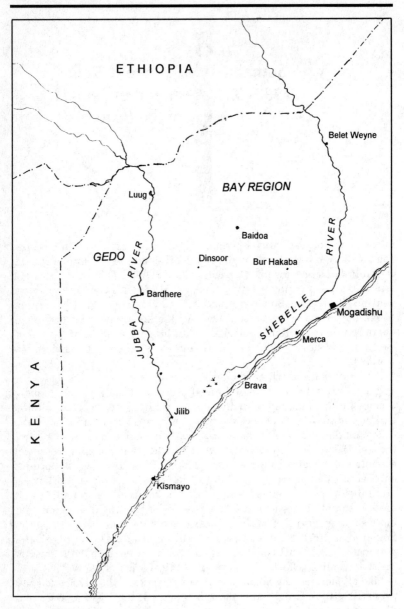

Southern Somalia

appeared to be escaping hunger altogether. In 1992 the main difference was that the inter-riverine Bay region became the worst hit. The first part of the chapter shows how this reflected power relations before and during the civil war.

Relief operations in Somalia manifested the best and the worst of the humanitarian international. Complete collapse of civil authority poses a challenge to the basic thesis of this book: how can humanitarian efforts support an anti-famine political contract if there is no civil politics at all? Surely, such a situation cries out for an emergency response, with the technical, organizational and if necessary military resources of the humanitarian international brought to bear on saving lives. The second part of the chapter explodes this claim: there were opportunities to build on nascent political contracts, which would have been both politically progressive and more technically effective.

Roots of the famine

One of the many ironies of Somalia is that in 1974–5 the government harnessed popular energies in an anti-famine campaign. Teams from the recently completed literacy programme were remobilized, and tens of thousands of drought-stricken pastoralists were airlifted to new settlement schemes. These projects were quick to suffer all the ills of Soviet-style central planning as well as political manipulation, but at the outset the general enthusiasm for participating in a struggle against poverty and backwardness was undeniable. Somalia also developed a cadre of relief professionals, who a few years later were to put their skills to work in refugee programmes. The Refugee Health Unit, for example, provided a much-admired quality of primary health care (Godfrey and Mursal, 1990).

Government commitment to inclusive social development evaporated after the Somali army was defeated in its war against Ethiopia in 1978. Promises of national unity, development and socialism were betrayed. The government of Siad Barre became grotesquely corrupt and utterly ruthless in its suppression of opposition, culminating in the near-genocidal destruction of the northern capital Hargeisa in 1988. All domestic structures that could have provided some pressure for accountability were crushed, so that for those who were excluded from power the only option was armed rebellion. Increasingly, the insurrections were mobilized along clan lines. This was not because of primordial identifications, but because Siad Barre deliberately and deftly used clan affiliation as the main instrument for his divide-and-rule tactics. After the destruction of Hargeisa, the flight of most of the northern population and the battlefield losses of half its fighting force in 1988, the rebel Somali National Movement (SNM) also fell back upon clan-based mobilization among its Isaaq supporters. The subsequent resistance fronts, the Hawiye-based United Somali Congress (USC) and the Ogaden-based Somali Patriotic Movement (SPM), followed suit in 1989.

International aid was complicit in Siad Barre's dismantling of Somali political society. In 1978 he decamped from the Soviet to the US side in the Cold War, and thereafter Somalia became the largest per head recipient of aid in Africa.[1] Little of this aid was used for its ostensible purposes of feeding refugees or developing industry and agriculture; rather, it sustained Siad Barre long after he would otherwise have fallen. The aid also sharpened conflict, as the government used it to selectively reward its followers and facilitate land-grabbing. By the time of Siad Barre's (overdue) overthrow in January 1991, Somalis were deeply cynical about the motives of any humanitarian or development assistance. The nature of aid as an incalculable resource continued to fuel war after Siad's fall. Official aid has the dual characteristics of being indeterminate in quantity and being awarded to sovereign governments. It is therefore something that admits little compromise: only the possessor of the symbols of sovereignty can control it. The struggle to control Mogadishu in 1991–2 can be seen in part as a struggle to control the keys to foreign aid. Factional leaders mobilized their troops by promising future reward (through looting and aid), not by tangible political reform or economic welfare. Even when there was virtually no aid in Somalia (1991 and much of 1992) it continued to exercise its influence by promoting external orientation and undermining domestic accountability.

The specific victimology of the famine can be seen in the history of political marginalization of the inter-riverine area of southern Somalia (principally the Jubba and Shebelle river valleys and Bay region). The famine was the legacy of long-standing power relations, not poverty as such. These regions are the most fertile part of the country, where almost all of Somalia's agriculture is concentrated. The peoples of the inter-riverine region are not accustomed to famine. One of their proverbs translates as: 'The drought that hits the south is not serious, but that of the north is terrible'. Agriculture boomed in the 1980s. But this natural wealth did not ensure the prosperity of the farmers. The inter-riverine people belong to several minority groups, with lower social and political status than the principal pastoralist Somali clans that have dominated the state since independence. The minorities include the Sab Somali (Digil and Rahanweyn clan families), enclaves of indigenous Cushitic peoples such as the Shebelle and Gabwing, and the Bantu. The latter consist of a number of groups, some of whom are descendants of the indigenous inhabitants of the area, and others who are descendants of slaves brought into the region in the nineteenth century. The Bantu are not part of the clan system at all: if the Sab clans are considered second-class citizens, the Bantu are third-class.

[1]Exempting small enclave countries such as The Gambia and Djibouti.

The history of these minorities has been one of marginalization and dispossession, dating back to pre-colonial times. None of these groups has been well represented politically. The Sab-dominated political party, Hizbia Digile Mirifle, was harassed and excluded from government in the 1960s. Few minority politicians ever held office, and very few Bantu even received an education.

Land is at the centre of the minorities' problems. The Italians confiscated large tracts of riverine farmland for foreign-owned banana plantations. After independence, a new class of Somali entrepreneurs also began acquiring irrigable land, using their government connections and, if necessary force. The largest and most systematic dispossession occurred in the 1980s, when thousands of civil servants, politicians, merchants and army officers seized huge tracts of riverine land, using provisions in the ostensibly progressive 1975 Land Reform Act to register land leases in their own names, while local smallholders were unable to navigate the bureaucracy or pay the bribes necessary to protect the land they and their parents had farmed. Some land was taken at gunpoint, other land was acquired by a mixture of coercion and trickery. Legal ceilings on landholdings could be circumvented by forming fictitious 'co-operatives', and much land was also taken directly by the government for large-scale irrigation schemes. A group of capitalist landowners established itself, creating in the process a class of indigenous smallholders and day labourers (African Rights, 1993c; Besteman and Cassanelli, 1996).

War and depredation 1991–92

The power relations of the 1960–90 period became starkly manifest after the fall of Siad Barre in January 1991. The inter-riverine farming minorities suffered from a combination of elements. One was that the Middle/Lower Shebelle, Lower Jubba and Bay region were each battlefields on one or more occasions during 1991–2. The second was that the local people were not well armed. The third was that armies and bandits were drawn to these fertile, sedentary and ill-defended areas because they could easily sustain themselves there by looting: a war economy developed. Fourthly, the forces that overthrew Siad Barre, styling themselves 'liberators', replicated the same power relations as their predecessors. Finally, the minority clans were last in line to receive local and international relief.

After Siad Barre fled from Mogadishu in January 1991, there was a mass exodus of residents, fearing the fighting and USC-led pogroms against the Darod clan, from whom Siad Barre and his lieutenants were drawn. Many people fled to the Shebelle valley, either to join their families or just because it was nearby. The population of some villages doubled, and food supplies rapidly ran short. The uprising also saw the beginnings of the banditry that was to become a feature of rural Somalia.

Retreating government soldiers and some local pastoral clans preyed on the villages. Some villagers bought weapons and organized patrols, others were unable to defend themselves and abandoned their villages. Then came the 'liberators' – members of the triumphant USC seeking to purge the Shebelle valley of former government supporters and in search of loot.

The Shebelle and Jubba valleys
The disarray among the USC, notably the failure of General Aidid and self-proclaimed Interim President Ali Mahdi Mohamed to agree upon a government, created a power vacuum in Mogadishu. In March, some of Siad Barre's lieutenants, together with SPM members who had fallen out with the USC in the inter-clan pogroms, mounted an offensive on the city. They marched up the Lower Shebelle and wreaked havoc. Unlike the bandits, these forces were well organized and quickly overran local resistance; many villages were looted of all their food and other possessions. They also took their revenge for the locals' 'disloyalty' and gratuitously burned, raped and killed. General Aidid then regrouped the USC forces, counter-attacked and drove the Darod forces back almost to the Kenyan border.

Aidid captured the town of Kismayo and overran the lower Jubba valley. This area suffered virtually continuous fighting and famine for the following eighteen months. When the USC first arrived, many Bantu leaders saw them as liberators, and provided them with recruits and intelligence. In fact, the USC were merely exploiting the gullibility of the Bantu, and when they withdrew in June, the Bantu were left to the mercies of the reoccupying Darod forces. The reprisals were brutal. Six months later the Darod forces themselves split and again turned the valley into a battleground. The militias looted to sustain themselves, storming villages at night and carrying away what they could, and exacting taxes at checkpoints on roads and villages.

The halt to production in the two river valleys in 1991 had ramifications throughout southern Somalia. Formerly, the valleys had provided seasonal work for tens of thousands of migrant workers from Bay region. With the collapse of employment, many poor would-be labourers found themselves without an income and reliant on the scant resources of the Bay itself. The granaries of Somalia were not producing, while commercial imports to the coastal towns and overland from Kenya and Ethiopia were inadequate. In mid-1991, the price of food shot up. It rose further when the November fighting in Mogadishu and the December battle in Kismayo closed the two main ports. Food disappeared altogether from many markets.

Bay region
The famine was slower to develop in Bay region. In February 1991, there were several fierce battles between the USC and SPM in which

Baidoa itself was partly destroyed. Most of the shops in the town were closed after being looted or burned (Asante *et al.*, 1991: 109). But then relative calm returned, until October, when Bay region's nightmare began. Siad Barre had set up his headquarters at Burdhubu on the Upper Jubba, from where he despatched a force of 3,000 militiamen, most of them from his own Marehan clan, towards Mogadishu. Baidoa was occupied. Bur Hakaba, between Baidoa and the Shebelle river, was ravaged. It was the front line, and Siad's troops fed themselves by looting, which was systematically organized. 'They would see the smoke from cooking, and come to that place and loot the food for themselves', said one inhabitant who had witnessed their actions. 'During Ramadhan, they would arrive at breakfast time and take the breakfast that had been prepared.' The looting was also commercial, particularly in the case of the large-scale theft of livestock, especially cattle, which were then exported to Kenya.

There was also an element of vindictive retribution in the behaviour of Siad's army. Many of the Rahanweyn were seen as allies of the USC, and their villages were singled out for destruction. In Baidoa itself, the militia hunted down people suspected of having collaborated with the USC during its administration of the town; they were killed and often the mutilated bodies were displayed in public. The Marehan followed an invidious strategy of 'divide and rule': they spared some villages, but these were later subject to reprisals from the Rahanweyn militia. Most of the population of Baidoa fled; no more than a sixth of the town's pre-war population of 60,000 remained (while other displaced people began to congregate there). To the west, in Bardhere, two-thirds of the pre-war population of 30,000 fled. A witness described how fear, not hunger, drove the people away: 'There were villages completely deserted. The people just ran away. They left their food, everything.' In this area, the people had long lived with the Marehan as neighbours; but the *modus vivendi* broke down, as many Rahanweyn saw the USC as a chance to liberate themselves from Darod supremacy. This led to five months of war between Marehan and Rahanweyn militiamen, in which many villages were destroyed and their people driven out.

It is difficult to exaggerate the suffering of Bay region. The famine that ensued was one of the most devastating on record. However, the destruction was localized. One Somali doctor commented, 'Even during the summer [of 1992] you could go a few kilometres outside Baidoa and find villages that were [full of] normal people.' Some villages came to agreements with the Marehan forces; they would pay a certain amount of animals or grain as tribute, or collect tribute from other villages, in return for being left in peace. One area that escaped relatively lightly was Dinsoor. The community leaders succeeded in persuading the Marehan forces that they were entirely neutral and had no wish to be involved in the conflict. They provided food to any forces that passed through, but escaped looting. As a result, according to a Somali aid worker in the area, Dinsoor and the twelve surrounding villages 'look like Somalia in 1988, in 1989 . . . there was no war at all'. One Somali aid worker estimated that about 40 per cent of the villages in Bay region were hit by the famine. 'It was a disaster, but it was not on everybody, everywhere; it was selective.'

The Bay region famine struck just as the Shebelle valley was beginning to recover. This meant that at least some succour was available for the famine migrants who made it as far as the river valley. In the middle of 1992 there were at least half a million displaced people in southern Somalia, excluding refugees in Kenya and Ethiopia and the 'invisible' displaced living with relatives. One survey in August 1992 estimated that Mogadishu alone hosted more than 300,000 people; Baidoa had over 45,000, Lower Shebelle 60,000, Kismayo 50,000 (Rogge, 1992). These refugees died in uncounted numbers. They suffered more than the host populations, but they also overwhelmed their hosts, bringing disruption, hunger and epidemic disease. In the first six months of 1992, malnutrition rates shot up again in the Lower Shebelle. The burden of the refugees deepened and prolonged the crisis in the Shebelle valley.

The 'liberators'

The famine was most directly caused by the devastation inflicted by the militias, chiefly the Darod. The Hawiye 'liberators' also played a role; their depredations were scarcely less violent. In the riverine areas, little of the land that had been confiscated in the previous decades was returned. Some intrepid farmers immediately reoccupied their land when the people who had seized it were driven out. More commonly, a new set of landlords, mostly Hawiye, claimed the spoils. One village elder in the Lower Shebelle summed up what had happened: 'The USC, the Habr Gidir, came to occupy the land. They said, "We have liberated this house, this land, this farm." And they even took more.'

Production began to restart in the Lower Shebelle in the rainy season following the April 1991 battles, but the farmers were not able to make full use of their time or their assets. The need for defence against potential looters meant that many young men were forced to spend their time guarding the entrances to villages, or watching over pumps and tractors whenever they were brought out for use. The villagers were unable to market most of their produce; one group described themselves as being 'locked up' by the impossibility of taking goods to market. Irrigation pumps that had not been looted had to be guarded at all times, or remain buried in secret locations.

In the Lower Jubba, there was virtually no production by the local people. Those who did cultivate had a minimal harvest. Most villagers ate wild foods only. The confiscated farms were able to produce throughout the famine. But a former employee at the Ministry of

Agriculture described how the new landowners in his village ran their 'liberated' farms.

> They never had sympathy with the old villagers. Never any co-operation. They punished people, even the hungry people. If the poor, the displaced people went inside the plantation that they took from the Italians or the well-to-do Somalis, the Darod and other clans, they killed them. They killed the displaced people who went inside the farm, for a single banana. And worse than that, they were displaying the corpses for others to see. Even if they are dying from hunger, they had to be made to fear more from the guns than from starvation. This is a well-known fact. If you went through the plantation area, you would see corpses. They didn't say 'Get out of the plantation!' They shot them just like wild pigs or monkeys.

Experiences were similar in the Lower Jubba and elsewhere. Not all rich farmers were so cruel. Some – especially those who had some connection with the communities dating from before the war – made genuine efforts to help the hungry. But all were mainly concerned with their own status, and protecting their property.

Another burden imposed on some villages was the payment of protection money. In one Shebelle village the farmers made a deal with the local militia whereby they paid 3 million shillings a day and were not raided. But this payment rapidly impoverished them.

The numbers who died from this famine are even more difficult to estimate than usual, because of the massive displacements of people and the extremely uneven impact of the disaster. Frank starvation was common in one or two places, especially Bay region in mid-1992, but as is normal, the principal killers were epidemic diseases, particularly measles, dysentery and latterly malaria. A cautious estimate would be 200,000 excess deaths.

In the second half of 1992, the famine began to wane. Maize prices began to drop from their peak of 4,000 shillings per kg in July, to 2,700 in August, 1,700 in September and 1,300 in October. Levels equivalent to production costs were reached in November. The main reason for the fall was undoubtedly that the Lower Shebelle was gathering good harvests: the first crops were harvested in September and good production was expected for January 1993. A second reason was the relief programme, which began to gear up for large-scale food deliveries from May-June. In the event, the deliveries were slower and smaller than hoped for, but confidence in the market was boosted by the start of the US Air Force airlift at the end of August. By early 1993, prices were well below production costs in the Shebelle valley, and farmers had large stores of grain unsold from the previous two harvests. Death rates also fell markedly in late 1992, though they remained above normal in the early months of 1993. In the Lower Shebelle and Mogadishu, a degree of normalcy had returned earlier in 1992; Baidoa remained the main famine-stricken region. Weekly death rates in Baidoa fell from a peak of 1,700 in early September to about 300 in mid-November, where they stayed on a plateau (Centers for Disease Control, 1992). In the Jubba Valley, conditions remained more precarious. Another Darod assault captured Bardhere in October, creating another round of looting and disrupting relief efforts. Most of the farmland in the Lower Jubba stayed uncultivated into mid-1993.

Protection and relief

Somalis waited many years for the fall of Siad Barre, hoping for a new era of peace and democracy. In the early months of 1991, there was optimism that the political struggles would be resolved and that these hopes would be fulfilled.

Siad's regime had destroyed any emergent political contracts that had existed in Somalia. The citizens had to start from scratch. But it does not follow that there was a complete vacuum which had to be filled by foreign aid agencies. The very absence of the state created opportunities for citizens' action and local political process, and for creative engagement by humanitarian organizations. Many Somalis took the first opportunity for sixteen years to set up independent organizations and begin to rebuild their country with a spirit of civic responsibility. Relief to displaced people and famine victims was one of the main channels for this renewed enthusiasm.

In the first year of the famine, the great majority of the relief distributed to the poor came from within the local community. There were many village committees, often organized around mosques, or generous individuals who set up feeding centres. Several relief associations were established, most of them built around energetic and charismatic individuals. One was the Karaan hospital, created within 24 hours in north Mogadishu on the day full-scale war broke out in the city in November 1991. A group of doctors, calling themselves the Health Emergency Committee, requisitioned a seafront villa as an operating theatre, made a collection of drugs and surgical equipment from private pharmacies and their own stores, joined a crowd that was looting a UNICEF warehouse containing infusions, and set to work on a voluntary basis without any external support. The challenges of hardship and isolation often brought out the best qualities in individuals.

The SRCS–ICRC operation

The most important Somali relief organization was the Somalia Red Crescent Society (SRCS), which was to become the partner of the ICRC in the latter's largest-ever relief operation, surpassing its previous record in Biafra. The SRCS was the only countrywide institution functioning during 1991 and 1992. In the ICRC it had a patron that was prepared to be extremely flexible and persistent in providing resources: between them the ICRC and SRCS handled more food relief in 1991–2 than all other relief agencies combined (a total of nearly 200,000 tonnes). The SRCS attracted a cadre of professionals and businessmen who were prepared to run exceptional risks and work extremely hard on behalf of the relief programme. Thirteen SRCS staff were killed during 1991–2 carrying out relief activities.

The ICRC mounted an extraordinary operation. In January 1992 it came to the conclusion that all Somalis in the centre and south of the country would be in need of food aid, and used all available means to supply relief. When the major ports were closed, it offloaded on to small boats that came ashore on the beaches of fishing villages. Seventeen landing points on the coast were used. When the monsoon changed, helicopters were used to offload the freighters. Cross-border relief was brought in from Kenya; negotiations were undertaken with every lineage and every faction. At its peak, the ICRC was providing food to 900 kitchens, and over 2 million people were believed to be receiving relief. The kitchen programme was based on the earlier initiative of a Somali woman, Dhahabo Isse, who began providing cooked food to destitute people in April 1991: its rationale was that cooked food was less attractive to looters than dry rations. The chief ICRC delegate, Peter Stocker, made an unequalled personal commitment which was reciprocated by his staff, Somali and expatriate alike. Two expatriates were killed during the programme. While food relief was the main component of the programme, the ICRC also undertook medical programmes, water and sanitation, agricultural and veterinary programmes, family tracing and visits to prisoners of war.

The SRCS–ICRC programme was exceptionally responsive to local demands. It reflected the strengths and weaknesses of Somali society in crisis. There were no formal mechanisms for holding the operation accountable to the people; instead there was energy, creativity and commitment. This worked for a while, and then began to face insurmountable problems.

The ICRC made some major compromises. Shortly after its return to the country in February 1991, it began hiring armed guards. This was a major break with a 130-year old ICRC tradition; it came about because it was simply not possible to rent a house or a vehicle without an accompanying guard. Another compromise was to tolerate high levels of looting and diversion. The monitoring of relief was so poor that it is impossible to ascertain exactly how much was diverted. The ICRC itself has spoken of 'unaccounted losses' of 10–15 per cent (Netherlands Development Cooperation, 1994: 166). This is optimistic. Preliminary field investigations indicate 50 per cent as a rough estimate (African Rights, 1993a: 2). 'Looting' covers many different activities. Some food was taken by guards, some by drivers, some by elders and kitchen supervisors. Much of this was by agreement: the ICRC paid most of its

24,000 employees and subcontractors in food. Some vehicles were held up at gunpoint. More often, contractors and elders used non-violent methods such as registering 'ghost' kitchens and 'ghost' villages; one list of 126 villages contained 10 invented names, one list of 65 kitchens included 15 'ghosts'. Alternatively, a group of people could pose as the representatives of a genuine village and take that village's consignment, which would then be sold. In one village investigated by the present author, the ICRC records indicated that regular deliveries of 24 tonnes were received every four days, but the villagers themselves estimated they received only 900 kg each time. In another village, 15 deliveries were made by the ICRC, and in each case about 75 per cent of the quota arrived. This compares with diversion rates of about 85 per cent of food destined for refugees in northern Somalia in the 1980s, as estimated by the US General Accounting Office (Askin, 1987).

Losses were high and many gunmen were fed. However, on the argument that 'flooding the country with food' would bring down the price and thus reduce the famine, all food that actually arrived in Somalia and reached the market could be considered as doing some good. Certainly, in January 1992, when 8,000 tonnes of wheatflour was looted from a CARE warehouse in Mogadishu port, the price of food dropped sharply and tension in the city was appreciably if briefly eased. While the food–violence relationship held for freelance gunmen, it is unclear whether it was the same for the factions themselves, which gained enormous financial benefits from the relief operations.

Another set of practices focused on financial extortion. Haulage and security contractors enforced high rates of pay, and could not be laid off without incurring severe risks. Throughout 1991 and into the early months of 1992, the relatively small number of aid agencies managed to maintain a cartel that fixed rates of pay. But with the arrival of many more relief agencies after May 1992, and also journalists, this system rapidly broke down.

These problems mounted as the relief programme continued, and the ICRC began to lose the initiative. The programme developed its own dynamic: the diversion and extortion became more systematic and the relief programme became drawn into a symbiotic relationship with the militias. The growth in other NGO operations accelerated this: all agencies suffered from the mistakes of each one. By the time of the military intervention, the ICRC was stretched to its limits as an institution; it had become enmeshed in a number of protection rackets that were placing staff in serious danger and threatening the basic principles of its mandate. It was becoming entangled in the war economy.

Nonetheless, the SRCS–ICRC operation was remarkable and unique. It has received some recognition. Senior officials of USAID nominated the ICRC for the Nobel Peace Prize and others have spoken of it in the highest terms. The Netherlands government review praised the ICRC but then questioned whether it would be advisable to mount such an operation again (Netherlands Development Co-operation, 1994). However, compared to the voluminous literature on the US–UN intervention, there is virtually nothing published on the ICRC programme as such. Clarke's bibliography does not contain a single item specifically concerned with the ICRC. As in the case of the cross-border operations to Eritrea and Tigray, there is need for a good theory to legitimate successful practice – not least so that the programme does not become mythologized, and its shortcomings overlooked. This problem is not helped by the secretiveness of the ICRC itself. Its head office in Geneva did not even supply documents to the Netherlands' official investigation, despite the Netherlands being one of the ICRC's major donors.

Some of the capabilities that made the SRCS–ICRC operation possible can be outlined. One was the close partnership between the two organizations, with each working to its strengths. ICRC delegates followed an open-door policy, encouraging Somalis to come to them with requests, complaints and suggestions. Meanwhile, the SRCS was the closest there came to a functioning civil organization in Somalia. Its representatives were responsive to the demands of local communities, and they were the leading players in the dynamics of the programme – in particular, its flexibility and relentless expansion. For the same reasons, SRCS involvement was also why the programme became so deeply enmeshed in local politics and resource flows, and provided an opportunity for some individuals to make themselves small fortunes.

Secondly, there was the decision-making structure of the ICRC itself, with the major decisions entrusted to the Somalia delegation (based first in Mogadishu and later in Nairobi), which in turn entrusted many decisions to offices in the regions. Linked to this was flexibility: the readiness to address each problem with a creative solution. The nature of the Somali crisis made this a uniquely appropriate management structure, and in its chief delegate, Peter Stocker, there was an individual with prior experience of Somalia who was able and willing to take the necessary decisions.

Finally, the operation was made possible by a regular but low level of coverage in the media. All the journalists who visited Somalia applauded the ICRC programme. But when news coverage became intense in mid-1992, the principal beneficiaries were the more conventional NGOs which had expatriate staff running feeding centres and clinics. The ICRC always assisted journalists in Somalia, but its operations were far more discreet and far less publicity-driven than those of most operational NGOs. A high level of media interest earlier in the famine might have led to a much larger international response and many more NGOs starting programmes, but almost certainly the ICRC would have been unable to compete for the spotlight and would not have run the operation that it did.

Could the SRCS–ICRC operation have been sustained? Could an aid-based political contract have become established? In the absence of a positive political process, it is improbable: the obstacles were simply too huge. But this shortcoming does not provide the argument for a conventional relief operation, such as the UN tried to mount. Rather, it is an argument for adopting a similar kind of flexible, responsive model, while recognizing its limitations.

International neglect 1991–2

The UN specialized agencies failed in Somalia throughout. Sensitivity to the realities on the ground is the essential prerequisite for any form of accountability, and the UN showed none in 1991–2. There was no political commitment by the UN, no sense of obligation on the part of its bureaucrats, and no possibility of Somalis enforcing its mandates. Only shame, mobilized by some journalists, the ICRC, USAID and some NGOs, finally moved the UN system to act. Then, some Somalis began to wonder if the inaction had not been preferable to the incompetence and bureaucratic infighting that paralysed the operation. The official relief programme cannot be said to have destroyed any national political contract – there was none – but it certainly did nothing to promote the sorts of political processes that might have brought such a contract into existence.

In December 1990, as security worsened in the final days of the Siad Barre government, the UN withdrew all its staff. In early 1991, UNICEF received a grant of over $3m. from USAID to begin rehabilitation work, but virtually none of this money was spent for twelve months. The UNDP employed a consultant to investigate whether the UN should return in mid-1991: he recommended that it should, but after an incident in September in which the expatriate staff were held at gunpoint and robbed, and three guards were killed, the decision was taken to withdraw again. There was simply no pressure for the UN agencies to be present. On the contrary, staff insurance rules and the comforts of living in Nairobi (and thereby also earning a daily $100 allowance for being away from post) ensured that most UN staff had little interest in returning.

At all levels, the UN looked the other way. The Secretariat refused to support the Djibouti Government's efforts to convene a reconciliation conference in July 1991. The UN's Special Emergency Appeal for the Horn of Africa requested $64m for Somalia, but there was no indication of how the funds might actually be spent. UNICEF refused to despatch staff members, and SCF (UK) produced an elaborate plan whereby it would fund, recruit and support a consultant to do UNICEF's work, hopefully as a prelude to a UNICEF presence. In June, the consultant arrived and UNICEF contributed a meagre $54,000 to SCF's budget. But the UN evacuation in September – ironically organized by the NGOs, as the UN had no workable evacuation plans – meant that this consultant

Camp for displaced people, Mogadishu (Panos: J. C. Tordai)

also had to leave. Asked whether UNICEF might pay local staff, the reply was, 'It's not our policy to pay incentives'.[2]

Such inaction outraged other aid institutions as well as journalists. In December, Pierre Gasman, ICRC Delegate-General for Africa, broke with that organization's customary discretion: 'How come UNICEF-Somalia has 13 people in Nairobi and no-one inside Somalia?' The deputy director of UNDP Somalia, Marco Barsotti, replied: 'In a situation of war, we don't operate'.[3] A few days later, Andrew Natsios of USAID was also unusually outspoken in his criticism. Referring to Barsotti's remark, he said, 'The United Nations is involved in six other civil wars in Africa. Are they going to pull out of those too?'[4] It was these public criticisms combined with press coverage of the Mogadishu war that finally sparked action from the UN Secretariat in January 1992.

In Somalia, the UN's operations were run on principles radically different from those of the ICRC. The clearest example of this is the attempt by WFP and CARE to deliver wheatflour to Mogadishu. USAID allocated the money for 12,000 tonnes in May 1991, the first shipment of a promised 40,000 tonnes. The ship docked in September. Some of the food was allocated to the ICRC, which distributed it immediately in rural areas close to the city. CARE made plans to begin systematic distributions in Mogadishu itself. It was a tense time in the city. CARE's plans consisted of 25-truck convoys distributing to neighbourhoods on a rotational basis – the antithesis of the small, rapid and flexible system already developed by the ICRC. The convoys incurred so much insecurity that the plan had to be changed, but it was still cumbersome, and 8,000 tonnes remained in the port when fighting broke out in the city on 17 November. These 8,000 tonnes stayed in the warehouse for two months while food prices rocketed and CARE tried to think of a way of distributing the food in relative safety. Its attempts to obtain agreement from a committee composed of members of all factions came to nothing. On 20 January 1992, the problem was solved when Hashamud militia opened the warehouse doors to all comers, and the city's markets were briefly full of wheatflour.

The ICRC and some other NGOs recognized lessons to be learned from this debacle: move food from the port as soon as it is offloaded, do not rely on negotiating with a single multi-faction committee, distribute rapidly and flexibly, and keep other options in reserve such as offloading in small ports. But when, on 20 April 1992, a 'Ninety-day consolidated inter-agency plan of action' was formally launched, CARE and WFP repeated the same procedure. By setting up a single nine-man port committee including representatives of all factions and refusing to

---

[2]Dr Hussein Mursal, former health co-ordinator, SCF, interviewed in February 1992.

[3]Jane Perlez, 'Somali fighting keeps aid from a suffering city', *The New York Times*, 11 December 1991.

[4]Jane Perlez, 'U.S. increases aid to Somalia after U.N. balks', *The New York Times*, 15 December 1991.

contemplate any alternative to using the deep-water port, the agencies made themselves hostages to the factions. This system never worked properly and finally broke down completely in November.

The UN agencies adhered to procedures established by central diktat, and CARE also tried to run a conventional expatriate-led operation. The attitude to Somali staff was in complete contrast to that of the SRCS-ICRC operation. A senior Somali employee of CARE, speaking anonymously, said (in the context of CARE's support for Operation Restore Hope):

> There were no consultations with Somali staff about the operation. We were not asked then, or since, what we think. They [the expatriates] believe that every Somali is just a part of these factions, whether they work for CARE or any of the other agencies . . . There were no meetings with Somalis working at CARE, not even the most senior staff. Nor are we ever consulted about political issues (Interviewed by Rakiya Omaar, January 1993).

The bitterness felt by the senior Somali staff of almost all agencies was never appreciated by the expatriate staff of NGOs, the UN, or the US military forces. When presented with evidence of how Somalis felt – including the most senior Somalis working for foreign organizations, speaking anonymously – the response by senior expatriates was to dismiss these reports out of hand, for instance as 'a shotgun, anecdotal approach to gathering evidence, based upon street interviews in Mogadishu and a few local towns' (Clarke, 1995: 120). The breadth of popular support for General Aidid's resistance to the US and the UN in mid-1993 caught the international organizations almost completely by surprise.

There was also extraordinary organizational infighting and straight-forward incompetence. UNDP refused to co-operate with either UNICEF or the 'co-ordination office' in Mogadishu set up by the DHA. At one point it even took away the office's fax machine. A 31-strong 'team of experts' made a tour in August 1992, after which it announced that most of the UN programmes were to be implemented by NGOs – without having consulted them. Only at the end of that month was the first UN co-ordination meeting held – and then it was chaired by UNICEF. The spark for the meeting was the US announcement of an imminent relief airlift, indicating, for the first time, major Western interest. Those present report a remark by the UNICEF head of mission, David Bassiouni, that became emblematic of the UN's response: 'We need to do something urgently; my career is at stake.' By the end of June, the entire UN system had delivered only about 12,000 tonnes of food. This was at the peak of the ICRC operation, which alone was delivering almost 20,000 tonnes per month. Mohamed Sahnoun, UN Special Envoy at the time, wrote later: 'Not only was the UN assistance program very limited, it was so slowly and inadequately delivered that it became counter-productive' (Sahnoun, 1994: 17).

A comparable accountability to remote patrons with obscure imperatives was also manifest in the failure to despatch UN troops to Mogadishu in April 1992. In early March, a ceasefire was achieved in the four-month-old fighting in Mogadishu between General Aidid and Ali Mahdi. The UN despatched a technical mission to Mogadishu to develop proposals for monitoring the ceasefire, and the US Administration rashly committed itself to abide by its recommendations. The mission proposed sending 500 UN troops to Mogadishu to protect humanitarian relief supplies, to be called the UN Operation in Somalia (UNOSOM), and to accompany 50 unarmed ceasefire monitors. Immediate despatch of the force could have transformed the situation, but in the event the ceasefire monitors were deployed only in July (after four months in which the ceasefire had held without a break), and the 500 soldiers (from Pakistan) arrived only between 14 September and 8 October, by which time the situation had completely changed.

The initial, crucial delay was caused by the US Administration. It had already signalled its lack of interest when it weakened the wording of a UN Security Council resolution on 23 January, insisting on removing the words 'ensuring the political normalization' of Somalia. Now it was concerned with the precedent of how to finance UN forces mandated to protect relief. The US wanted UNOSOM to be funded as a humanitarian initiative (for which UN member states made voluntary contributions, with the US part set at about 25 per cent), and not as a normal peacekeeping force (financed by set-rate levies, under which the US paid 30 per cent). The difference amounted to about $500,000 for the first six months of UNOSOM. This was the new global *Realpolitik*: fiscal economy and control over multilateral institutions.

Ambassador Mohamed Sahnoun
In April 1992, the UN Secretary General appointed a veteran Algerian diplomat, Mohamed Sahnoun, as his special representative in Somalia. In his six months in the post, Sahnoun was to gain universal respect from Somalis and enormous stature internationally. In a manner comparable to the ICRC relief programme, Sahnoun and his 'strategy' have become mythologized.

It is not easy to detail Sahnoun's 'strategy', not least because he had to spend an inordinate amount of time dealing with his 'bitter experience' with the UN (quoted in *The* [London] *Independent*, 30 October 1992). In one among many examples, he was caught unprepared by the sudden announcement on 20 August of the expansion of UNOSOM to 3,500 men – a decision which caused serious problems with General Aidid, who was deeply distrustful of the UN agenda. On another occasion, an Ilyushin aircraft, still carrying UN insignia from its previous contract, flew military supplies and currency to Ali Mahdi. Sahnoun instructed the UN not to use Ilyushins until an investigation had been completed, but two months later senior UN officials chartered an Ilyushin to fly to meet Aidid. Other problems were with the specialized agencies. For example, Sahnoun had to renegotiate the demilitarization of the airport after UNICEF inadvertently violated the previous agreement made by the NGOs. On another occasion, he asked the relief agencies not to hire warehouses (which were prone to armed attack) near the residential quarters of the UN and NGO staff. Immediately afterwards, UNICEF rented a large warehouse barely fifty yards from the main UN residence. Despite this, UNICEF was the sole agency that Sahnoun exempted from his public critique. These criticisms drew the ire of the Secretary General, who forced Sahnoun to resign on 26 October.

Some elements in Sahnoun's approach to the Somali social and political crisis stand out. The first was its inclusiveness. Sahnoun's personal demeanour was humble and open, and his diplomatic style was informal. Like the ICRC, his office had an open door. This was appreciated by all Somalis.

> He would talk with any Somali who approached him. He was the first who came and saw there were alternatives. He was the first to meet the elders of the Hawiye clans, the neutral clans, who are not involved in the fighting. Also he was talking with women. He used to reason like Somalis.[5]

Sahnoun spoke often about 'civil society', and repeatedly stressed the need to support a wide range of non-factional initiatives. Speaking to the international donors, he stressed the need 'to move as fast as possible to create a responsible civil society.'[6] Between August and October 1992, there were a number of promising signs of new confidence among the Hawiye elders, who were meeting to prepare inter-clan reconciliation conferences, planning to involve the factional leaders only as they gathered momentum. Sahnoun later wrote of the support he received from such people:

> What sustained our hope was the encouragement we had received from the elders in all regions as well as some former social, political, and administrative officials, including former police officers, and women leaders at both the national and community level. These leaders approached us sometimes with tears in their eyes, offering to work closely with the UN to bring Somalia out of the mess it was in. . . . The UNOSOM team pursued a strategy of putting the clan system to work for Somalia. (Sahnoun, 1994: 25)

Sahnoun encouraged whatever initiatives he could. He convened a meeting in the Seychelles of Somali intellectuals from a range of clans, a modest but successful attempt to open a dialogue. He also spent much time with General Aidid, trying to win his confidence and ensure his co-operation with the deployment of troops. The main criticisms made of Sahnoun by the Mogadishu factions are that he failed to condemn the

---

[5]Dr Hussein Mursal, interviewed in Mogadishu, December 1992.
[6]Presentation to the Donors' Conference, Geneva, 12 October 1992, point 188.

crimes of the other side. His strategy was not so much one of marginalizing the warlords as of including the non-warlords as well in political discussions.

Most tributes to Mohamed Sahnoun, both from Somalis and from foreigners present in Somalia, are extraordinarily fulsome. This is partly a tribute to his personal and diplomatic qualities, but also to the way in which he came to embody a set of ideals that Somalis had almost given up believing in. Without appreciating the way in which so many hopes were vested in this one man, it is not possible to understand the extent of his influence during his brief tenure, the universal esteem in which he was held, and the dismay that followed his departure. Sahnoun set out to personify peacemaking and civil society. Hence it was essential for him to gain the personal trust of those with whom he was negotiating, and those whose hopes he represented. In many more ways than simply talking to elders, Sahnoun was 'making the clan system work for Somalia'. Though much maligned for creating social and political divisions, the clan system was also a powerful force for loyalty and cohesion; along with the commitment to basic human values symbolized by the SRCS and other voluntary groups, it was the only existing structure for providing security and a measure of social welfare. If a political contract were to have emerged, it would have done so through such a strategy.

Perhaps most fundamentally, Sahnoun allowed his agenda to be dictated by the needs of Somalis, and not by the demands of the UN system. In an informal but genuine way, Sahnoun was accountable to the Somalis. His readiness to criticize the UN was central to that shift in agenda, and it cost him his position. On 26 October, the interference and lack of support from the UN Secretariat at last became too much, and Sahnoun resigned.

Implications

As implied by the title of Mohamed Sahnoun's book, *Somalia: The Missed Opportunities*, the absence of a Somali state did not entail hopelessness. The myriad clan, civil, political, commercial and military structures that superseded the state created as many opportunities as problems for peacemaking, civil reconstruction and famine relief. Amid the war, plunder and extreme human suffering, there were signs of a political process that might have begun to resuscitate structures that were accountable to the people. In the self-declared Republic of Somaliland (formerly north-west Somalia) considerable success was achieved with minimal external assistance. In Somalia itself, no such opportunity was provided. Those institutions within the humanitarian international which were least accountable to the Somali people gained the ascendancy and instigated an extraordinary experiment in philanthropic imperialism: Operation Restore Hope.

9

**Humanitarian
Impunity**

Somalia 1993
& Rwanda 1994

An official of UNICEF described Somalia as 'the greatest failure of the UN in our lifetime.' That was in the middle of 1992, when the famine was at its nadir and the UN was simply not there. Its failure consisted largely of acts of omission. This absence reflected a deeper failing on the part of the UN and some major NGOs, namely immunity from account-ability to the ostensible subjects of their concern. They prospered institutionally, and their staff advanced their careers, despite a dismal performance in meeting real human needs. Meanwhile, international humanitarians wielded unprecedented power and were able to advocate what would have been unthinkable only a few years previously: the military occupation of an independent country on humanitarian grounds. Even more remarkably, they got what they asked for.

The hard interests of relief agencies coincided with emerging strategic US foreign policy concerns. The US military wanted to prove its role in 'Operations Other Than War'. The US State Department wanted to set a precedent for humanitarian intervention. Meanwhile, the UN Secretariat saw this as an opportunity for expansion in size and mandate. These hard interests could not be stated baldly in public. They needed justification. Bosnia promised to be too tough; Somalia was the candidate. Hence the same US concern with precedent that had slowed action earlier in the year now speeded it up. Starting in August 1992, there were serious discussions at the UN and in Washington about an international takeover of Somalia. It is possible that a high-level decision to make Somalia a test case was taken as early as September, although the actual shape of the operation was not determined until the last moment. Unfortunately for the proponents of intervention, their campaign coincided with signs of political optimism in Somalia and the waning of the famine. A series of distortions of the situation ensued, followed by lies and provocations, designed to justify the intervention – but which also ensured its failure.

Philanthropic imperialism, manifest in military intervention, is the

179

Dead refugee and survivors in Merca, Somalia; bodies collected once a day (Panos: J. C. Tordai)

starkest manifestation of the power of the humanitarian international. In the abstract, there is a strong *prima facie* case for external intervention in a country without any form of political contract, in order to provide basic protection and assistance. The realities are very different. As this chapter makes clear, intervention is the antithesis of politically progressive local accountability which is the essence of protection against famine.

The drumbeat for intervention in Somalia

The first casualty of the agenda for intervention was the UN Special Representative, Mohamed Sahnoun. Although the full reasons for his fall from favour with the UN Secretary General are not known, the circumstantial evidence is strong. Sahnoun's replacement was an Iraqi diplomat, Ismat Kittani, who immediately adopted a confrontational approach and ordered the deployment of the UNOSOM troops at the airport even before his own arrival. This duly sparked a political and security crisis, with threats against and attacks on expatriate aid workers, and an ultimatum from Aidid to UNOSOM to withdraw from the airport. Kittani did nothing to cool the tension; during his entire tenure he had only two meetings each with Ali Mahdi and General Aidid.

A more central player in the plan was Philip Johnston, President of CARE-US He made up his mind as early as September: 'the international community, backed by UN troops, should move in and run Somalia, because it has no government at all' (letter to *The Guardian* (London), 15 September 1992). Although Johnston was not always fully in accord with some of his senior staff, on this he reflected the considered policy of the organization; William Novelli, Vice-President of CARE-US, later spoke of 'the NGO drumbeat we built up [for intervention]' (quoted in Odling-Smee, 1993). Malcolm Fraser, President of CARE-International, repeated the call in October. His description of 'naked anarchy, wanton destruction and total collapse of social, economic and political structures' (letter to *The Guardian*, 31 October 1992) contradicted Sahnoun's picture and efforts. The CARE view was in the ascendant, however. That month, Johnston was seconded to the UN to head the new 'Hundred Day Action Programme for Accelerated Emergency Assistance'. (In the event, despite the launch of Operation Restore Hope on day 56, the programme took 140 days to reach its targets.) He arrived just as Sahnoun was removed and promptly instigated a new hard line in humanitarian politics:[1]

> We have to fight the Somalis themselves. There's plenty of food and the agencies are willing to deliver it. But we have to dodge firefights

[1]Quoted in: Jane Perlez, 'Food Piling up in Somali Port as Many Starve', *The New York Times*, 2 November 1992.

to do it, and deal with those Somalis who want to rip off the system and deprive these children.

A few days later, Johnston threw down the gauntlet to the militia roadblocks in Baidoa. CARE despatched a large convoy on the night of 11/12 November from Mogadishu, with instructions to cut out the USC governor entirely from any payment and deliver all the food to representatives of the different neighbourhoods of Baidoa. Anticipating a battle, the Somali employees were reluctant to go, and aid staff in Baidoa hunkered down behind their sandbags. The battle duly occurred. The Somali staff of CARE paid off the first checkpoint but were prevented from paying off the second by orders from above. The staff member responsible later commented, 'CARE was a bit strict, which may have cost the convoy'. In the shoot-out, five people were killed (three looters and two guards) and fourteen injured. Most of the trucks turned round and drove back to Mogadishu; one made it through to Baidoa. Was this a deliberate provocation of the militia? Was it a test of whether a 'normal' distribution was possible? Or was it simply an act of naiveté on the part of CARE and the UN? Whatever the motives, this convoy set international alarm bells ringing. Immediately, lurid reports of a huge battle were circulated to the international press, some of which reported that 40 people had been killed, including relief workers.[2] No-one would later admit to having been the source of the exaggeration.

By this point CARE's programme was becoming extremely expensive. For example, its expatriate staff commuted daily by aeroplane from Nairobi to Baidoa. As with other agencies at this time, most expatriate staff were new to Somalia. A bunker mentality developed, consultation with Somalis declined and expatriates were increasingly taking major decisions based on rumour and fear. This coincided with the first significant increase in daily shootings in Mogadishu since the March ceasefire. For different reasons, both factional leaders were trying to stir up trouble – Ali Mahdi to provoke an international intervention, Aidid to prevent one and also to quell internal dissent. The civil initiatives that had shown promise in October made no progress in November. More importantly for subsequent developments, the nine-man port committee set up by the UN to supervise WFP shipments finally became deadlocked. The agencies denied responsibility: 'The port was never shut by either CARE or WFP in November 92; delays were imposed on outloading only by Aidid and Ali Mahdi' (CARE, 1993), Somalis believed that a little more flexibility in negotiations could have kept the port open. One of the UN's senior Somali staff explained how and said: 'It was the UN that closed the port'. In fact, the ICRC continued to use the port, relying on its own system of bilateral negotiations with each faction. One ICRC shipment was unloaded on 10 November and another was due a month later, and the ICRC expected no problems.

[2] '40 die in Somalia aid convoy raid'. *The Independent*, 14 November 1992.

In mid-November, the first concrete plans for military intervention began to surface. Fred Cuny, an adviser to USAID and one of the most influential humanitarian strategists in the US, proposed the creation of armed relief enclaves. The US National Security Council discussed the possibility of intervention on 19 November, when Admiral David Jeremiah, Vice Chairman of the Joint Chiefs of Staff, said that the logistics were 'do-able'. The same day, prominent Washington columnists began to talk up intervention, with Leslie Gelb of *The Washington Post* advocating 'shoot to feed'. The momentum was gathering by the Thanksgiving weekend of 23–24 November. Three events came together to make the pressure unstoppable. One was the (un)luckiest artillery shot of the war. On 24 November, a shell was fired from one of Ali Mahdi's positions at a WFP ship as it entered the port. For months, Ali Mahdi's artillerymen had been trying to hit Aidid's headquarters and weapons dumps, but, despite the aid of street maps and constant practice, they had never managed it. But on 24 November they hit a moving target at long range with a single shell. Some of Ali Mahdi's ministers claimed responsibility for the shot,[3] others denied it, blaming 'irresponsible elements'.[4] But it served their aims well. The shot reverberated in New York in the Security Council meeting the next day.

The second event was Ismat Kittani's letter to the Secretary General, for that same Security Council meeting. The contrast with Sahnoun's approach was total. Kittani claimed that 2 million Somalis faced starvation, and that 'in the absence of a government or a governing authority capable of maintaining law and order, Somali "authorities" at all levels of society compete for anything of value' (quoted in *The Washington Post*, 26 November 1992). Most crucially, he claimed that 70–80 per cent of relief food was being looted. This figure later became notorious. The US State Department and the UN Secretariat repeatedly quoted '80 per cent' as fact, but its origins are untraceable. Sahnoun had estimated 15–40 per cent losses in October.[5] MSF argued that 'nobody could seriously claim that such a large proportion was not getting through' (Martin, 1993: 2). SCF-UK reported having distributed 4,000 tonnes without losing a single bag.[6] The ICRC was silent but its staff privately claimed diversion rates of 15–20 per cent. The WFP disagreed, but justified its silent endorsement of the exaggeration by saying 'we were never asked to correct it'.[7] CARE was also silent at the time, but later said, 'CARE's proud claim was that, overall, not more than 20 per cent was looted, despite the appallingly dangerous circumstances' (CARE, 1993). (These claims were certainly over-optimistic, but they

---

[3]Mohamed Qanyare, speaking on the BBC Somali Service, 24 November 1992.

[4]Prof. Mohamed Hassan, speaking to the present author, 18 March 1993.

[5]Presentation to the Donors' Conference, 12 October 1992, point 23.

[6]Nicholas Hinton and David Shearer, SCF press conference, London, 3 December 1992.

[7]Paul Mitchell, WFP spokesman, quoted in Mark Huband, 'When Yankee Goes Home,' *Africa Report*, March/April 1993, p. 21.

were the only information available at the time, as no monitoring systems were in place.) In short, Kittani's claim was a fiction that suited the UN and the US State Department.

On 25 November, the Security Council permitted military intervention. The third key event was a press conference held in Washington DC the following day by three US agencies, CARE, Oxfam-America and the International Rescue Committee (IRC), at which they threatened to pull out of Somalia unless greater security could be provided. This press conference had a profound impact in the US: it seemed that Somalia's saviours were about to quit, and reportedly this was instrumental in swinging President George Bush behind the plan to intervene. In fact, Oxfam-America was not operational in Somalia at the time; it was a funding conduit for other agencies. The IRC had just begun a small programme in Gedo region, working cross-border from Kenya, and had not yet opened its first office inside Somalia. It did not consult its staff in Somalia before making the statement. Only CARE had a significant programme in the country, and it had made up its institutional mind several months earlier.

Among international NGOs, only SCF-UK spoke out publicly against the intervention. Uniquely, SCF had a Somali (Dr Hussein Mursal) in a senior management position, and he volunteered his negative opinion on the action. But as the consensus in favour became overwhelming, SCF succumbed and finally dropped its public opposition.

Underpinning these misrepresentations was a more insidious manipulation of visual imagery. A characteristic genre of iconography of Somali apocalypse became identifiable from mid-1992. One strand was images of sleek gunmen on their technicals (jeeps mounted with heavy machine guns) amid the ruins. Some of the most potent examples are the pictures of Dan Eldon, the young British–Kenyan photographer killed in Mogadishu in July 1993; some of his photographs are staged, virtually all are highly selective in what they represent (Eldon, 1994). Another strand was pathetic pictures of the victims. The phrase 'disaster pornography' was coined to describe this, the pictorial product of disaster tourism (Rakiya Omaar, letter to *The Independent on Sunday*, 31 August 1992). Often, newspapers ran pictures with only the briefest accompanying text, and in many television news features words were almost redundant. The emotive impact of such pictures cannot be overestimated.

The 'victim' pictures were also selective, and as the months passed, became increasingly so. Dr Hussein Mursal described a conversation he held with another television journalist:

> He just said to me, 'Pick the children who are most severely malnourished'. I asked, 'You go into a feeding centre with a thousand children. Two hundred are bad, and some of those are very bad. Why do you just select the two hundred – or the smaller number who are severely malnourished?' [The journalist] replied, 'I am doing this to

raise funds'. I said, 'So you tell lies to get people to pay money?' He was just silent after that.

Both the media and most NGOs were insensitive to Somali opinion – including their own staff – and often careless with the facts. By the time the drumbeat for intervention reached its crescendo, the vision of 'Somalia' in which the US Marines were intervening was wholly different from the real Somalia experienced by Somalis.

The humbling of UNOSOM

An extraordinary amount of money went on this fantastic enterprise. Between December 1992 and October 1993, $2 billion was spent on Operation Restore Hope, and $1.55 billion was budgeted for the subsequent UN Operation in Somalia (UNOSOM II). (In the event, the amounts spent were much larger because of the war with General Aidid.) Over $300m. went on civil infrastructure to support UNOSOM, mostly its headquarters compound. By contrast, the UN specialized agencies asked for a total of $166m. at the Humanitarian Conference for Somalia in March 1993, of which about $35m. had been disbursed by November. Somalia's gross domestic product was less than $1 billion.

The intervention was ill-conceived from the outset. The very fact of such an enormous action transformed Somali politics by feeding inflated expectations of the return of the aid machine that had sustained Siad Barre. This was compounded by blunders made by the US and UN in the first weeks. The full story of the intervention has yet to be told. The present analysis will concentrate on the way in which the lack of accountability of the humanitarian international led rapidly to its logical endpoint: impunity for war crimes committed in the name of the humanitarian community.

The mandate of the US led Unified Task Force (UNITAF) was to 'create a secure environment for the delivery of humanitarian relief'. This indicated that the formal focus of the effort was on the relief agencies and not the subjects of their concern. (Fortuitously, the Marines landed just as the famine was abating, so that it was a straightforward task to declare victory over starvation.) The *de facto* priorities were still further removed from Somali realities: to produce good television pictures in the weeks before Christmas, and to withdraw without American casualties. UNITAF achieved both of these, but at the price of making a series of agreements that set the course for a political collision later on. In particular, the US Special Envoy, Robert Oakley, made warm overtures to General Aidid. He rented a house from Aidid's financier, Osman 'Ato', and most of the US commercial deals were made with Aidid supporters. Later, when the UN, with US backing, decided to marginalize Aidid in the political process, it could not do so without a confrontation. To win in such a showdown, a record of invincibility was needed.

The bluff was called in February 1993 when forces commanded by General Mohamed Sayed Hersi 'Morgan' occupied the town of Kismayo, defeating the Somali National Alliance (SNA) militiamen of Aidid's ally, Colonel Omer Jess. Morgan infiltrated his troops into the town by night, and used crowds of civilians to shield the attack. The Belgian UNITAF troops had the choice of opening fire on the crowds or standing by while the battle proceeded. They chose the latter, and after two battles in a three-week period, Morgan was in complete control of the town. When news of the first assault was announced on the BBC, crowds in Mogadishu took to the streets in an anti-UNITAF protest, believing that a secret deal had been made to deliver the town to Morgan. There is no evidence for this, but Ambassador Oakley made no public speech to rebut this line or to reassure the crowds. Some of the UNITAF troops opened fire and caused casualties among the demonstrators. This was a turning point for the intervention (wholly ignored in Oakley's own account of what happened) (Oakley and Hirsch, 1995). The militias learned that the war could continue despite the presence of international troops, and General Aidid began to distrust the US deeply.

The confrontation between Aidid and the UN duly occurred on 5 June, when 23 Pakistani members of UNOSOM were killed when searching the Radio Mogadishu compound and two other registered weapons sites belonging to the SNA (Drysdale, 1994). This led to a bloody four-month war in Mogadishu in which several thousand people were injured or killed. In October the US was forced to admit that it could not win and to settle for a truce.

The collapse of the intervention can only be understood in the context of the routine brutality and impunity of many of the military contingents, which antagonized many Somalis who would otherwise have been supportive. The Belgian troops in Kismayo were a case in point. They harassed, beat and killed many Somalis, some of them unarmed and without provocation (African Rights, 1993b). Speaking anonymously, Belgian soldiers were frank: 'You know, if someone had been killed, you just left him there. In the end, all you thought about was the red tape it would cause [to report it]. . . . [a]t the very end, we would shoot straight at them, straight away.'[8] After the abuses became public, the Belgian army set up an internal inquiry. Its first report was very superficial, with a few remarks on seven incidents (Commission d'enquête Somalie, 1993). It then investigated 268 incidents, including 58 cases of killing or serious injury (Reuters, 21 December 1994). (On the numbers killed, one paratrooper commented, 'You can multiply the official figure by about four or five. At the minimum.'[9]) Only one case came to court: three paratroopers accused of manslaughter. No Somalis came to the Belgian courtroom to testify. The three were acquitted.

[8]Interview on BRT, Belgian Radio, 25 August 1993.
[9]Interview on BRT, Belgian Radio, 25 August 1993.

The US army, the Italians, French, Nigerians and others also committed abuses. Only the Canadian contingent was subject to a thorough inquiry, that led to prosecutions and reforms within the army.

The Geneva Conventions and the war against Aidid

The war against Aidid saw the UN set an important precedent: the non-applicability of the Geneva Conventions to UN forces. Several times, UN forces undoubtedly violated the laws of war. The UN acknowledged the facts but claimed immunity. This was a development of immense importance which passed almost unnoticed amid the media spotlight on the war.

At first, the UN forces simply lied to try to cover up their violations. When Pakistani UN troops opened fire on a crowd in the centre of Mogadishu on 12 June, they simply denied the incident had occurred, despite the presence of many foreign journalists who witnessed the killings. The Pakistanis then claimed they had been fired on from the crowd. Journalists established that the Pakistani troops, under no serious threat, opened fire with a heavy machine gun and killed at least ten people.[10]

A well-documented violation was the attack on Digfer Hospital on 17 June, when UNOSOM forces were pursuing Aidid from his headquarters (African Rights, 1993b). The present author, having gathered evidence on this incident, confronted the US Provost Marshall and asked him whether the forces considered themselves bound by the Geneva Conventions. No answer was provided, but the following day the UN issued instructions that 'If this individual is seen in UNOSOM facilities he should be detained'.[11] With regard to the attack, an unnamed UN official was quoted as saying 'The normal rules of engagement do not apply in this nation'.[12]

Another incident was a helicopter raid on a house belonging to one of Aidid's senior aides on 12 July, described by the UN as a 'command and control centre' for the SNA; 73 people were killed. Ann Wright, a UN legal adviser, addressed a strong memorandum to Admiral Howe the next day in matchless lawyerly prose:

> This UNOSOM military operation raises important legal and human rights issues from the UN perspective. The issue boils down to whether the Security Council Resolution's directive authorising UNOSOM to 'take all necessary measures' against those responsible for attacks on UNOSOM forces meant for UNOSOM to use lethal force against all persons without possibility of surrender in any building suspected or known to be SNA/Aidid facilities or did the

---

[10]See Mark Huband, 'Marchers died in battle between hidden gunmen and UN troops', *The Guardian*, 17 June 1993.

[11]UNOSOM Military Information Office, 'UNOSOM FHQ [Field Headquarters] Morning Briefing Notes for 11 Jul[y] 1993', p. 2.

[12]Quoted in Liz Sly, 'UN raises the ante in Somalia attacks', *Chicago Tribune*, 20 June 1993.

Security Council allow that persons suspected to be responsible for attacks against UNOSOM forces would have an opportunity to be detained by UNOSOM forces and explain their presence in an SNA/Aidid facility and then be judged in a neutral court of law to determine if they were responsible for attacks against UNOSOM forces or were mere occupants (temporary or permanent) of a building, suspected or known to be an SNA/Aidid facility.[13]

UNOSOM had decided, implicitly, that the Security Council had indeed authorized the more drastic measures. Admiral Jonathan Howe, head of UNOSOM, stated: 'We hit a key military planning cell of key Aidid advisors. . . . This is where they have done their plotting for their terrorist attacks. We knew what we were hitting. It was well planned.'[14] He claimed that the evidence for the official version of events was not forthcoming because the camera on their helicopter had jammed. Meanwhile, another of the UN's legal advisers developed the argument that it was illegal for Somalis to fire on UN troops, even in self-defence, because the latter were acting on behalf of the world's highest legal authority, the UN Security Council.

After one incident on 9 September, in which a helicopter opened fire on a crowd and killed over 60 people, the UN spokesman, Major David Stockwell, said, 'There are no sidelines or spectator seats – the people on the ground are considered combatants.'[15] Later, questions were asked by journalists about the legal status of 55 Somalis detained without charge by the UN forces.[16] David Ijayala, legal adviser to UNOSOM, stated that the UN was drawing its authority from legal codes accepted in 'civilized countries' and that detainees were 'being held for security reasons, and the authority is under chapter seven [of the UN Charter], no other legal code'.[17] In short, the Security Council can authorize UN forces to violate international humanitarian law. The implications of this for humanitarian action can scarcely be overemphasized.

Humanitarian impunity

The UN violations of the Geneva Conventions in Mogadishu were the culmination of the evolution of international law over the immediate

---

[13] Ann Wright, 'Legal and Human Rights Aspects of UNOSOM Military Operations', Memorandum to the Special Representative of the Secretary-General from UNOSOM Justice Division, 13 July 1993.
[14] Quoted in Keith Richburg, 'U.S. raid reportedly killed Aidid aides', *International Herald Tribune*, 16 July 1993.
[15] Quoted in Keith Richburg, 'UN defends firing on Somali crowd', *The Washington Post*, 11 September 1993.
[16] Keith Richburg, 'Somalis' imprisonment poses questions about UN role', *The Washington Post*, 7 November 1993.
[17] Quoted in Mark Huband, 'UN forces deny Somali detainees legal rights', *The Guardian*, 25 September 1993.

post-Cold War period, which saw a significant, if little noticed, re-writing of international humanitarian law at the UN Security Council. This was a necessary counterpart to the concept of humanitarian intervention: the gradual emergence of a concept of humanitarian impunity. In a succession of resolutions concerned chiefly with Iraq, Bosnia and Somalia, the right of 'humanitarian access' and the privileged status of humanitarian organizations and UN forces were reinforced. At the same time, these concepts were subtly changed, so that material relief was given legal pre-eminence over human rights; assistance was given priority over protection.

The history of the concept of 'humanitarian access' is a manifestation of the humanitarian Gresham's Law. As explained in Chapter 7, the laws of war provide only weak and conditional guarantees for relief agencies. These laws are much tougher on the use of starvation as a method of warfare. However, in the 1990s, the right of 'humanitarian access' has come to refer primarily to the desire of humanitarian agencies to be operational in conflict zones. The needs of the relief agency are conflated with those of the suffering civilians. Two influential analysts, Larry Minear and Thomas Weiss, write:

> In fact, humanitarians have come to resemble the objects of their labors. Those who work for the Red Cross or the United Nations often are denied *their* right of access, harassed and held hostage, injured and killed. Long-established symbols no longer command automatic respect or assure implicit protection. In many conflicts, relief convoys have been hijacked or blocked, drivers wounded or killed, and emergency assistance activities commandeered or shut down. International humanitarian actors suffer indignities differing only in degree from those experienced by distressed civilian populations. (Minear and Weiss, 1995: 3. Emphasis added)

This description would not be recognized by the inhabitants of Sarajevo, Mogadishu or Juba, but reflects the consensus that relief workers should be privileged under the laws of war. As a consequence, international military intervention in Somalia and Bosnia was primarily aimed at protecting aid givers, rather than the populace in the area. The 'PRO' in UNPROFOR referred to protecting the humanitarian effort, not the Bosnian people.

The privileging of humanitarian agencies has gone hand in hand with the emasculation of their duties to ensure impartiality and non-abuse of aid. The right of humanitarian access found in the Geneva Conventions is workable only if the agencies submit to the belligerent government's regulation or regulate themselves, and in particular if they are ready to withdraw if the belligerents violate the principles. Historically, the ICRC has been ready to delay starting its operations and to withdraw if necessary. But competition among relief agencies now precludes this, driving them to jettison principles in favour of being seen to be present on the ground. Non-entry or withdrawal is seen as the very last resort, rather than the agencies' most important card in ensuring that humanitarian principles are upheld. In the Horn of Africa the only cases of withdrawal on principle are MSF-France in Ethiopia in 1985 and Community Aid Abroad in Somalia in 1989.[18]

What this has meant in practice is the development of a new doctrine in international law.

> The UN resolutions adopted in connection with the flight of the Kurds and the Yugoslav and Somali conflicts all refer to the protection of aid convoys – a new doctrine in humanitarian action – while not one mentions the victims. The civilian population is regarded solely as the recipient of aid, which is lavishly provided with the best of intentions, even if it never reaches its intended target. Preoccupation with logistics eclipses concern for human beings, as if soap or milk powder could prevent bombs from falling on hospitals, or generosity could offer protection against murder and expulsion. (Bouchet-Saulnier, 1993: 128)

The wider phenomenon has been called the 'Kouchner Doctrine' after the founder of Médecins Sans Frontières and subsequent Minister for Humanitarian Affairs in France. A more precise description would be 'humanitarian impunity', summarized as the automatic legal privileging of *all* actions by *all* humanitarian agencies. The law is thus rendered void in favour of the practice of operational presence whatever the cost.

Humanitarian impunity has primarily benefited the UN specialized agencies. NGOs have benefited too, and have maintained their demands for equal privilege. The 1994 Red Cross/Red Crescent-NGO Code of Conduct commits the signatory agencies to following international humanitarian law, but it seems improbable that they would submit to the articles which authorize to the belligerents to restrict relief supplies if they suspect they may provide military advantage to the adversary. The Code calls upon host governments to 'recognize and respect the independent, humanitarian and impartial actions of NGHAs [nongovernmental humanitarian agencies]'. However, the agencies themselves have only to sign the Code of Conduct to entitle themselves to this privileged status. There are no mechanisms for investigating their credentials or enforcing their adherence to the principles, or indeed the law.

The reaction of the humanitarian international to the Somali debacle illustrates the wider ramifications of the principle of humanitarian impunity. By mid-1993 it was evident that the intervention had gone horribly wrong. The US Government initiated a review which concluded that troops should be sent abroad only when vital national interests were at stake. Western military authorities also studied the implications of what the Somalis called 'high-tech search and low-tech hide'. By contrast, many humanitarians did not even recognize that they

---

[18]MSF's expulsion was probably involuntary. See Chapter 6.

had lessons to learn. As the Mogadishu war intensified, the agencies that had clamoured for troops in November now tried to distance themselves from the consequences of their action. CARE belatedly became a critic of the intervention and said the UN had strayed too far from its humanitarian mandate.

Rwanda 1994: humanitarianism unbound

In 1994, Rwanda suffered genocide, not famine. The genocide of the Rwandese Tutsi would be literally incredible had it not happened. More than 800,000 people were murdered in less than a hundred days on the orders of a Hutu extremist government (African Rights, 1994b). There is one major reason for including the Rwandese genocide and its aftermath in this account. It is this: if famine reflects a failure of accountability, genocide can be said to be the most extreme manifestation of lack of accountability. Genocide is a state crime perpetrated against a group which the state does not even believe has the right to exist. The response of the humanitarian international to the most political of all human crises is a test case for its capacity to deal with political crimes; arguably, if it fails on this one, it can never succeed with the less clear-cut case of famine.

The humanitarian international did fail in Rwanda. It failed to prevent the genocide, it did not intervene to halt it, and it even failed to discourage the perpetrators. There was a massive humanitarian response, too late and aimed at people who fled the country (Hutu civilians and their political masters, including the former Rwandese army and militia and thousands of those responsible for the genocide). Survivors of the genocide were almost wholly ignored at the time and have been largely neglected since. The response was of uneven competence and proved politically regressive, assisting the genocidal extremists. This type of response was remarkable, given the fact that, in the early days of the genocide, senior staff in the established relief agencies came to a broadly similar view that genocide was a political crime which demanded something other than a conventional humanitarian reaction. Almost uniquely for such a crisis, human rights information and political analysis *preceded* humanitarian action and were able to be used to inform it from the outset.

The fundamental reason for this 'counterfeiting' of humanitarian action was the institutional instincts and interests of the relief agencies. After the 'refugee' crises began, the humanitarian Gresham's Law came into operation with a vengeance, in several respects. First, the agencies' own priorities were identified with those of the Rwandese themselves. Secondly, in the Western media 'humanitarian' analyses tended to drive out all others, and the more sensationalist and 'debased' humanitarian analyses drove out the more politically informed ones. These in turn strongly influenced the international political response. Thirdly, humanitarian action was made to stand in place of political action. The result was a political paralysis that allowed the genocide to continue, and a 'debased' relief response that may have delivered some essential services, but at enormous political cost.

This process was not driven solely, or even primarily, by humanitarian agencies. The Western media and political leadership share responsibility. Some aid agency staff protested about the way the media portrayed the crisis and the way in which the UN Security Council and the major Western powers used relief agencies as their principal policy instruments. The relief agencies were remarkably united in their criticisms of the French military intervention, when it was first floated. Many members of the humanitarian international recognized that something was deeply wrong, and some of them said so. Others happily went along with the manipulation and energetically sought the media limelight. The concern here is not to cast aspersions on the integrity of individuals, some of whom struggled hard against both the logistical and the political obstacles they faced in the field, and against the tendencies of their institutions. Rather it is to ask why the humanitarian international reacted in a way that contradicted much of its own analysis of the situation.

Genocide and humanitarian neutrality
The first compromise made by the humanitarian international was to introduce and elevate the principle of neutrality. This arose from experience in other countries (such as Somalia) and institutional priorities. It led the humanitarian response astray at the outset.

The genocide in Rwanda could scarcely be more different from the protracted crisis of state collapse in Somalia. Before the genocide, virtually the only thing the two countries had in common was that both were culturally, linguistically and religiously homogeneous societies of about 7 million people. Somalia suffered a collapsed state, Rwanda a state of such strength and cohesion that it could organize genocide. There was no disintegration in Rwanda, but instead a powerful state with a unique ideological legacy:

> Rwanda was a country with a mystique. Keeping all due precautions in mind, one has to see it in the company of Cuba, Israel, North Korea and the Vatican, that is an ideological state where power is a means towards the implementation of a set of ideas at least as much as a *de facto* administrative structure for governing a given geographical territory. (Prunier, 1995: 80)

This state carefully organized the murder of at least 10 per cent of its own citizens. The state did not collapse. Instead, in the end the genocidal government was militarily defeated by a well-disciplined army, the Rwandese Patriotic Front (RPF).

How were organizations dedicated to the relief of suffering to deal with a government whose *raison d'être* was the infliction of suffering? Though on an unprecedented scale, this issue was not new. There were similarities in Cambodia in 1979–80, in Ethiopia in the 1980s, in Iraqi Kurdistan, and perhaps most significantly, in Uganda. The relief operation in the Luwero Triangle in Uganda in 1983–4 raises the moral issue of whether a relief agency should speak out about human rights abuses or continue its operations in silence. At the time, the government of Milton Obote was engaged in abuses against the mainly Baganda people of Luwero that amounted to genocide. At least 300,000 were killed in massacres intended to deter support for Yoweri Museveni's National Resistance Army. Relief agencies active in Luwero chose to remain silent, fearing that to speak out would not affect international acquiescence in Obote's crimes but would merely remove a source of sustenance for the people. One reason for this silence was that the agencies themselves were not threatened by government abuses; a second was that they had programmes elsewhere in Uganda that they did not want to endanger. Staff members of Oxfam, to name one agency, remain scarred by this experience and the agency's decision to stay silent. Having gone to the extreme of passionate advocacy in Biafra, the operational NGOs went to the other extreme in Luwero. It remains a little known and rather dark chapter in NGO history.

During the genocide there were few international humanitarian operations of any note inside Rwanda. The ICRC stayed and MSF tried to set up a medical programme in Butare but closed it before the genocide began there, following threats to its staff and killings in the hospital wards. Caritas also tried to deliver supplies. Most humanitarian organizations simply watched, frustrated by their inability to do anything meaningful. One of these was Oxfam, the most active of the agencies of the English-speaking world.

Oxfam was among the first to use the term 'genocide' in Rwanda. In late April 1994, Oxfam began to campaign publicly for greater international involvement in Rwanda, chastising the UN for its abrupt withdrawal of troops the day after the genocide was launched. Oxfam called for an end to the killings, and correctly distinguished between the genocide of Tutsi civilians and the war between the Rwandese army and the RPF. How the killings were to be halted, it did not specify. More concretely, Oxfam also called for a ceasefire, UN military intervention, and humanitarian access. Inside the organization, these were seen as the minima that would have a (modest) effect and the maxima that a charity could advocate. Outside – given the vacuum of international political action – Oxfam gave the impression that these measures would have stopped the genocide.

A ceasefire would have stopped the war but not the genocide. The major instruments of killing were the army, the gendarmerie and extremist *interahamwe* militia operating away from the battle lines. The main constraint on the killing was the military advance of the RPF. A ceasefire would have frozen the battle lines, enabling the army and militia to continue killing with impunity in the larger part of the country controlled by the interim government. A ceasefire as a prelude to a negotiated settlement to the war would have entailed extending some form of legitimacy or recognition to the interim government responsible for the genocide. This would have entrenched the extremists in power in much of Rwanda and prevented bringing those responsible for the genocide to trial.

The contradiction is heightened by the fact that in the same statement as it called for a ceasefire and political negotiation, Oxfam named the crime 'genocide'. This call appears to have been made for three reasons. One was that a ceasefire was a precondition for the despatch of UN troops. A second was that the fighting was causing human suffering and impeding the delivery of humanitarian relief. Thirdly and most significantly, *not* to call for a ceasefire would have appeared to be compromising the organization's reputation for neutrality. This reflected a confusion of peacemaking with human rights: the appropriate human rights statement would have been to call for adherence to the Geneva Conventions and the Genocide Convention. Charitable law does not require a commitment to ending combat; Oxfam was not required to press for a ceasefire in Ethiopia or Kuwait, let alone in World War II.

Waging war on the interim government was the only form of military intervention that would have contributed to stopping the genocide. No major military power was ready to undertake this; intervention would have to follow another model. One option was akin to traditional peacekeeping. The UN Assistance Mission to Rwanda (UNAMIR) pursued this and spent most of its diplomatic resources during the genocide in vain pursuit of a ceasefire. A second model was protecting humanitarian agencies, as in Somalia – an all but irrelevant proposal. Feeding the captive Tutsi populations, mainly in churches and football stadiums, would not have prevented the massacres. (In the RPF-controlled zones there were destitute and displaced people needing assistance, who could be reached without any protection other than RPF escort, but very few agencies pursued this option, largely so as not to jeopardize their 'neutrality.') A third model was the armed protection of enclaves of threatened people. A force with these objectives could perhaps have saved tens of thousands of lives, but might have been drawn into a political deal that legitimized the interim government. When French troops were despatched on 'Operation Turquoise' in June ostensibly to protect those at risk of genocide, the result was precisely as follows: about 13,000–14,000 displaced Tutsis were protected in Nyarushishi camp and elsewhere in the 'Safe Humanitarian Zone',[19]

[19]The French army erroneously claimed to have saved 80,000–100,000 lives. (see OECD, 1996; 154).

while small-scale killings continued in the rural areas, but the killers were also provided with a safe haven for refuge and reorganization. Had the 'Safe Humanitarian Zone' included the national capital, the interim government would have retained power.

The RPF advance brought the genocide to an end. The humanitarian international did not support the RPF advance; on the contrary, the UN and the NGOs repeatedly called on the RPF to observe a ceasefire. Part of the reason for this was so that UN troops could be despatched to protect civilians. Hence, the humanitarian proposals would not have halted the genocide and would almost certainly have contributed to further slaughter, the legitimation of the genocidal government, and impunity for genocidal criminals. Although the policies were wholly inappropriate, they were acceptable within the limits of humanitarian discourse. The demands of 'neutrality' overrode those of fighting against genocide. 'Neutrality' was the moral lever that toppled the possibility of an effective response to the genocide.

Although some agency staff rapidly came to an understanding of the Rwandese crisis, they did not develop a strategy for action. Events unfolded too fast, institutions proved inert and slow to learn, and there was no international political response. In fact, after the first fortnight, the level of understanding within agencies appeared to *regress*, probably because more staff were becoming involved who had neither the time nor the inclination to study the politics. Media stereotypes of 'anarchy' and 'state collapse' were imposed, or imported by staff moved from programmes such as Somalia.

Counterfeit humanitarianism
The extremists laid a trap for the humanitarian international, and sprang it twice. First, 300,000 'refugees' fled to Ngara District of Tanzania at the end of April. Secondly, nearly one million 'refugees' moved to Goma in Zaire in early July, and another 300,000 or so to Bukavu, also in Zaire. These enormous exoduses were the largest since those from Bangladesh in 1971. They were not the familiar unplanned flight of civilians caught up in a war, but rather the planned exodus of a population under political direction, to seek sanctuary abroad and provide a base from which the architects of the genocide could regroup and attack Rwanda again. The exodus included the flight of virtually the entire extremist government and most of the Rwandese armed forces. The term 'refugee' has been universally but carelessly used to describe these people. Few fit the legal definition of a refugee. Many are fugitives from justice. Many are migrants, persecuted by the same political leaders who crossed the border with them. But this fundamental legal point was considered an irrelevant nicety by humanitarian agencies in the rush to assist 'people of concern to UNHCR'. (Only in mid-1996 were the first serious proposals made for withdrawing the refugee label from people known to be implicated in the genocide.)

The extremists who had mounted the genocide aimed at depopulating Rwanda, so that the victorious RPF would inherit a deserted country. One broadcast on the extremist radio station, Radio Télévision Libre des Milles Collines, taunted the RPF leader, General Paul Kagame:

> The country is the inhabitants, not the mountains, not the animals in the parks. It is clear that if he adds animals, parks and snakes and frogs . . . *[fades]* He [Kagame] has no half of the country – the population have fled him. One governs people, not owls and all [other] animals. . . . Has he got half the population? Not at all. (quoted in African Rights, 1994b: 658)

The extremists also knew they could rely on the humanitarian international to respond with material assistance for the 'refugees', and that there would be few if any efforts to isolate them from the mass of the population. They thus forced people to flee and then diverted enough assistance from relief agencies to consolidate their power. In both cases the trap worked to perfection. The 'irreducible residue of naiveté' meant that the agencies felt they had no moral choice but to respond to massive human suffering, even though it meant supporting the extremists' strategy. The humanitarian Gresham's Law meant that the moral complexities were hidden away and a simple charitable imperative (Give!) was presented through the media.

The response to the 'refugee' crises, particularly at Goma, was extraordinary by any standards. Tens of millions of dollars were raised and spent in a few weeks. Dozens of private agencies arrived in response to a blitz of publicity. They then cultivated that publicity, stationing press officers at Goma airport to seize on visiting journalists and emblazoning their logos in every prominent position. In the longer term, although most of the funds spent in the camps came from Western governments, the relatively smaller amount from the general public had a profound influence: it set the political tone of the assistance programme. The pressures to 'be there' were overwhelming for all agencies. John Seaman of SCF-UK commented:

> If you stand back not far from a crisis like Rwanda, it is clear that NGOs behave like rabble. In a concentration of NGOs such as Goma there is such an imperative to establish a trademark and territory, and all technical standards go to the wall.
>
> For Save the Children Fund, it is a difficult question of either competing or staying away – in which case we lose out on both media coverage and money. We have not yet decided how to face the problem over the next few years. (Seaman, 1995b)

The non-operational agencies suffered particularly in this rush to be visible 'on the ground'. The relative slowness with which they could disburse funds made them the targets of cheap criticism that they were not helping fast enough. This in turn pushed them to deal with local 'partners' in an indiscriminate fashion. This was particularly problematic for church agencies, because senior figures in all the mainstream churches in Rwanda were implicated, to a greater or lesser degree, in the genocide. European churches (Roman Catholic, Anglican and Baptist) have preferred to forgive their Rwandese brethren quietly, with the result that individual churchmen who openly sympathized with the extremists remain in post, sometimes benefiting from humanitarian aid. This form of local ecclesiastical accountability has worked against humanitarian principle.[20]

Though international relief organizations did not directly support the genocidal government inside Rwanda, the moment government forces had decamped to Zaire the familiar synergy between an abusive authority and humanitarian relief became established. Much of the assistance was simply stolen. Some of the relief agencies present delivered direct to the soldiers, either on the grounds that they had no option, or because they considered the soldiers needy as individuals. Many extremist professionals, including doctors, nurses, civil servants and journalists, sought and obtained employment with aid agencies.

Almost the only coherent ethical defence of the agencies' actions has been given by Hugo Slim, who argues that the agencies could not be held responsible for any future violence by the recuperated extremists, on the grounds that the extremists make their own moral choices.

> To have withheld humanitarian assistance in the hope that the regime might not be able to regroup and might not choose violence again would have meant working on the principle of 'doing evil that good may come' – a principle that has consistently been objected to in Christian moral theology and which would make an absurdity of the humanitarian mandate of relief agencies. (Slim, 1996: 12)

The countervailing principle is found in the Geneva Conventions: relief should be given only when there are assurances that it cannot be abused.[21] Following this principle would have led to preventable deaths among the 'refugees', but could have restrained the ongoing killing campaign directed against genocide survivors in Rwanda and local Tutsis in eastern Zaire.

For the humanitarian international and its donors, the 'refugees' obscured the genocide and justice. After the mass exodus, the issues of genocide and justice slipped down Oxfam's agenda: an immediate humanitarian response for the 'refugees' became its priority (both in lobbying and in its own operations). This could be interpreted cynically: Oxfam needed to work in the camps because it was an unmissable fund-raising opportunity, and a programme for 'refugees'

---

[20]The ICRC's relationship with the Rwandese Red Cross was also problematic. Before the genocide, the Rwandese Red Cross had been working extensively with war-displaced people, many of whom had been recruited to the extremists' cause.

[21]Especially Article 23 of the Fourth Geneva Convention. While not strictly applicable to the Rwanda conflict, it expresses the norm that should be adhered to.

entailed not offending their extremist political leadership. A more generous reading is that the genocide was now over (in fact it was not), and that the agency's urgent priority was saving the lives of 'refugees'. Oxfam's policy adviser wrote: 'Oxfam believes in the indivisibility of all rights: the right to relief, for example, is neither greater nor less than the right to protection from physical attack'. (Cairns, 1995: 8). This statement is perhaps more revealing than its author intended: it is in fact an *elevation* of the 'right to relief' to the same level as fundamental rights such as protection from execution or genocide – a legal innovation.[22] Moreover, the work of relief agencies' is based precisely on the *separation* of the 'right to relief' from other rights. Agencies deliver on the 'right to relief' where other rights are not enforced. Their advocacy concentrates on it. Given the *de facto* separability of these rights, Oxfam's argument implies that it can be justifiable to compromise other basic rights in order to fulfil the 'right to relief'. This is precisely what happened in Rwanda: the 'right to relief' took priority over the search for justice. The agencies fulfilled the charitable imperative but violated the spirit of international law.

This episode illustrates how an aid agency's portrayal of a situation can not be divorced from its institutional interests. Ironically, Oxfam is a substantial target for criticism precisely because it went further than other agencies in developing a political and ethical approach to the genocide. If it had confined itself simply to service delivery and ignored human rights issues, it would have avoided much of the criticism. But it could not escape from its institutional (including legal and fund-raising) constraints, and the contradiction was exposed.

The contradictions matter so much because the Western media and Western governments thrust the humanitarian agencies into such an exposed position. The agencies can argue with some justification that they were betrayed or manipulated by higher powers: they were used to cover the nakedness of Western policy. But this very prominence (wanted or not) indicates the humanitarians' political significance.

Most humanitarian agencies revelled in their prominence and ignored their political responsibilities. Most fund-raising appeals were unashamedly emotive and simplistic. Some agencies put out astonishing descriptions of their roles. A publication by Feed the Children (FTC)[23] explained how the agency responded to genocide (Feed the Children, 1995). A box in the left-hand corner marked 'acts of genocide' was accompanied by the text 'emergency alert'. An arrow then led to a second box marked 'fleeing to camps', accompanied by the text 'field surveys and aid preparation'. Seven boxes later we arrive at 'revival of community life' and finally 'normalcy', whereupon 'FTC hands over to

---

[22]In practice, as argued above, the 'right to relief' means 'humanitarian access', which privileges the agencies themselves.

[23]Feed the Children should not be confused with the Save the Children Fund. It has subsequently changed its name to Children's Aid Direct.

nationals at local level'. What can only be described as a deception was further compounded by the agency's almost exclusive concentration on the events in Kibeho in April 1995 (see below), with the 1994 genocide relegated to the background. A French Red Cross publicity campaign appealed for funds to 'save the victims of genocide from cholera'. Genocide victims and survivors (by definition almost exclusively Tutsi) were not among the fugitives and migrants who had fled to Goma (the exception being rape victims taken by force by the men who held them captive). In Western countries, advertising standards authorities prohibit such misleading claims. But for most agencies, refugee or displaced persons camps are the very essence of aid; they are a visible sign of comprehensible and concentrated human need for charity.

The NGOs competed intensely for funds. They spent the great majority of their resources in the 'refugee' camps. In twelve months, over US$800m., more than two-thirds of all the assistance provided for Rwanda, was allocated for the 'refugee' programmes. Oxfam spent more than 90 per cent of its Rwanda funds in the 'refugee' camps. Approximately 100 NGOs were operational in Goma alone. Many of these had not worked in emergencies before; some were newly formed in response to the charitable opportunities presented by the crisis. About 60 were present only briefly. An independent evaluation team commissioned by the OECD was unable to trace many of them.[24] The collapse of standards was most evident for the most 'debased' agencies, but even the best established ones (including UNICEF and CARE-Germany) followed the same logic. The team was disturbed by the inflated claims of success made by agencies, and 'came across examples of agencies telling, if not falsehoods, then certainly half-truths'. It also noted 'a remarkable lack of attempts by agencies to seek the views of beneficiaries on the assistance being provided'. (OECD, 1996: 152–4) In short, 'hard' institutional interest overrode both professional and ethical standards.

The Kibeho incident
After the defeat of the extremist government the humanitarians ran amok inside Rwanda as well. In late 1994, when the new government tried to register the more than 180 NGOs that claimed to be operational in the country, it faced obstruction at every turn. The registration procedure was largely a formality, but most NGOs co-ordinated their opposition to it. In particular, they objected to the requests that their accounts be audited in Rwanda and their expatriate staff be subject to Rwandese law. To give just one example, the Danish NGO Børnefonden asked that 'The Organization's expatriate staff is granted criminal

---

[24]In the light of the immense media interest in humanitarian action in 1994 it is noteworthy that no major news outlet even mentioned the five-volume OECD review when it was publicly released in March 1996.

immunity while working for the Organization in Rwanda. Accordingly no criminal charges can be brought against an expatriate staff-member and MINIREISO [the Ministry of Rehabilitation and Social Integration] is responsible to the Organization that such immunity against criminal charges is not violated by the Rwandan authorities.'[25] Demands similar to these were backed by donors including ECHO and the German Government.

The majority of the humanitarian agencies concentrated their efforts on the displaced camps inside the 'Safe Humanitarian Zone' after the withdrawal of the French army. These camps were, politically speaking, extensions of the 'refugee' camps, largely controlled by the extremists and containing thousands of hard-core criminals. But because they were within Rwandese territory, the new government claimed jurisdiction, and began to close them. The camps had little humanitarian or economic justification, but they served both the extremists and the humanitarian agencies well, albeit for different reasons. The extremists could organize without interference from the new government and its army; the NGOs welcomed the camps as visible justifications of the continued need for their presence. The last camp remaining open was Kibeho. When the Rwandese Patriotic Army (RPA) moved in to close it in April 1995, it came into confrontation with both the extremists and the NGOs. The camp was closed with bloodshed and international outcry.

The government maintained that the closure was necessary and that 'several hundred' people were killed, some by the extremists in the camp and some by RPA soldiers who opened fire after coming under attack. With remarkable speed and unanimity, the international NGOs produced an alternative version of events. According to this, the 'Tutsi' government had made a premeditated assault on innocent 'Hutu refugees', killing 8,000 in cold blood. This was implicitly (and sometimes explicitly) called a 'second genocide'. One of the most strident advocates of this view was John O'Shea, director of the Irish aid agency Goal:

> The butchering of 8,000 members of the Hutu tribe by the governing Tutsi can only lead to increased violence . . . It is silly to think we should help the Tutsi-dominated Rwandan Government to establish itself. Our Government should not now send the £1 million aid it has promised that regime.
>
> The dispute is ethnic . . . The Tutsi are now bent on revenge. The 8,000 deaths at the weekend are just the start.[26]

This statement could have been drafted by the extremists themselves. Feed the Children wrote:

[25]Letter to the Minister of Rehabilitation and Social Integration, 23 August 1995.
[26]Quoted in Michael O'Regan, 'Rwandan Bloodshed', *Irish Times*, 24 April 1995.

The closing of these camps means that over 250,000 Hutus are on the move again, many dying as they travel. There are at least 100,000 children within this desperate throng. These children have already moved from camp to camp, their parents and extended families dying back all the time. Now they are left to make it alone. In this *landscape of genocide* many 'returnees' are therefore children. (Feed the Children, 1995: 2. Emphasis added)

A reader not familiar with Rwanda might be forgiven for inferring that the genocide was committed *against* the former residents of Kibeho.

The NGOs also accused the government of stopping their access to the survivors of Kibeho. The five branches of MSF wrote jointly to the government:

MSF demands from the government that they keep the promise that the removal of the people from the camps will be done in a safe and non violent way. . . . MSF demands from the government the following:

1. To guarantee immediate access for MSF to the people who need medical assistance, especially in the Kibeho hospital.
2. To guarantee access for the people to the health facilities where MSF is working.[27]

The readiness of the MSFs to demand action of a sovereign government reflects their self-confidence. The letter ignores the fact that the breakdown of order during the removal process was not wholly the fault of the RPA.

The NGOs' account was faithfully reproduced by the international media, which largely used the contrast with the government's claims to imply or state outright that the government was lying. Later, an independent commission, including representatives from the UN, the Organization of African Unity, seven Western countries and the Government of Rwanda, investigated the events. The commission's report is the closest to an independent assessment that exists, and should have caused no little embarrassment to the NGOs. The commission members concurred that there had been 'an urgent need to close the IDPs [internally displaced persons] camps' and that Kibeho camp 'appeared to be a center of hostility and a threat to internal security' (Brisset-Foucault *et al.*, 1995: 4). A procedure for closing the camps was worked out between the government, UNAMIR and the donors, and an Integrated Operations Centre established to supervise this process. However, in the words of the commission:

[Some NGOs] actively contradicted the policies of the Government of Rwanda by encouraging IDPs to remain in Kibeho camp and by pursuing discriminatory hiring practices. Moreover, the decision of a

[27]MSF joint letter to President and Vice-President of the Republic of Rwanda, dated 26 April 1995.

number of NGOs not to cooperate with the closure operation once it began exacerbated the humanitarian crisis. (ibid.: 11)

After slow progress, the army was deployed around the remaining camps. Contradicting the claims of a 'second genocide', the commission stressed that 'There is no evidence to suggest that the operation was intended to eliminate a certain category of people, especially those belonging to one ethnic group' (ibid.: 7). The closure operation, however, quickly degenerated into a battle, with panicked RPA soldiers (untrained in riot control and not equipped with non-lethal weaponry) firing into a stampeding crowd, while armed extremists within the camp also opened fire and attacked with machetes. Deaths were caused by gunshots, machetes, trampling and in some cases hunger and exposure. The commission criticized the RPA's use of excessive force and also blamed the 'hard core' of extremists within the camp for the killings. It did not produce its own estimate of the number of deaths but referred to 'overestimation in the initial fatality counts and estimates' (ibid.: 10). A later UN investigation put the death toll at between 800 and 1,200, a figure close to the government's initial estimate of several hundred fatalities.[28]

But the relief agencies almost achieved impunity. Despite the independent commission's findings, no agency made a retraction or a public apology for its erroneous statements, nor even a correction in subsequent public reports. The government finally took its only effective sanction, and in December 1995 expelled 38 agencies (114 remained).

Rwanda and the future of humanitarianism

The men and women who bear overwhelming responsibility for the plight of the Rwandese people are the Hutu extremists who planned and implemented the genocide of 1994. Their crime is so huge that the culpability of any other actor pales by comparison. Since 1994, the overriding issue is whether the Hutu extremists will enjoy impunity for their crime, or even try to complete their genocide (the killings have not stopped) (African Rights, 1996). Rwanda needs a new political dispensation that guarantees protection from mass murder. Creating a new political contract from scratch is an immense task and one that can only be accomplished by the Rwandese themselves.

Many people within the relief agencies recognize the political imperatives in Rwanda and the limits to their role. Some acknowledged these from the start. Nonetheless, the humanitarian international has, collectively, contributed little towards resolving Rwanda's basic political problems. In many respects, it has been an impediment. Not

---

[28]Alex Belida, 'Rwanda/Kibeho', *Voice of America*, transcript, 7 November 1995.

only have agencies proved incapable of assisting a process of justice, but some have become the tactical allies of the extremists.

The Rwanda crisis has led to an unprecedented level of criticism of NGOs. Richard McCall, chief of staff to the Administrator of USAID, has written:

> One gets the same sense that the pursuit of resources drives far too many institutions. With declining resources for development and sizeable resources devoted to complex emergencies, agencies are packaging programmes in order to capture humanitarian relief dollars. It is not only time to review the mandates of all institutions involved in humanitarian relief and rehabilitation efforts in order to rationalise the system more effectively, but it is also time to really decide which institutions are no longer relevant to the challenges posed by reality. (McCall, 1995)

The stirrings of a backlash are also evident in the very different context of Somalia. In private, US politicians and generals became more sceptical about the pretensions of the relief agencies – a scepticism that contributed to the US opposition to intervention in Rwanda. Bitterness at the way they were treated by foreign humanitarians contributed to the readiness of Somalis to confront UNOSOM.

McCall's suggestion of reviewing mandates and eliminating the worst offenders would certainly improve matters. But the malaise runs deeper. In Rwanda, *all* relief agencies were subjected to the pressure to counterfeit humanitarianism. Even Oxfam – among the most thoughtful and politically informed of agencies – ended up contradicting its stated principle of supporting justice. The problem is not the integrity or intelligence of agency staff, nor the free entry to the relief industry, but the institutional and political position that relief agencies find themselves in. This crisis is partly of their own making, partly not. Whoever shares the blame for getting them into this mess, the humanitarians have a responsibility for getting themselves out of it.

10

| Eastern | The Fundraisers' |
| Zaire 1996 | Catastrophe |

In November 1996, a dramatic episode in eastern Zaire illustrated the nature of the humanitarian mode of power. The focus was the plight of Rwandese refugees (more properly labelled externally displaced persons or EDPs) in camps near to Goma and Bukavu. This chapter will not document the history and politics of eastern Zaire and the Rwandese EDPs, except in passing; instead, it focuses on how they were co-opted as subjects of humanitarian discourse for a brief but significant moment. For approximately one week – 7–15 November – the feared deaths of a million Rwandese EDPs dominated world news. Richard Dowden, Africa editor of *The Economist*, wrote:

> Catastrophe! Disaster! Apocalypse! For once the words are the right ones. Eastern Zaire is the latest zone of death in a continent where such disasters have become commonplace. And it could be the biggest . . . hundreds of thousands are going to die of hunger and disease.[1]

Within days of this narrative becoming a consensually accepted representation by most of the media, Western governments and relief agencies, it was rather spectacularly shown to be false. There was no humanitarian tragedy of the scale or nature claimed.

Rather than realities in eastern Zaire, this humanitarian narrative was anchored in the institutional imperatives of the humanitarian international, compounded by a clever game played by France (partly on behalf of its friends in the region, the Rwandese extremists and President Mobutu Sese Seko). The humanitarian agencies needed money. In October 1966, there were disasters of various proportions in Sierra Leone and Liberia, Sudan, Burundi, Chechnya, Iraqi Kurdistan, Afghanistan and North Korea; a cyclone hit India and an earthquake struck Peru. None of these disasters appeared quite to fit the bill for the humanitarian fund-raisers: the agencies would not have sufficient

[1]'Good intentions on the road to Hell', *The Independent*, 3 November 1996.

access or freedom of action, and the visual imagery of the crisis would not be compelling enough. Not having run a successful appeal since the summer of 1994, agencies with large emergency departments (Médecins Sans Frontières, Oxfam and a host of lesser-known ones) were facing a financial squeeze, so much so that the present author wrote:[2]

> Be warned – you will soon be called upon to reach into your pockets and give to disaster relief charities in response to a big human tragedy. My advice is to think hard before you give.
> The early warning signs are clear. I am not referring to deepening drought in the Sahel or thousands of refugees on the move in the Middle East, but simply to the fact that the run-up to Christmas is the fundraising season for aid agencies. In America it is even more pronounced than here: the seven weeks between the presidential election and Christmas is the prime time to schedule a media-friendly disaster. . . . It is a safe bet that the agencies will do their best again this year.

It was a somewhat cynical analysis, and some staff in relief NGOs said so. They argued that, over the previous two years, agencies had absorbed many lessons, and that critiques such as *Humanitarianism Unbound* (African Rights, 1994a) no longer held good. Some relief workers had indeed taken much of the criticism to heart: their understandings and motives were not in question. But the institutional capacity of humanitarian organizations to change remained open to challenge.

The war in eastern Zaire

Since their flight to Zaire in July 1994, the Hutu extremist forces had been planning their return to power and the completion of the genocide of the Tutsis. They had done so from the safety of EDP camps, notably Mugunga, near Goma. The extremists levied a 15 per cent 'war tax' on all rations received by the EDPs, in addition to receiving rations themselves and diverting unknown amounts (unpublished UN Report, September 1996). As they reorganized, the killing campaign against Rwandese Tutsis was stepped up; by early 1996, dozens of survivors and witnesses of the genocide were being killed each week in incursions from Zaire (African Rights, 1996). The extremists also extended their campaign to eastern Zaire, where Zaireans of Tutsi origin were killed, mutilated or expelled from their land. A series of killings at Masisi, west of Goma, in early 1996 proved a turning point: several hundred Zaireans of Tutsi origin were massacred without international protest. Other Zaireans suffered as well.

---

[2]*The Observer*, 20 October 1996. A sub-editor gave the article the misleading title, 'Sorry St Bob, It's time we banned aid'.

Western diplomats and aid agencies recognized that the political and human rights problems of the region could not be resolved until the extremist militia were separated from the wider EDP population. In 1995, some half-hearted attempts were made to enforce this, using the Zairean army. But the extremists bribed the soldiers, and by 1996, the Zairean army had become a partner in the ethnic cleansing of eastern Zaire. This element of the extremists' strategy contained the seeds of their own downfall, however: Zaireans of Tutsi origin took up arms. In early October, the deputy governor of South Kivu ordered that all Tutsis should leave the country within a week. 'For those of them who defy the order . . . [they] will be exterminated and expelled.'[3] This was the spark for a rapid rebel offensive, and their armed struggle quickly spread to encompass a coalition of other anti-government forces in the region. They received support from the governments of Rwanda and Burundi, and sympathy more widely in the region and beyond.

As the offensive gathered pace it began to threaten French interests. France already believed it had 'lost' Rwanda from the francophone bloc, and was in the process of losing Burundi. Zaire was the greatest prize, and there was now the prospect of the fiercely anti-French rebel leader Laurent Kabila overrunning eastern Zaire, at a time when President Mobutu was on the point of physical and political demise. Loyalty to old friends has been a consistent feature of French policy in Africa: it is wedded to notions of the prestige of *la francophonie* and global influence rather than material interests as such (Chipman, 1989). In addition, the French Government was not eager for evidence about its past role in Rwanda to come to light. The task of the troops would have been to 'stabilize' the situation – in other words, prevent the defeat and demise of old friends. But sending in troops unilaterally was difficult: a pretext and a diplomatically acceptable mechanism were needed.

The humanitarian pretext

The French Government used humanitarian need as the pretext for its mission, which it presented as a purely humanitarian enterprise to save a million refugees from starving to death. This was a shameless fabrication, but it nearly worked. As the Zairean rebels advanced, a series of EDP camps were overrun and the *interahamwe* defeated and driven out. Aid workers were evacuated from Bukavu on 22 October. The militia and former Rwandese army concentrated in Mugunga, the largest camp, which was quickly surrounded by the rebel forces. The last international aid agencies withdrew.

Until the moment of withdrawal, the EDPs had been very well cared for by African refugee standards. They had received regular rations (the

<hr>

[3]Lwasi Ngabo Lwabanji, quoted in Chris McGreal, 'Trapped in a bloody triangle of terror', *The Guardian*, 21 October 1996.

last two weeks' worth of rations were distributed just days before the agencies withdrew), and had excellent water and sanitation systems. The camps had become cities, with a thriving economic life. As elsewhere in the continent, the camp residents had developed their own coping strategies: some had acquired land (by various means including violence), others were engaged in petty commerce. The EDPs had never been counted: it is probable that the total numbers were inflated, so that the payment of the 'war tax' and diversion did not affect the adequacy of the general ration. Over the years, enough has been learned of coping strategies during food shortages to be confident that the EDPs would survive with little difficulty, at least for a month or more, whether they remained in the camps or dispersed to the surrounding villages and forests.

The French Foreign Minister, Hervé de Charette, preferred to describe the situation in the following terms: 'Perhaps the most disastrous humanitarian crisis the world has seen'.[4] Some of France's allies in the international community echoed the sentiment. Emma Bonino, European Commissioner for Humanitarian Affairs, was first off the mark: 'Five hundred thousand people today, probably a million in a few days, are dying of hunger'.[5] Boutros Boutros-Ghali introduced a legal innovation: 'We are facing, let me call it, genocide by starvation'.[6] Sadako Ogata of UNHCR said she feared 'a catastrophe greater than the one we knew in 1994'.[7] Catherine Bertini of the World Food Programme was the least pessimistic, 'People are already starting to die and we estimate that by the end of the month over 80,000 children under three will die'.[8]

For their own reasons, the private aid agencies were already drumming up the crisis. 'Aid was needed yesterday. The situation is shaping up to be genocide by disease,' one MSF doctor said.[9] An MSF advertisement stated, 'For the people in Goma, as well as the hundreds of thousands of refugees out of reach of the [single MSF relief] convoy, the situation becomes more desperate by the hour'.[10] Oxfam said that 'Up to one million people in Eastern Zaire are dying from starvation and disease',[11] and 'Starvation, thirst and disease will kill them, even if the

[4]Speaking on the BBC, 8 November 1996.

[5]Quoted in Stephan Buckley, 'Disaster in Making', *International Herald Tribune*, 30 October 1996.

[6]Press conference at the UN, 8 November 1996.

[7]Quoted in Chris McGreal, 'Fearful flight from Zaire', *The Guardian*, 28 October 1996.

[8]Quoted in 'UN calls for food corridors to save 80,000 starving children', *The Guardian*, 8 November 1996.

[9]Quoted in Mary Braid, 'UN stalls over Zaire nightmare', *The Independent on Sunday*, 10 November 1996.

[10]'Yesterday, he was beyond help. Today is a new day', MSF advertisement in *The Independent*, 12 November 1996.

[11]'Oxfam: Save lives in Central Africa', advertisement in *The Independent*, 10 November 1996.

bullets don't'.[12] CARE said 'Over one million lives are at risk'.[13] Even the Save the Children Fund, one of the few large agencies that was most level-headed during November 1996 (it did not call for military intervention), ran a commercial that began: 'The crisis in Central Africa threatens to become the worst this century'.[14] Almost every large agency joined in.

Many journalists bought the line. Others' scepticism was watered down by editors, who ran inflammatory headlines. The distinction between people 'at risk' and 'about to die' became blurred to vanishing point. When a doctor reported cholera in a camp of 250,000 people, newspaper headlines ran: 'Cholera epidemic "could wipe out 250,000" '.[15] (The following day's denials got almost no attention.)

No agencies or journalists were present in eastern Zaire: the claims were based on no evidence at all. If true, they would have represented death rates of a level wholly unprecedented in demographic history. For one million people all to die in two months requires death rates more than seven times as high as the worst mortality levels recorded in camps during the 1983–5 famine in Ethiopia. Even for 80,000 to die in three weeks implies the worst-case scenario of the entire EDP population suffering those levels of mortality: an unparalleled deterioration in health and nutrition. The latter is the hypothetical limit of reasonable pessimism or defensible exaggeration, and most relief agencies went an order of magnitude beyond it. In short, any nutritionist or demographer with five minutes to consider the evidence would have concluded that the numbers were wild exaggerations.

This was compounded by a confusion – in some cases deliberate – about the political and human rights dimensions of the crisis. Boutros Ghali insidiously counterposed the 1994 genocide of the Rwandese Tutsis with the genocide by starvation of the Hutu refugees. Relief workers implied that the Zairean rebels were planning or carrying out a genocide aimed at the Hutu EDPs. With an ominous echo, Oxfam and MSF wrote that 'Unless security is secured on the ground in a matter of days, the refugee question of Central Africa will have found its final solution'.[16] The term 'refugee' was universally used, in some cases conjoined to the claim that the camp residents should enjoy political asylum and that attacking a refugee camp was an abrogation of the Geneva Conventions.[17] (Under international law, refugee camps should

---

[12]'Oxfam: Tragedy in Eastern Zaire', advertisement in *The Guardian*, 5 November 1996.

[13]'Central African emergency', CARE advertisement in *The Guardian*, 9 November 1996.

[14]'Central Africa: Frightened children need your help', SCF advertisement in *The Guardian*, 11 November 1996.

[15]*The Guardian*, 13 November 1996.

[16]David Bryer, Director of Oxfam, and Anne-Marie Huby, Executive Director of MSF-UK, 'Dead Refugees cannot be Saved', Open letter to Prime Minister, John Major, 8 November 1996.

[17]E.g. David Welch, Concern, speaking on BBC Radio Scotland, 'Speak Out', 14 November 1995.

be demilitarized: the EDP camps, of course, were not.) The ethics and politics of the crisis were blurred, even inverted.

The call for intervention

France needed a diplomatically acceptable way to send its troops to Zaire. This meant gaining the consent of the US Government and the Organization of African Unity. American co-operation could not be contemplated until after the 5 November Presidential election. The ground was prepared in the previous fortnight,[18] and on the day of the election itself, the French diplomatic campaign began in earnest. The first move was to persuade the Kenyan Government to propose at a special one-day OAU summit that Zaire be permitted to invite European Union (i.e. mainly French) troops in. Other African governments, notably Ethiopia (outgoing chairman of the OAU), objected. To avoid splitting the OAU, the matter was referred to the UN Security Council.

Two days later, Boutros Ghali salvaged the proposal at the UN, but discussions were slow. Under pressure (over EU business), the British Government swallowed its scepticism and agreed to participate. Then the Canadian Government unexpectedly took up the cause, when Prime Minister Jean-Pierre Chrétien became personally enthused. The Canadian military was anxious to redeem its international reputation after the scandal of abuses by its soldiers in Somalia. Finally, under intense domestic and foreign pressure, the US agreed. But all this took much longer than the French wanted: in the meantime their clients were losing the war.

On 4 November, Jacques de Miliano, the vice-president of MSF-International, spearheaded the call for military intervention. Oxfam followed immediately. Both agencies dissociated themselves from the French initiative: they pointedly criticized Operation Turquoise and said that a force would have to disarm the extremists.[19] But, overall, their demand gave humanitarian credentials and political momentum to the French plan. Others, notably Refugees International and InterAction, joined the chorus.

Western generals knew exactly what disarming the *interahamwe* or separating them from civilians would entail – fighting a war – and had no intention of doing so. It was naive to suppose that any UN force would take on such a mandate. John Dinger, speaking on behalf of the US State Department, said that the force would work with the extremists for their mutual 'humanitarian interests'.[20] Others spoke of

---

[18]'Situation d'urgence à l'est du Zaïre', *Le Monde*, 23 October 1996; 'Zaïre: demain l'apocalypse: L'impuissance internationale et l'offensive du Rwanda annoncent une catastrophe humanitaire', *Liberation*, 31 October 1996. A French government minister first publicly floated the idea of intervention on 3 November 1996.
[19]Oxfam press release, 13 November 1996.
[20]Speaking on BBC Radio, 'The World Tonight', 13 November 1996.

'stabilizing' the situation: the force would establish a ceasefire and negotiate with the extremists. This would have recreated the status quo in the camps and made the problem more intractable, while the killings continued. It was exactly the same formula that would have prolonged the genocide in 1994, had it been implemented then. When the forces mandate was announced, no relief agency publicly revoked its support for intervention: they merely re-iterated their futile hopes of what it might achieve.

The crisis is resolved

Fortunately, the EDP crisis was resolved before any international troops could arrive. On the announcement of UN approval of the intervention, the Zairean rebels broke their ceasefire, advanced on the extremists' base at Mugunga, and in a brief but fierce battle, scored a decisive victory. The *interahamwe* fled to the hills. Their military plan succeeded. About 600,000 EDPs decided *en masse* to return to Rwanda. They had survived the aid cut-off with little difficulty, and now took matters into their own hands, contradicting the agencies' portrayal of complete helplessness.

As the EDPs abandoned Mugunga, surprised journalists reported on their nutritional status: there were no signs at all of starvation. There were some old, sick or wounded people, but the returnees showed little sign of malnutrition, let alone starvation. Though there were certainly some deaths, there was no evidence that overall death rates had risen. Even the most optimistic predictions were proving pessimistic; arguably, there was no humanitarian disaster at all. 'We have been very lucky,' was the aid agencies' response.[21] It would have been more honest to have said, 'We were wrong: we should have known better'. Either, it was a spectacular failure of competence in nutritional and demographic science compounded by a failure of political intelligence, or it had been a highly cynical exercise throughout.

A process of covering tracks then began. Some aid staff argued that the fitter people would arrive in Rwanda first and the starving would be at the back of the long queue: 'What we are witnessing is the survival of the fittest', claimed the MSF press officer. There were no starving people at the back. The few cases of suspected cholera and malnutrition were seized upon. Most absurdly, the claim was made that the extremists had fled Mugunga because they feared the arrival of the international troops.[22] A former French minister blamed the relief agencies, accusing them of 'lying'.[23] The French role too was scrutinized. By 19 November,

[21]Anne-Marie Huby, MSF speaking on BBC Radio 5, 16 November 1996.

[22]Phil Bloomer, Oxfam, speaking on BBC Radio 4 'Today', 16 November 1996.

[23]Pierre Mesmer, quoted in Joseph Fitchett, 'Zaire crisis easing, France takes heat for sounding alarm', *International Herald Tribune*, 19 November 1996.

the idea of an intervention force with a combat mandate had been abandoned.

A new numbers game then started over how many EDPs were 'missing' or 'unaccounted' for in Kivu. Estimates ranged from zero (the Rwandese and US Governments) to 750,000 (UNHCR and some NGOs). Agencies still called for military intervention; some accused those who disputed the high figures of racism.[24] In mid-December, UNICEF raised the alarm that vast numbers would die before Christmas. The reality was that some – an estimated 120,000–150,000 – were the routed extremist army and its camp followers, who scarcely warranted the privileges extended to refugees. About 100,000 others duly turned up in Western parts of South Kivu, who by February 1997 were suffering high rates of malnutrition. For this discussion what is more significant is that relief agencies, whose claims for EDP camps such as Mugunga had been disproven just days before, continued to use exactly the same strategy: huge figures, the use of words such as 'refugee' without nuance, and appeals for military intervention. Two elements were notable by their absence. One was the near-total failure to mention the needs of the local Zairean population, many of whom were displaced, impoverished and hungry on account of the war and the depredations of the extremists. The second was a failure to recognize that the prospects for gaining relief access were being undermined by the publicity strategy and especially by the call for military intervention. Kabila was unlikely to agree to foreign agencies' plans while they were so openly accomplices in a military strategy designed to halt his advance. Hence the over-dramatized humanitarian narrative impeded the prospects for doing what was needed.

Implications for the humanitarians

The crisis in eastern Zaire in November 1996 is likely to prove a seminal event in modern humanitarianism. It presents some major challenges for disaster relief agencies. First, the hopes for massive fund-raising were not fulfilled. Although major donors did provide more resources for Rwanda and Zaire programmes, this was no salvation for agencies highly reliant on emergency fund-raising. Secondly, it was a test of the credibility of the disaster relief agencies' commitment to reform. The encouraging signs of internal debate and admission of mistakes had raised hopes. In this case, at least, the hopes were dashed.

At the outset of the crisis, at least one aid worker, speaking anonymously, welcomed the opportunity: 'the absence of television cameras in the cut-off camps might mean this time that short-term

[24]Nick Stockton, 'Rwanda, Rights and Racism', paper presented at VOICE/ECHO forum, Dublin, December 1996.

decisions about the crisis will be avoided and a more lasting solution found'. He continued: 'People will undoubtedly die. But perhaps this time we will get a proper solution. Hard decisions must be taken.'[25] But these lessons and options appeared to be forgotten the moment one agency (in this case, MSF) had seized the initiative with apocalyptic predictions and the call for military intervention. For the fund-raisers and chief executives of other agencies, the priority was not so much how to provide for needy people in Zaire, but how to manage the challenge thrown down by MSF, and the publicity and fund-raising opportunity this entailed. The humanitarian Greshams Law functioned: the most dramatic characterization prevailed. Most major agencies rather dramatically failed the test of their commitment to reform, notably MSF, Oxfam, and all the UN specialized agencies.

The crisis revealed hard humanitarian interests in stark form. Relief agencies called for 'political solutions' and mentioned the limitations on their own roles. But their characterization of the crisis impeded any such solution. The Zairean rebels' offensive was an imminent solution to the problem of the *interahamwe*, and some agency staff privately welcomed it. Publicly, everything the agencies did worked against the offensive achieving its aim. The exaggeration ('a million dead by Christmas') drew Western public attention to the crisis, but implicitly demanded extreme measures (such as military intervention) that were incompatible with any realistic political solution.

The agencies called for military intervention: this had elements of institutional self-interest. Large emergency-oriented agencies have become so dependent on government money that they can no longer act on the basis of public subscription alone: they need commitments from governments before going in. This means engaging governments' interest. Calling for military intervention is an ideal way of doing this: if the government sends troops, it will also want to spend money on relief, and if it does not send troops, it will want to justify this by saying it is supporting relief efforts. Aid agency lobbyists may not think so cynically, but there can be no doubt that their hard interests cloud their judgement.

In conclusion, the crisis in Zaire was the beginnings of a solution for the residents of central Africa, but an unprecedented crisis of credibility for the disaster relief agencies. Events on the ground in eastern Zaire were not out of control: rapid political progress was being made (albeit by military means), at remarkably low human cost. It was the disaster relief agencies that were out of control, and they nearly succeeded in inflicting the disaster they were predicting on eastern Zaire.

[25]Anonymous aid worker quoted by Mary Braid, 'France urges EU to intervene in Zaire', *The Independent*, 4 November 1996.

11

Political Contracts & Humanitarian Dilemmas

The last fifteen years or so have not been good for famine prevention in Africa. Robust successes based on political contracts have been exceptional. Successful models seem more remote than they were in the 1970s. But there should be no pieties about a 'return' to benevolent state-led public policy and cohesive communal mobilization; in most cases these are chimera, and always were. Neither should there be calls for universalistic templates for political or economic reform. No grand formulas for 'democratization' or 'development' have yet worked in Africa.

The first step towards freedom is to recognize the inevitable. At least for the coming decade, the prospects of dramatic economic growth and inclusive political contracts are remote. Governments have a tendency towards authoritarianism; it is rare to see strong and consistent pressures resisting this. Neo-liberal economic reforms are unlikely to be reversed. The erosion of state-provided public services will not be halted. Where war economies based on asset-stripping have become entrenched, they will probably remain so. Western governments are becoming less and less interested in sub-Saharan Africa and more ready to find pretexts for non-involvement. Media coverage is declining in both quality and quantity. Humanitarian agencies are reluctant to change. Their stock remains remarkably high with Western governments and the donating public, and pressure for radical reform is still a minority concern.

In short, a general overview indicates that there are no easy solutions to hand. But a wide focus is misleadingly pessimistic: signs of optimism are evident only when the focus shifts to become more local and specific. By its nature, popular accountability involves responding to such local and specific pressures.

A political agenda in Africa

The conclusions of this book are primarily addressed to African citizens and politicians. It is the abdication of responsibility for fighting famines by most African leaders – albeit under pressure and with no clear alternatives – that has made possible the slide into the current impasse. If there are to be successful future initiatives to conquer famine in Africa, they must come from African citizens. This is not because Africans have some deep understanding of the mysteries of Africa that is denied to outsiders, or that foreign ideas are irredeemably alien or inappropriate, but because it is only through forms of popular accountability and political contract that famine will be conquered. Such accountability and political contract cannot be implanted, let alone imposed, from outside (though they can be supported from outside). People must mobilize and impose their own political priorities. They must seize moral ownership of the issues. They may do this through resistance to outside domination, possibly including resistance to philanthropic imperialism. Solutions cannot come from anyone other than Africans themselves. This book has given some instances of this happening. Sadly, they are too few and too fragile, but they are better than what is on offer from Washington, New York, Geneva or London. Famine in Africa can be defeated by Africans and only by Africans.

This returns us to the analytical heart of this book: the notion of political contract against famine. The right to be free from famine is socially and historically determined and politically negotiated. There is no single route to this. Empirically, guarantees of liberal civil and political rights assist freedom from famine. Once people have the right to assemble, freedom of information, and can remove a government by democratic means, it is probable that they will then guarantee that their basic interests are looked after. But it is not certain: famine must be politicized, minorities must be represented, and technical capacity must exist.

The internationalization of responsibility for fighting famine is not a positive development. It has given both an unprecedented hegemony and a large measure of practical power to institutions that are remote and unaccountable. The challenge is to reverse this process.

'Africanizing' responsibility for famine might seem another pious naiveté: nice as rhetoric but impractical. Worse, it might seem to give *carte blanche* to authoritarian African governments with spurious claims to authenticity – such as the Sudan Government, which masks its own ethical bankruptcy with denunciations of Western imperialist plots. It need not be so. Responsibility can be re-localized in the context of pressures to forge political contracts. Creating this pressure is the task for Africans concerned with human rights, democratic accountability and freedom from famine. It requires political mobilization. The famine-vulnerable are a numerous but politically weak constituency. Many of them are ethnic or political minorities. Organizing them is a challenge, which is different in each country.

A central (if often implicit) theme of this book is that the concept of a right to be free from famine can be a mobilizing principle. Freedom from famine can be a right that can be legitimately asserted and successfully won. Many tactics suggest themselves to further this strategy. It is improbable that famine-vulnerable people themselves have enough leadership, cohesion or clout to form an effective political bloc. Alliances with others will be necessary. In turn, this requires making famine an issue of concern to those who are not directly affected: treating its prevention as a barometer of political legitimacy, and its occurrence as a political scandal. Tactics can include more public engagement in the processes that can prevent, warn of and relieve famine, and demanding commissions of inquiry into political culpability when famines have struck. A more modest proposal, attractive to those who are reluctant to move directly into the political arena, is the appointment of an ombudsman for professional standards. Important in their own right, the actions of an ombudsman would also begin to point towards political responsibilities for famine prevention.

A donor agenda

The re-localization of responsibility for famine is not a pretext for Western governments to desist from activities that can have a beneficial impact (debt forgiveness, for example). Western governments are more often than not accomplices in famine – more interested in managing (or containing) famines and refugee crises than solving them.

Again, it would be easy to compile a list of grand proposals for political action, economic reform and technical improvement. The following list is more modest, concerned with establishing some basic principles and setting up structures to increase accountability that should, by their very existence, create pressures for progressive reform.

Two pieces of legal symbolism could be important. One is an expansion of the mandate of the international criminal tribunal to cover the investigation of famine crimes. Currently the tribunal is focusing only on crimes committed in former Yugoslavia and Rwanda, and – especially in view of its faltering progress – it is unrealistic to expect it to take on a much wider mandate. But a statement that its remit expressly includes violations of laws of war that create starvation and famine would be a significant symbolic step. The second is a clear commitment to bringing back the supremacy of international humanitarian law: the Security Council should stop bestowing impunity on international forces and humanitarians. Humanitarianism is about much more than delivering food and medicine: it is about respecting and, where possible, enforcing the letter and spirit of the 1948 Genocide Convention, the 1949 Geneva Conventions and the 1951 Refugee Convention, among others.

Donors have recognized the need for improved regulation and professionalism in relief operations. It is important that this translates into institutional structures that improve accountability rather than intensify the elitism of the citadel of expertise. Donors have a clear interest in ensuring that their money is well spent. Aid bureaucracies also have professional pride at stake in their effectiveness. To be effective, the privatization of international social welfare needs to have a more rigorous regulatory authority, to ensure minimum standards of professionalism, co-ordination and assessment for those organizations that receive public funds. It also needs a more open tendering procedure that allows local organizations, local government departments and commercial service providers to compete fairly with international NGOs.

It will be difficult for foreign organizations to submit themselves to genuinely rigorous forms of local accountability to recipients. An important step can be taken, however: improving transparency. The most obvious form this can take is the appointment of some sort of international famine relief commissioner with quasi-judicial powers to examine the records of international organizations and all others who have been involved in any relief operation.

It is self-interest that ultimately drives Western governments. Embarrassment at the hands of the media and voluntary organizations may intermittently cause tactical policy shifts, but rarely a fundamental reorientation. The basic Western agenda is towards disengagement from sub-Saharan Africa. In most respects this is welcome, and an essential precondition for re-localizing political responsibilities. But some forms of Western involvement will continue, and continue to cause problems: for example, demands for repayment of debts, manipulation of the world markets for agricultural goods, aggressive sale of armaments. The idea of simply letting crises in Africa 'burn themselves out' as though they were forest fires is neither realistic nor moral (Slim, 1996: 10); the metaphor is inaccurate as conflicts can continue without Western involvement. Even a writer like Robert Kaplan, whose writings are widely credited with encouraging the US Administration's unwillingness to intervene in Rwanda, argues that the West cannot cut itself off from trouble-stricken regions of Africa (Kaplan, 1996). The profusion of international interest in mechanisms for conflict prevention and resolution attests to the West's growing concern that the human embers of faraway conflicts can be blown across the world and ignite problems at home. This is not a charter for routine intervention or involvement. Conflicts in Africa can have local solutions, military or political: it can be better to do nothing.

Western governments and their electorates *do* have a fundamental interest in not merely containing crises in Africa, but solving them. That interest should, logically, compel governments to scrutinize the mechanisms currently employed for containing crises – principally the humanitarian international – and initiate major reform. But, without domestic pressure, this is unlikely to come about. This is where Western humanitarians and the agendas of human rights activists can be most constructive.

A humanitarian agenda

Contemporary international humanitarianism works, but not for famine-vulnerable people in Africa. High-profile 'debased' humanitarianism works to extend the institutional reach of relief agencies, to create an attractive narrative for the media and to provide a political alibi for Western governments. The future of famine prevention does *not* lie with today's international relief agencies, until they have been radically reformed. On the contrary, while fighting famine remains entrusted to today's humanitarian international, famine will continue.

It is tempting simply to ignore the professional humanitarians in the conclusion of this book. But, while international humanitarian agencies remain in business, they should not be ignored. They are self-proclaimed agents of change within the international system: while this role is over-stated, it has been the case in the past and can potentially become so again. Some humanitarians are more amenable to persuasion than the media, Western foreign ministries and aid departments, African governments and military commanders. (Many are not.) But three caveats are in order. One, we should not overestimate the power of humanitarian agencies: though more visible, their influence is less than that of arms manufacturers, civil servants in donor treasuries and a host of others. Two, we should be careful not to reinforce the humanitarians' moral ownership of other people's suffering and the legitimacy of their intrusion into other societies. Three, we should not mistake vigorous debate by middle management and public policy researchers for real institutional reform: the humanitarian international is a master at *appearing* to change, and the emergency fund-raising culture remains robust. The director of Children's Aid Direct, replying to criticisms of his agency's fund-raising methods (see Chapter 9), moaned: 'Don't knock a campaign that seeks to maximise public awareness, that has six seconds to do its work . . . Don't knock the massive good that aid achieves. . . .'[1] While such attitudes persist, 'knocking' aid will always be justified. The November 1996 'crisis' in eastern Zaire, coming after

[1]David Grubb, 'Don't knock the benefits of aid', letter to *The Observer*, 3 November 1996. The following week, CAD began a high-profile marketing campaign on the crisis in eastern Zaire.

two years of supposed internal reform in aid agencies, showed just how little had actually changed.

International disaster relief organizations face real dilemmas as to which direction to move in. The basic option is between being public service contractors (the 'third force' path) and trying to be embodiments of citizens' moral sense (the 'first force'). Both these options are acceptable in different ways: the middle way, of continuing in ambiguity, is not. Counterfeiting thrives on the ambiguity, and agency identity moves closer to manifestations of the Victorian charity ethic than to concern with genuinely serving the poor and marginalized.

Public service contracting and professional standards
At a technical and managerial level, disaster relief can be treated as a public service provision like any other. Public service providers – state-run or private, charitable or commercial, local or international – are necessary for famine prevention and relief. International NGOs have an obvious role here, subject to reforms. Probably, as in the 'development' arena, international agencies will find it hard to compete with local agencies, government departments and commercial companies. As discussed above, professional standards and proper co-ordination can be established through regulation, and adherence to standards can be investigated and enforced by an ombudsman or relief commissioner.

The difficulties with a regulatory framework are political. One objection is that it would destroy the voluntary ethos. This is absurd. If a voluntary agency does not want to co-ordinate with others or be obliged to meet minimum standards, then it should not receive public funds or provide essential public services. More seriously, regulation would prove retrogressive if it meant putting more power in the hands of unaccountable, repressive or self-aggrandizing institutions. Regulation by General Omer al Bashir or the UN Secretariat is highly undesirable. The problem lies not with regulation as such, but with the nature of the authority that controls it: the challenge of regulation is inseparable from the political context of humanitarian action. (This problem often shrinks under scrutiny. It is precisely where no progressive and accountable authorities exist – or they have no power – that unregulated humanitarianism is allowed or encouraged. Debased humanitarianism flourishes on political decay in recipient countries. Similarly, the most inefficient international donors are the least able to regulate, and the most debased agencies are the most resistant to regulation.)

There is a similar challenge for formerly state-provided public services, as reformed under neo-liberal auspices. The problem is not the privatization of welfare provision as such, but the decline of political accountability that has accompanied structural adjustment. The key is to establish a regulatory framework that is accountable to famine-vulnerable people, or at least transparent to them.

Where a political contract against famine exists, the task is relatively straightforward. Foreign humanitarians should respect the contract by allowing popularly accountable institutions to regulate relief activity. They should support it by material resources and political advocacy. The successes of the Botswana Drought Relief Programme and ERA and REST were all founded on such political contracts. Public service provision under the aegis of such an authority can be both technically effective and politically progressive.

Supporting the struggle for political contract
As a rule, humanitarian successes are attributable to discreet professional operations that run under the aegis of accountable local institutions. Cases from Eritrea, Tigray and Somalia have been detailed. When a local organization is accountable – in a social or political sense – to the people, then international organizations can be confident that it will regulate their activities in an acceptable way. For the international agency, this may mean foregoing publicity and being unable to claim the credit. Formal financial accounting may be more difficult under such circumstances: it is the task of international organizations to turn the social accountability of the local organization into the formal accountability required by donors.

This is where long-term solutions lie. It is fine as rhetoric, and a salutary reminder of priorities. But putting it into practice is more of a challenge. Can humanitarians support an incipient political contract? Can they act on behalf of famine-prone people and create pressures for political contract?

This depends on two factors. One is the kind of agency. They should be of the 'first force' citizens' movement kind, rather than being service contractors; they should be ready to work in an explicitly political manner. The political character of the agency is crucial. Agencies that are wedded to an ethos based on drama and self-publicity have no serious contribution to make. Those embedded in more thoughtful and politically progressive constituencies, ready to act without publicity from a sense of solidarity, can do a great deal.

Secondly, it depends on local circumstances; there must be local organizations with a progressive social agenda. It is rare that there is no opportunity at all to press for some sort of political contract. Northern Sudan under the National Islamic Front is one such case, but even here there are institutions that will outlast the current regime and can lay the foundations of a future contract. The danger is to support such an institution, and then become trapped as it becomes ineffective or co-opted. Strict rules are needed to counteract the tendencies to preserve programmes under all circumstances. There is also a danger that 'political progressiveness' will become another fashionable criterion to be bandied about to justify funding programmes.

Genuine political contracts tend to emerge where there is little or no aid. An aid relationship makes it much more difficult for people to forge political contracts: aid corrupts. Involvement under these circumstances is a matter of good political judgement, and rather few agencies have shown themselves consistently capable of this. The dangers are at least as great as the benefits that can be gained: the burden of proof should be on those who advocate support.

Where there is no political contract
Unfortunately cases of established or incipient political contracts are rare. Far more common are cases where there is no political contract (especially in civil war). This is the growth area for the humanitarian international: less able to compete in 'development' or peacetime relief under the auspices of African governments, international NGOs and UN agencies are driven to precisely the places where no political contracts exist, and hence there is little or no regulation or competition. These are the places where the ethical challenges are greatest, and the political dangers of ill-conceived advocacy (such as calling for Western military intervention) are most serious.

It is morally unacceptable to allow people to suffer and die on the grounds that relieving their suffering will support an obnoxious government or army. The big question is therefore: Can humanitarian agencies save lives in the absence of any form of political contract? Can they act in a technically proficient and politically inoffensive way, while others struggle to create political contracts or resolve political crises?

This is much, much harder than it sounds. Most relief agencies would argue that this is precisely what they do now and have done all along. But claims to being neutral or politically inoffensive can no longer be taken at face value. Major changes are essential if this mode of action is to be possible: things must *not* continue as at present.

There are some basic rules that would minimize the political damage done by contemporary humanitarian intrusion. Success would be much easier with a more accurate and sensitive international press and an end to the readiness of politicians to use humanitarianism as an alibi. Regulatory and investigatory schemas are essential.

But the humanitarians cannot escape responsibility for taking some far-reaching initiatives. The following three rules are more to do with the representation of humanitarian action than with the action itself. The first is: do not obscure power relations. In other words, be frank that relief agencies are service contractors to Western donors, are pursuing their own institutional interests and are implicitly supporting the host authorities. The second is, do not claim to have long-term solutions. Do not speak about 'justice' or 'long-term development', and still less make any claims that current humanitarian activity is helping to achieve these goals. The third is, do not seek the media limelight. A high media profile risks the severe danger that humanitarian action will be misrepresented, for example it will be inflated, distorted or used as an alibi by donors. Once relief is 'mediatized', there is little space for the kinds of political action required. It is simple hypocrisy to make a claim that one million people will die unless aid is provided, and then complain that no coherent political action is forthcoming.

In war, the rules established by the ICRC have proved their value. The reasons why they are being discarded are not to do with their intrinsic value, but because they are incompatible with the publicity-seeking humanitarianism that generates funds. There are some specific changes to the ICRC's rules that are in order – for example, how to respond in cases of genocide – but the overall framework remains as valid as ever. In particular, the rule that aid should not be provided where there is a reasonable chance of a belligerent party obtaining substantial material advantage from it should be reinstated.

These are relatively straightforward rules that should not deter the honest service provider. But the twin requirements of regulation and modest publicity will have far-reaching implications. Deprived of impunity and the capacity to invent their own rules, and the ability to inflate the record, the humanitarians will no longer be subject to their Gresham's Law to anything like the same degree. This will mean that many agencies will not survive in their current form.

Telling the truth
In *La Peste*, Albert Camus puts the following words in the mouth of Dr Rieux: 'It's not a matter of heroism, it's a matter of honesty. It's an idea that may seem laughable, but the only way of fighting the plague is honesty.' The same is true of fighting famine.

The greatest harm done by the humanitarian international is to create delusion. Western governments and donating publics are deluded into believing the fairy tale that their aid can solve profound political problems, when it cannot. The humanitarians deceive themselves about their own importance. Most significantly, local people ('recipients' or 'beneficiaries') are deluded into believing that salvation can come from other than their own actions. Some tangible material benefits (many fewer than are commonly believed) are delivered, but at the cost of sustaining this tremendous, institutionalized delusion. Meanwhile, the real reasons why people survive and conquer famine are obscured.

The minimum duty of the humanitarian is therefore to tell the truth. The problem of famine will be solved by political action, and humanitarians must never hint otherwise, nor allow their existence or actions to be used to imply otherwise. They must not inflate the marginal contribution they make to saving lives and livelihoods. Any humanitarian agency that cannot survive on this basis should die, and famine-vulnerable Africans will not regret its passing.

Aall, Cato, 1970, 'Relief, Nutrition and Health Problems in the Nigerian/Biafran War', *Journal of Tropical Paediatrics* 16: 70–90.

Africa Watch, 1990, 'Sudan: Nationwide Famine', *News from Africa Watch*, November.

Africa Watch, 1991, *Evil Days: Thirty Years of War and Famine in Ethiopia*. London: Africa Watch.

African Rights, 1993a, *Somalia: Operation Restore Hope: A Preliminary Assessment*. London: African Rights, May.

African Rights, 1993b, *Somalia: Human Rights Abuses by the United Nations Forces*. London: African Rights, July.

African Rights, 1993c, *Land Tenure, the Creation of Famine and Prospects for Peace in Somalia*. London: African Rights Discussion Paper No. 1, October.

African Rights, 1994a, *Humanitarianism Unbound? Current Dilemmas Facing Multi-Mandate Relief Operations in Political Emergencies*. London: African Rights Discussion Paper No. 4, November.

African Rights, 1994b, *Rwanda: Death, Despair and Defiance*. London: African Rights, September.

African Rights, 1995a, *Sudan's Invisible Citizens: The Policy of Abuse against Displaced People in the North*. London: African Rights, February.

African Rights, 1995b, *Facing Genocide: The Nuba of Sudan*. London: African Rights, July.

African Rights, 1996, *Killing the Evidence: Murder, Arrests and Intimidation of Survivors and Witnesses*. London: African Rights, April.

African Rights, 1997, *Food and Power in Sudan: A Critique of Humanitarianism*. London: African Rights, May.

al Turabi, Hassan, 1983, 'The Islamic State', in John L. Esposito (ed.), *Voices of Resurgent Islam*. New York: Oxford University Press.

Alagiah, George, 1992, 'A Necessary Intrusion', *The Independent on Sunday*, 23 August.

Alemayehu Lirenso, 1987, *Grain Marketing and Pricing in Ethiopia: A Study of the Impact of Grain Quota and Fixed Grain Prices on Grain Producers*. Addis Ababa: Institute of Development Research.

Alemneh Dejene, 1990, *Environment, Famine, and Politics in Ethiopia: A View from the Village*. Boulder, CO: Lynne Rienner.

Allen, Charles A., 1989, 'Civilian Starvation and Relief during Armed Conflict: The Modern Humanitarian Law', *Georgia Journal of International and Comparative Law* 19: 1–85.

Ambirajan, S., 1976, 'Malthusian Population Policy and Indian Famine Policy in the Nineteenth Century', *Population Studies* 30: 5–14.

Amnesty International, 1989, *Sudan: Human Rights Violations in the Context of Civil War.* London: Amnesty International, December.

Archer, Robert, 1994, 'Markets and Good Government', in Andrew Clayton (ed.), *Governance, Democracy and Conditionality: What Role for NGOs?* Oxford: Intrac.

Arnold, David, 1988, Famine: Social Crisis and Historical Change. Oxford: Blackwell.

Article 19, 1990, *Starving in Silence: A Report on Famine and Censorship.* London: Article 19.

Asante, Kofi, Coultan, Vince, Davies, Rick and Laskey, Charles, 1991, *A Report of the Assessment Mission to Mogadishu, Hiran, Bay, Middle Shebelle and Lower Shebelle Regions.* London: Inter-NGO Committee for Somalia.

Askin, Steve, 1987, 'Food Aid Diversion', *Middle East Report*, March–April: 38–40.

Autier, P., 1988, 'Nutrition Assessment through the Use of a Nutritional Scoring System', *Disasters* 12: 70–80.

Balsvik, Randi Rönning, 1985, *Haile Selassie's Students: The Intellectual and Social Background to Revolution, 1952–1977.* East Lansing, MI: Michigan State University Press.

Bantje, Hans, 1980, 'Floods and Famines: A Study of Food Shortages in Rufiji District'. University of Dar es Salaam, Bureau of Resource Assessment and Land Use Planning, Research Paper No. 63.

Bauer, Peter, 1991, *The Development Frontier: Essays in Applied Economics.* Brighton: Harvester Wheatsheaf.

Baulch, Bob, 1987, 'Entitlements and the Wollo Famine of 1982–1985', *Disasters* 11: 195–204.

Baxter, Paul T. W., 1993, 'The "New" East African Pastoralist: An Overview', in John Markakis (ed.), *Conflict and the Decline of Pastoralism in the Horn of Africa.* London: Macmillan.

Beckman, Björn, 1992, 'Empowerment or Repression? The World Bank and the Politics of Adjustment', in Peter Gibbon (ed.), *Markets, Civil Society and Democracy in Kenya.* Uppsala: Nordiska Afrikainstitutet.

Benthall, Jonathan, 1993, *Disasters, Relief and the Media.* London: I.B. Tauris.

Best, Geoffrey, 1995, *War and Law since 1945.* Oxford: Clarendon Press.

Besteman, Catherine and Cassanelli, Lee V., 1996, *The Struggle for Land in Southern Somalia: The War behind the War.* Boulder, CO: Westview Press and London: Haan.

Bhatia, B. M., 1967, *Famines in India: A Study of Some Aspects of the Economic History of India, 1860–1965.* Bombay, Asia Publishing House (second edition).

Black, Maggie, 1992, *A Cause for Our Times: Oxfam: The First Fifty Years.* Oxford: Oxford University Press.

Bonar, J., 1895, *Malthus and his Work.* London: Macmillan.

Borton, John, 1989, 'Overview of the 1984/85 National Drought Relief Programme', in T. E. Downing, K. W. Gitu and C. M. Kaman (eds), *Coping with Drought in Kenya: National and Local Strategies.* Boulder, CO: Lynne Rienner.

Bouchet-Saulnier, Françoise, 1993, 'Peacekeeping Operations above International Law', in F. Jean (ed.), *Life, Death and Aid: The Médecins Sans Frontières Report on World Crisis Intervention.* London: Routledge.

Bratton, Michael, 1987, 'Drought, Food and the Social Organisation of Small Farmers in Zimbabwe', in M. H. Glantz (ed.), *Drought and Hunger in Africa: Denying Famine a Future.* Cambridge: Cambridge University Press.

Brietzke, P. H., 1982, *Law, Development and the Ethiopian Revolution.* Lewisburg, PA: Bucknell University Press.

Brisset-Foucault, Marc, *et al.*, 1995, *Report of the Independent International Commission of Inquiry on the Events at Kibeho, April 1995*, Kigali, 18 May.

Brooke, C., 1967, 'The Heritage of Famine in Central Tanzania', *Tanzania Notes and Records* 67: 15–22.

Brown, Richard, 1988, 'A Background Note on the Final Round of Economic Austerity Measures Imposed by the Numeiry Regime: June 1984–March 1985', in T. Barnett and A. Abdelkarim (eds), *Sudan: State, Capital and Transformation*. London: Croom Helm.

Brown, Richard, 1992, *Private Wealth and Public Debt: Debt, Capital Flight and the IMF in Sudan*. London: Macmillan.

Bryceson, Deborah, 1980, 'The National Grain Supply Problem in Tanzania, 1961–78'. Seminar paper, Dar es Salaam, September.

Bryceson, Deborah, 1987, 'A Century of Food Supply in Dar es Salaam', in Guyer (ed.) *Feeding African Cities: Studies in Regional Social History*. Manchester: Manchester University Press.

Bryceson, Deborah, 1990, *Food Insecurity and the Social Division of Labour in Tanzania, 1919–85*. London: Macmillan.

Buchanan-Smith, Margaret, 1990, 'Drought, Income Transfers and the Rural Household Economy'. Study Paper No. 2 in Food Studies Group.

Buchanan-Smith, Margaret, and Davies, Susanna, 1995, *Famine Early Warning and Response – The Missing Link*. London: Intermediate Technology Publications.

Cairns, Ed, 1995, 'A Dilemma', *Index on Censorship*, issue 2.

Callwell, Col. C. E., 1996, *Small Wars: Their Principles and Practice*. Lincoln, NE: University of Nebraska Press, third edition (originally published 1896).

CARE, 1993, 'CARE International in Somalia', November, mimeo.

Center for Economic and Social Rights, 1996, *UN Sanctioned Suffering: A Human Rights Assessment of United Nations Sanctions on Iraq*. New York: CESR, May.

Centers for Disease Control, 1992, 'Population-Based Mortality Assessment – Baidoa and Afgoi, Somalia, 1992', *Morbidity and Mortality Weekly Report* 41.49, December: 913–17.

Chambers, Robert, 1983, *Rural Development: Putting the Last First*. London: Longman.

Childers, Erskine and Urquhart, Brian, 1991, 'Towards a More Effective United Nations', *Development Dialogue* 1–2.

Chipman, John, 1989, *French Power in Africa*. London: Blackwell.

Clarke, Walter, S., 1995, *Humanitarian Intervention in Somalia: Bibliography*. Carlisle, PA: Center for Strategic Leadership.

Clay, Jason, and Holcombe, Bonnie, 1985, *Politics and the Ethiopian Famine, 1984–1985*. Cambridge, MA: Cultural Survival.

Clough, Michael, 1992, *Free at Last? U.S. Policy toward Africa and the End of the Cold War*. New York: Council on Foreign Relations.

Collins, R. O., 1971, *Land Beyond the Rivers: The Southern Sudan 1898–1918*. New Haven, CT: Yale University Press.

Commission d'enquête Somalie, 1993, *Rapport*. Brussels, 14 November.

Constable, M., 1984, *Ethiopian Highlands Reclamation Study: The Degradation of Resources and an Evaluation of Actions to Combat it, Vol II*. Addis Ababa: FAO and Ministry of Agriculture.

Cornia, G. A., Jolly, R. and Stewart, F. 1987, *Adjustment with a Human Face*. 2 Vols, Oxford: Oxford University Press.

Currey, Bruce, 1978, 'The Famine Syndrome: Its Definition for Relief and Rehabilitation in Bangladesh', *Ecology of Food and Nutrition* 7: 87–98.

Cutler, Peter, 1988, 'The Development of the 1983–85 Famine in Northern Ethiopia', PhD thesis, London School of Hygiene and Tropical Medicine.

de St Jorre, John, 1972, *The Brothers' War: Biafra and Nigeria*. Boston, MA: Houghton Mifflin.

de Waal, Alex, 1987, 'On the Perception of Poverty and Famines', *International Journal of Moral and Social Studies* 2: 251–62.

de Waal, Alex, 1989a, *Famine that Kills: Darfur, Sudan, 1984–1985*. Oxford: Clarendon Press.

de Waal, Alex, 1989b, 'The Sudan Famine Code of 1920: Successes and Failures of the Indian Model of Famine Relief in Colonial Sudan', London: ActionAid.

de Waal, Alex, 1990a, *Famine Survival Strategies in Wollo, Tigray and Eritrea: A Review of the Literature*. Oxford: Oxfam.

de Waal, Alex, 1990b, *Tigray: Grain Markets and Internal Purchase*. Oxford: Oxfam.

de Waal, Alex, 1991a, 'A Human Rights Agenda to Prevent Starvation in Africa', *Peace and Democracy News* 2 (Summer).

de Waal, Alex, 1991b 'Famine and Human Rights', *Development in Practice* 1 (2) (Summer).

de Waal, Alex, 1993a 'Starving out the South', in M. W. Daly and A. A. Sikainga (eds), *Civil War in the Sudan*. London: British Academic Press.

de Waal, Alex, 1993b, 'War and Famine in Africa', *IDS Bulletin* 24 (4): 33–40.

DeMars, William, 1995, 'Waiting for Early Warning: Humanitarian Action after the Cold War', *Journal of Refugee Studies* 8: 390–410.

Deng, Francis M., 1993, *Protecting the Dispossessed: A Challenge for the International Community*. Washington, DC: The Brookings Institution.

Dessalegn, Rahmato, 1987, *Famine and Survival Strategies: A Case Study from Northeast Ethiopia*. Addis Ababa, Institute of Development Research.

Dessalegn, Rahmato, 1989, 'Famine in Peasant Consciousness: Aspects of Symbolic Culture in Rural Ethiopia'. Paper prepared for the Fifth Annual Seminar of the Department of History, Addis Ababa University, July.

Drèze, Jean, 1990a, 'Famine Prevention in India', in J. Drèze and A. Sen (eds), *The Political Economy of Hunger, Vol II: Famine Prevention*. Oxford: Clarendon Press.

Drèze, Jean, 1990b 'Famine Prevention in Africa: Some Experiences and Lessons', in J. Drèze and A. Sen (eds), *The Political Economy of Hunger, Vol. II: Famine Prevention*. Oxford: Clarendon Press.

Drèze, Jean and Sen, Amartya, 1989, *Hunger and Public Action*. Oxford: Clarendon Press.

Drysdale, John, 1994, *Whatever Happened to Somalia? A Tale of Tragic Blunders*. London: Haan.

Duffield, Mark, 1994a *Complex Political Emergencies, with Reference to Angola and Bosnia: An Exploratory Report for UNICEF*. New York: UNICEF, March.

Duffield, Mark, 1994b 'Complex Emergencies and the Crisis of Develop-mentalism', *IDS Bulletin* 25 (3): October.

Duffield, Mark and Prendergast, John, 1994, *Without Troops and Tanks: Humanitarian Intervention in Ethiopia and Eritrea*. Lawrenceville, NJ: Red Sea Press.

Economist Intelligence Unit, 1983, *Quarterly Economic Report for Sudan, 1983*, No. 2.

Edwards, Michael and Hulme, David, 1995a, 'NGO Performance and Account-ability: Introduction and Overview', in M. Edwards and D. Hulme (eds), *Non-Governmental Organisations – Performance and Accountability: Beyond the Magic Bullet*. London: Earthscan.

Edwards, Michael and Hulme, David, 1995b, 'Beyond the Magic Bullet: Lessons and Conclusions', in M. Edwards and D. Hulme (eds), *Non-Governmental Organisations – Performance and Accountability: Beyond the Magic Bullet*. London: Earthscan.

Eide, Asbjorn, 1989, 'Right to Adequate Food as a Human Right', New York: United Nations, E.89.XIV.2.

Eldon, Dan, 1994, *Somalia.* Nairobi: Rotary Club.

English, John, Bennett, Jon, Bruce, Dick and Fallon, Caroline, 1984, *Tigray 1984: An Investigation.* Oxford: Oxfam, January.

Federation of International Red Cross and Red Crescent Societies, 1995, 'Code of Conduct for the International Red Cross and Red Crescent Movement and NGOs in Disaster Relief', *Refugee Participation Network* 19: May.

Feed the Children, 1995, *From Survival to Revival: Rwanda's Children of War.* Reading: Feed the Children, April.

Feierman, Steven, 1990, *Peasant Intellectuals: Anthropology and History in Tanzania.* Madison, WI: University of Wisconsin Press.

Finucane, Aengus, 1993, 'The Changing Roles of Voluntary Organizations', in K. M. Cahill (ed.), *A Framework for Survival: Health, Human Rights and Humanitarian Assistance in Conflicts and Disasters.* New York: Basic Books.

Firebrace, James and Smith, Gayle, 1982, *The Hidden Revolution: An Analysis of Social Change in Tigray (Northern Ethiopia) Based on Eyewitness Accounts.* London: War on Want.

Food Studies Group, 1990a, *Drought and the Rural Economy in Botswana: An Evaluation of the Drought Programme, 1982–90, Major Conclusions and Recommendations.* Oxford: Queen Elizabeth House, June.

Food Studies Group, 1990b, *Drought and the Rural Economy in Botswana: More Development with Less Rain.* Oxford: Queen Elizabeth House, June.

Fowler, Alan and Biekart, Kees, 1996, 'Do Private Agencies Really Make a Difference?' in D. Sogge (ed.), *Compassion and Calculation: The Business of Private Foreign Aid.* London: Pluto Press.

Fraser, Lovat, 1911, *India under Curzon and After.* London: Heinemann.

Gibbon, Peter, 1992a, 'Markets, Civil Society and Democracy in Kenya', in Peter Gibbon (ed.), *Markets, Civil Society and Democracy in Kenya.* Uppsala: Nordiska Afrikainstitutet.

Gibbon, Peter, 1992b, 'Structural Adjustment and Pressures toward Multi-partyism in Sub-Saharan Africa', in Peter Gibbon (ed.), *Markets, Civil Society and Democracy in Kenya.* Uppsala: Nordiska Afrikainstitutet.

Gill, Peter, 1986, *A Year in the Death of Africa: Politics, Bureaucracy and the Famine.* London: Paladin.

Godfrey, Nancy and Mursal, Hussein M., 1990, 'International Aid and National Health Policies for Refugees: Lessons from Somalia', *Journal of Refugee Studies* 3: 110–34.

Gooch, Toby and MacDonald, John, 1981a,'Evaluation of 1979/80 Drought Relief Programme'. Gaborone.

Gooch, Toby and MacDonald, John, 1981b, 'Evaluation of Labour Related Projects in Drought Relief and Development'. Gaborone.

Government of China, 1991, 'White Paper on Human Rights', cited in *Beijing Review*, 4–10 November.

Government of Sudan, 1920, *1920 Famine Regulations* (reissued 1937). Khartoum.

Griffin, Keith and Hay, Roger, 1985, 'Problems of Agricultural Development in Socialist Ethiopia: An Overview and a Suggested Strategy', *Journal of Peasant Studies* 13: 37–66.

Guyer, Jane (ed.), 1987, *Feeding African Cities: Studies in Regional Social History.* Manchester: Manchester University Press for the International African Institute.

Hall-Matthews, David, 1996, 'Historical Roots of Relief Paradigms: Ideas on Dependency and Free Trade in India in the 1870s', *Disasters* 20: 216–30.

Hardin, Russell, 1995, *One for All: The Logic of Group Conflict.* Princeton, NJ: Princeton University Press.

Harrison, Paul and Palmer, Robin, 1986, *News Out of Africa: Biafra to BandAid*. London: Hilary Shipman.

Hendrie, Barbara, 1991, 'The Tigrayan Refugee Repatriation, 1985–1987', *Journal of Refugee Studies* 4: 200–18.

Hewitt, K., 1983, 'The Idea of Calamity in a Technocratic Age', in K. Hewitt (ed.), *Interpretations of Calamity, from the Viewpoint of Human Ecology*. Boston, MA: Allen and Unwin.

Hitchens, Christopher, 1993, review of Noam Chomsky's *The Culture of Terrorism*. in: *For the Sake of Argument*. London: Verso.

Hoben, Allan, 1996, 'Paradigms and Politics: The Cultural Construction of Environmental Policy in Ethiopia', in M. Leach and R. Mearns (eds.) *The Lie of the Land: Challenging Received Wisdom in African Environmental Change and Policy*. London: James Currey and Portsmouth (NH): Heinemann, for the International African Institute.

Hodson, Roland, 1992, 'Small, Medium or Large? The Rocky Road to NGO Growth', in M. Edwards and D. Hulme (eds), *Making a Difference: NGOs and Development in a Changing World*. London: Earthscan.

Hogg, Richard, 1985, 'The Politics of Drought: The Pauperisation of the Isiolo Boran', *Disasters* 9: 39–43.

Hogg, Richard, 1986, 'The New Pastoralism: Poverty and Dependency in Northern Kenya', *Africa* 56: 319–33.

Holm, John D. and Morgan, Richard G., 1985, 'Coping with Drought in Botswana: An African Success', *Journal of Modern African Studies* 23: 463–82.

Hoskins, Eric, n.d., 'The Impact of the Gulf War on Public Health', mimeo.

Huband, Mark, 1993, 'When Yankee Goes Home', *Africa Report*, March/April.

Human Rights Watch, 1992, *Indivisible Human Rights: The Relationship of Political and Civil Rights to Survival, Subsistence and Poverty*. New York: Human Rights Watch, September.

Ikiara, Gerrishon K., Jama, Mohamed and Amadi, Justus O., 1995, 'The Cereals Chain in Kenya: Actors, Reforms and Politics', in Peter Gibbon (ed.), *Markets, Civil Society and Democracy in Kenya*. Uppsala: Nordiska Afrikainstitutet.

Iliffe, John, 1990, *Famine in Zimbabwe, 1890–1960*. Harare: Mambo Press.

International Commission of Jurists, 1985, 'Siracusa Principles on the Limitation and Derogation Provisions in the International Covenant on Civil and Political Rights', *Review of the International Commission of Jurists* 36: 47–56.

International Institute for Strategic Studies, 1989, *The Military Balance, 1989– 1990*. London: Brassey's.

International Law Association, 1984, 'The Paris Minimum Standards of Human Rights Norms in a State of Emergency', *Report of the Sixty-First Conference* 58–76.

Jackson, J. C., Collier, P. and Conti, A. , 1987, *Rural Development Policies and Food Security in Zimbabwe*. Geneva: ILO Employment and Development Department.

Jansson, Kurt, Harris, Michael and Penrose, Angela, 1987, *The Ethiopian Famine*. London: Zed Press.

Jayne, T. S. and Chisvo, M., 1991, 'Unravelling Zimbabwe's Food Insecurity Paradox', *Food Policy* 16 (1).

Jean, François, 1986, *Du Bon Usage de la Famine*. Paris: Médecins Sans Frontières.

Jespersen, E., 1992, 'External Shocks, Adjustment Policies, and Economic and Social Performance', in G. A. Cornia, R. van der Hoeven and T. Mkandawire (eds), *Africa's Recovery in the 1990s*. New York: St. Martins.

Jones, Stephen, 1992, 'Dilemmas of Agricultural Marketing Reform under Structural Adjustment in Zimbabwe: Maize Marketing Policy'. Oxford: Food Studies Group, mimeo.

Kane, P., 1988, *Famine in China 1958–61: Demographic and Social Implications*. New York: Macmillan.

Kanyinga, Karuti, 1995, 'The Politics of Development Space in Kenya', in J. Semboja and O. Therkildsen (eds), *Service Provision under Stress in East Africa*. London: James Currey.

Kaplan, Robert, 1996, *The Ends of the Earth: A Journey at the Dawn of the Twenty-First Century*. New York: Random House.

Karadawi, Ahmed, 1988, 'Refugee Policy in the Sudan, 1967–1984'. DPhil thesis, University of Oxford.

Karadawi, Ahmed, 1991, 'The Smuggling of the Ethiopian Falashas to Israel through Sudan', *African Affairs* 90: 23–49

Karim, Ataul, Duffield, Mark *et al.*, 1996, *Operation Lifeline Sudan: A Review*. Birmingham: CURS.

Kashasha, D. A. R., 1989, 'The Tanzanian Crop Monitoring and Early Warning System', in T. E. Downing, K. W. Gitu and C. M. Kaman (eds), *Coping with Drought in Kenya: National and Local Strategies*. Boulder, CO: Lynne Rienner.

Keen, David, 1991, 'Targeting Emergency Food Aid: The Case of Darfur in 1985', in S. Maxwell (ed.), *To Cure all Hunger: Food Policy and Food Security in Sudan*. London: Intermediate Technology Publications.

Keen, David, 1994, *The Benefits of Famine: A Political Economy of Famine in South-Western Sudan, 1983–1989*. Princeton, NJ: Princeton University Press.

Kelly, Marion and Buchanan-Smith, Margaret, 1994, 'Northern Sudan in 1991: Food Crisis and the International Relief Response', *Disasters* 18: 16–33.

Kent, Randolph C., 1987, *Anatomy of Disaster Relief: The International Network in Action*. London: Frances Pinter.

Kevane, Michael and Gray, Leslie, 1995, 'Local Politics in the Time of Turabi's Revolution: Gender, Class and Ethnicity in Western Sudan', *Africa* 65: 271–96.

Knuttson, Karl Eric and Selinus, Ruth, 1970, 'Fasting in Ethiopia: An Anthropological and Nutritional Study', *American Journal of Clinical Nutrition* 23: 40–9.

Korn, David A., 1986, *Ethiopia, the United States and the Soviet Union*. London: Croom Helm.

Korten, David C., 1990, *Getting to the 21st Century: Voluntary Action and the Global Agenda*. West Hartford, CT: Kumarian Press.

Kumar, B. G., 1990, 'Ethiopian Famines 1973–1985', in J. Drèze and A. Sen (eds), *The Political Economy of Famine: Vol. II: Famine Prevention*. Oxford: Clarendon Press.

Lawyers Committee for Human Rights, 1986, *Zimbabwe: Wages of War, A Report on Human Rights*. New York: Lawyers Committee for Human Rights.

Leach, Melissa and Mearns, Robin, 1996, 'Environmental Change and Policy: Challenging Received Wisdom in Africa', in M. Leach and R. Mearns (eds), *The Lie of the Land: Challenging Received Wisdom on the African Environment*. Oxford: James Currey and Portsmouth (NH): Heinemann, for the International African Institute.

Lefort, René, 1983, *Ethiopia: An Heretical Revolution?* (trans. A. M. Bennett), London: Zed Press.

Leonard, E. M., 1900, *The Early History of English Poor Relief*. Cambridge: Cambridge University Press.

Leys, Colin, 1996, *The Rise and Fall of Development Theory*. London: James Currey.

Leys, Roger, 1986, 'Drought and Drought Relief in Southern Zimbabwe', in P. Lawrence (ed.), *World Recession and the Food Crisis in Africa*. London: James Currey.

Linden, Ian, 1977, *Church and Revolution in Rwanda*. Manchester: Manchester University Press.

Little, Peter D., 1985, 'Absentee Herd Owners and Part-Time Pastoralists: The

Political Economy of Resource Use in Northern Kenya', *Human Ecology* 13: 131–51.

Macrae, Joanna and Zwi, Antony, 1994, 'Famine, Complex Emergencies and International Policy in Africa: An Overview', in J. Macrae and A. Zwi (eds), *War and Hunger: Rethinking International Responses to Complex Emergencies*. London: Zed Press.

Madras Presidency, 1905, *Famine Code*. Madras: Government Press.

Malkki, Liisa H., 1995, *Purity and Exile: Violence, Memory, and National Cosmology among Hutu Refugees in Tanzania*. Chicago and London: University of Chicago Press.

Mallory, W. H., 1926, *China: Land of Famine*. New York: American Geographical Society.

Malthus, Thomas R., 1926, *First Essay on Population*, originally published 1798, London: Macmillan.

Malwal, Bona, 1991, 'Questions the SPLA Can No Longer Ignore', *Sudan Democratic Gazette*, June.

Mansour Khalid, 1985, *Nimeiri and the Revolution of Dis-May*. London: Kegan Paul.

Martin, Dominique, 1993, untitled, *Médecins Sans Frontières International Newsletter*, March.

Maxwell, Simon, 1990, 'Food Security for Developing Countries: Issues and Options for the 1990s', *IDS Bulletin* 21 (3): July: 2–13.

Maxwell, Simon, Swift, Jeremy and Buchanan-Smith, Margaret, 1990, 'Is Food Security Targeting Possible in Sub-Saharan Africa? Evidence from North Sudan', *IDS Bulletin* 21 (3) July: 52–61.

McCall, Richard, 1995, 'Confronting the New World Disorder', *DHA News*, May–June.

McCann, James, 1987, 'The Social Impact of Drought: Oxen, Households, and Some Implications for Rehabilitation', in M. H. Glantz (ed.), *Drought and Hunger in Africa: Denying Famine a Future*. Cambridge: Cambridge University Press.

Médecins Sans Frontières, 1992, *Populations in Danger*. Paris: MSF.

Meillassoux, Claude, 1974, 'Development or Exploitation: Is the Sahel Famine Good for Business?' *Review of African Political Economy* 1: 27–33.

Menkhaus, Ken, 1994, 'Getting Out vs. Getting Through: US and UN Policies in Somalia', *Middle East Policy* 3: 146–63.

Mesfin Wolde Mariam, 1986, *Rural Vulnerability to Famine in Ethiopia, 1958–1977*. London: Intermediate Technology Publications.

Minear, Larry and Weiss, Thomas G., 1995, *Mercy Under Fire: War and the Global Humanitarian Community*. Boulder, CO: Westview Press.

Mockaitis, Thomas R., 1990, *British Counterinsurgency 1919–60*. London: Macmillan.

Molutsi, Patrick P., 1991, 'The Political Economy of Botswana: Implications for Democracy', in Mpho G. Molomo and Brian T. Mokopakgosi, (eds), *Multi-Party Democracy in Botswana*. Harare: SAPES.

Monson, Jamie, 1996, 'Canoe Building under Colonialism: Forestry and Food Policies in the Inner Kilombero Valley, 1920–1940', in G. Maddox, J. Giblin and I. N. Kimambo (eds), *Custodians of the Land: Ecology and Culture in the History of Tanzania*. London: James Currey.

Moseley, P., Harrigan, J. and Toye, J., 1991, *Aid and Power, The World Bank and Policy-Based Lending in the 1980s*, Vol. II. London: Routledge.

Moskoff, William, 1990, *The Bread of Affliction: The Food Supply in the USSR during World War II*. Cambridge, Cambridge University Press.

Netherlands Development Co-operation, 1994, *Humanitarian Aid to Somalia: Evaluation Report 1994*. The Hague: Operations Review Unit.

Nolan, L., 1974, *The Forgotten Famine*. Dublin: Mercier.

Oakley, Robert and Hirsch, John, 1995, *Somalia and Operation Restore Hope: Reflections on Peacekeeping and Peacemaking*. Washington, DC: US Institute of Peace.

Odling-Smee, James, 1993, 'Aid Agency Denies "Gross Irresponsibility" Charge', *Third Sector*, 4 November.

OECD, 1990, *Geographical Distribution of Financial Flows to Developing Countries*. Paris: OECD.

OECD, Joint Evaluation of Emergency Assistance to Rwanda, 1996, *The International Response to Conflict and Genocide: Lessons from the Rwanda Experience, Vol. 3, Humanitarian Aid and Effects*. Copenhagen: OECD.

Osmani, Siddiq, 1991, 'The Food Problems of Bangladesh', in J. Drèze and A. Sen (eds), *The Political Economy of Hunger, Vol. III: Endemic Hunger*. Oxford: Clarendon Press.

Otlhogile, Bojosi, 1991, 'How Free and Fair?' in Mpho G. Molomo and Brian T. Mokopakgosi (eds), *Multi-Party Democracy in Botswana*. Harare: SAPES.

Oxfam, 1995, *The Oxfam Poverty Report*. Oxford: Oxfam.

Pankhurst, Alula, 1990, 'Settling for a New World: People and the State in an Ethiopian Resettlement Village', PhD Thesis, University of Manchester.

Patel, Maresh, 1994, 'An Examination of the 1990–91 Famine in Sudan', *Disasters* 18: 313–31.

Pilger, John, 1989, *Heroes*. London: Pan Books.

Plattner, Denise, 1996, 'ICRC Neutrality and Neutrality in Humanitarian Assistance', *International Review of the Red Cross* 311: 161–80.

Polanyi, Karl, 1946, *The Great Transformation: The Political and Economic Origins of Our Time*. New York: Beacon Press.

Provost, René, 1991, *Starvation as a Weapon: Legal Implications of the United Nations Food Blockade against Iraq and Kuwait*. New York: Human Rights Watch.

Prunier, Gérard, 1995, *The Rwanda Crisis: History of a Genocide, 1959–94*. London: Hurst.

Ram, N., 1990, 'An Independent Press and Anti-Hunger Strategies: The Indian Experience', in J. Drèze and A. Sen (eds), *The Political Economy of Hunger, Vol. I: Entitlement and Well-Being*. Oxford: Clarendon Press.

Rangasami, Amrita, 1985, ' "Failure of Exchange Entitlements" Theory of Famine: A Response', *Economic and Political Weekly* 20: 41–2.

Ravallion, Martin, 1985, *Markets and Famines*. Oxford: Clarendon Press.

Refugee Policy Group, 1994, *Hope Restored? Humanitarian Aid in Somalia 1990–1994*. Washington, DC: RPG, November.

Relief and Rehabilitation Commission, 1985, *The Challenge of Drought: Ethiopia's Decade of Struggle in Relief and Rehabilitation*. Addis Ababa: RRC.

Report of the Famine Commission 1880, 1880, London: HMSO.

Robinson, Mark, 1992, 'NGOs and Poverty Alleviation: Implications for Scaling up', in M. Edwards and D. Hulme (eds), *Making a Difference: NGOs and Development in a Changing World*. London: Earthscan.

Rogge, John R., 1992, '*The Displaced Population in South and Central Somalia and Preliminary Proposals for their Re-integration and Rehabilitation*. Manitoba, WI: University of Manitoba/UNDP, September.

Sahnoun, Mohamed, 1994, *Somalia: The Missed Opportunities*. Washington, DC: US Institute for Peace.

Sandoz, Yves, 1993, ' "Droit" or "Devoir d'Ingérence" and the Right to Assistance: The Issues Involved', *International Review of the Red Cross* 287: 215–27.

Saxby, John, 1996, 'Who Owns the Private Aid Agencies?' in D. Sogge (ed.), *Compassion and Calculation: The Business of Private Foreign Aid*. London: Pluto Press.

Seaman, John, 1995a, 'The International System of Humanitarian Relief in the "New World Order"', in John Harriss (ed.), *The Politics of Humanitarian Intervention*. London: Frances Pinter.

Seaman, John, 1995b, comment in *International NGOs and Complex Political Emergencies: Perspectives from Anthropology*. Report on the RAI/ESRC exploratory workshop, London School of Economics, 9 January.

Seaman, John and Holt, Julius, 1975, 'The Ethiopian Famine of 1973–4. I. Wollo Province', *Proceedings of the Nutritional Society* 34: 114A.

Sen, Amartya, 1981, *Poverty and Famines: An Essay on Entitlement and Deprivation*. Oxford: Clarendon Press.

Sen, Amartya, 1982, 'Food Battles: Conflicts in Access to Food'. New Delhi: Coromandel Lecture.

Sen, Amartya, 1990, 'Individual Freedom as a Social Commitment', *New York Review of Books*, 14 June.

Shawcross, William, 1984, *The Quality of Mercy: Cambodia, Holocaust and Modern Conscience*. London: Deutsch.

Shepherd, Andrew, 1988, 'Case Studies of Famine: Sudan', in D. Curtis, M. Hubbard and A. Shepherd (eds), *Preventing Famine: Policies and Prospects for Africa*. London: Routledge.

Slim, Hugo, 1996, 'Doing the Right Thing: Relief Agencies, Moral Dilemmas and Moral Responsibility in Political Emergencies and War'. Oxford: Oxford Brookes University, Centre for Development and Emergency Planning, unpublished paper.

Smillie, Ian, 1995, *The Alms Bazaar: Altruism under Fire – Non-Profit Organizations and International Development*. London: Intermediate Technology Publications.

Smith, Gayle, 1983, *Counting Quintals*. Utrecht: Dutch Inter-Church Aid.

Smith, K., 1951, *The Malthusian Controversy*. London: Routledge, Kegan Paul.

Sobhan, Rehman, 1982, *The Crisis of External Dependence: The Political Economy of Foreign Aid to Bangladesh*. Dacca: Dacca University Press.

Sobiana, Neal W., 1988, 'Pastoralist Migration and Colonial Policy: A Case Study from Northern Kenya', in D. H. Johnson and D. M. Anderson (eds), *The Ecology of Survival: Case Studies from Northeast African History*. London: Lester Crook.

Solway, Jacqueline, 1995, 'Drought as a "Revelatory Crisis": An Exploration of Shifting Entitlements and Hierarchies in the Kalahari, Botswana', *Development and Change* 25: 471–96.

Sperling, L., 1987, 'Food Acquisition during the African Drought of 1983–1984: A Study of Kenyan Herders', *Disasters* 11: 263–72.

Stewart, Frances, 1995, *Adjustment and Poverty: Options and Choices*. London: Routledge.

Stremlau, J. J., 1977, *The International Politics of the Nigerian Civil War, 1967–1970*. Princeton, NJ: Princeton University Press.

Survival International, n.d., *Unquiet Pastures: The Nomadic People of North East Kenya Today*. London: Survival International.

Swift, Jeremy, 1996, 'Desertification: Narratives, Winners and Losers', in M. Leach and R. Mearns (eds), *The Lie of the Land: Challenging Received Wisdom on the African Environment*. Oxford: James Currey and Portsmouth (NH): Heinemann, for the International African Institute.

Tabor, Steven, 1983, *Drought Relief and Information Management: Coping Intelligently with Disaster*. Gaborone: USAID, June.

Thompson, Carol B., 1993, *Drought Management Strategies in Southern Africa: From Relief Through Rehabilitation to Vulnerability Reduction*. Harare, SADC Food Security Unit and Nairobi, UNICEF.

Thompson, E. P., 1980, *The Making of the English Working Class*. London: Penguin.

Tomasevski, Katerina, 1994, 'Human Rights and Wars of Starvation', in J. Macrae and A. Zwi (eds), *War and Hunger: Rethinking International Responses to Complex Emergencies*. London: Zed Press.

Toye, John, 1992, 'Interest Group Politics and the Implementation of Structural Adjustment Policies in Sub-Saharan Africa', in P. Gibbon, Y. Bangura and A. Ofstad (eds), *Authoritarianism, Democracy and Adjustment: The Politics of Economic Reform in Africa*. Uppsala: Scandinavian Institute for African Studies.

Trinquier, Roger, 1964, *Modern Warfare: A French View of Counterinsurgency*. (trans. D. Lee), New York: Praeger.

UN General Assembly, 46th Session, Agenda item 143, A/46/182, 'Strengthening of the Coordination of Humanitarian Assistance of the United Nations', 19 December 1991.

UNOSOM Military Information Office, 1993, 'UNOSOM FHQ [Field Headquarters] Morning Briefing Notes for 11 Jul[y] 1993'.

Uvin, Peter, 1994, *The International Organization of Hunger*. London: Kegan Paul.

Valentine, Theodore R., 1993, 'Drought, Transfer Entitlements, and Income Distribution: The Botswana Experience', *World Development* 21 (1): 109–26.

Vaughan, Megan, 1987, *The Story of an African Famine: Gender and Famine in Twentieth Century Malawi*. Cambridge: Cambridge University Press.

Wallis, Malcolm, 1990, 'The Institutional Response to Drought', Study Paper No. 5 in Food Studies Group, 1990a.

Walton, John and Seddon, David, 1994, *Free Markets and Food Riots: The Politics of Global Adjustment*. Oxford: Blackwell.

Watkins S. C. and Menken, J., 1985, 'Famines in Historical Perspective', *Population and Development Review* 11: 647–76.

Watts, Michael, 1983, *Silent Violence: Food, Famine and the Peasantry in Northern Nigeria*. Berkeley, CA: University of California Press.

Webb, Patrick, and von Braun, Joachim, 1994, *Famine and Food Security in Ethiopia: Lessons for Africa*. New York: John Wiley.

Woodham Smith, Cecil, 1962, *The Great Hunger, Ireland 1845–49*. New York: Harper and Row.

World Bank, 1986, *Poverty and Hunger: Issues and Options for Food Security in Developing Countries*. Washington, DC: World Bank.

World Bank, 1989, *Sub-Saharan Africa: From Crisis to Sustainable Growth*. Washington, DC: World Bank.

World Food Programme, 1989, 'WFP Emergency Aid for Drought Victims in Kenya', in T. E. Downing, K. W. Gitu and C. M. Kaman (eds), *Coping with Drought in Kenya: National and Local Strategies*. Boulder, CO: Lynne Rienner.

Wright, Ann, 1993, 'Legal and Human Rights Aspects of UNOSOM Military Operations', Memorandum to the Special Representative of the Secretary-General from UNOSOM Justice Division, 13 July.

Young, Helen and Jaspars, Susanne, 1995, *Nutrition Matters: People, Food and Famine*. London: Intermediate Technology Publications.

Young, John, 1994, 'Peasants and Revolution in Ethiopia: Tigray 1975–1989', PhD thesis, Simon Fraser University, Burnaby BC.

Zimbabwe Grain Marketing Board, 1991, *Report and Accounts, 1991*. Harare, September.